99.62 (aet) Bartfield 5-67 (Stufferin)

# ORIGINAL NARRATIVES
# OF EARLY AMERICAN HISTORY

REPRODUCED UNDER THE AUSPICES OF THE
AMERICAN HISTORICAL ASSOCIATION

General Editor, J. FRANKLIN JAMESON, Ph.D., LL.D., Litt.D.

DIRECTOR OF THE DEPARTMENT OF HISTORICAL RESEARCH IN THE
CARNEGIE INSTITUTION OF WASHINGTON

ORIGINAL NARRATIVES
OF EARLY AMERICAN HISTORY

No. 4

# WINTHROP'S JOURNAL

## "HISTORY OF NEW ENGLAND"

### 1630—1649

EDITED BY

JAMES KENDALL HOSMER, LL.D.

CORRESPONDING MEMBER OF THE MASSACHUSETTS HISTORICAL SOCIETY
AND OF THE COLONIAL SOCIETY OF MASSACHUSETTS

VOLUME II

New York

BARNES & NOBLE, INC.

PRINTED IN THE UNITED STATES OF AMERICA

# CONTENTS

## WINTHROP'S JOURNAL

## "HISTORY OF NEW ENGLAND"

### EDITED BY JAMES KENDALL HOSMER

### 1640

### 1641

# CONTENTS

viii CONTENTS

1645

1646

# CONTENTS

# WINTHROP'S JOURNAL

## "THE HISTORY OF NEW ENGLAND"

1630–1649

Vol. II

# WINTHROP'S JOURNAL
## "THE HISTORY OF NEW ENGLAND"

1630–1649

---

## 1640

(3.) (*May*) 13.]  THE court of elections was at Boston, and Thomas Dudley, Esq., was chosen governor. Some trouble there had been in making way for his election, and it was obtained with some difficulty; for many of the elders labored much in it, fearing lest the long continuance of one man in the place should bring it to be for life, and, in time, hereditary. Beside, this gentleman was a man of approved wisdom and godliness, and of much good service to the country, and therefore it was his due to share in such honor and benefit as the country had to bestow.  The elders, being met at Boston about this matter, sent some of their company to acquaint the old governor with their desire, and the reasons moving them, clearing themselves of all dislike of his government, and seriously professing their sincere affections and respect towards him, which he kindly and thankfully accepted, concurring with them in their motion, and expressing his unfeigned desire of more freedom, that he might a little intend his private occasions, wherein (they well knew) how much he had lately suffered (for his bailiff, whom he trusted with managing his farm, had engaged him £2500 without his privity) in his outward estate.  This they had heard of, and were much affected therewith, and all the country in general, and took course, (the elders agreeing upon it at that meeting,) that supply should be sent

3

in from the several towns, by a voluntary contribution, for free-
ing of those engagements; and the court (having no money to
bestow, and being yet much indebted) gave his wife three
thousand acres of land, and some of the towns sent in liberally,
and some others promised, but could perform but little, and
the most nothing at all.  The whole came not to £500 whereof
near half came from Boston, and one gentleman of Newbury,
Mr. Richard Dummer, propounded for a supply by a more
private way, and for example, himself disbursed £100.[1]

This first court there fell some difference between the governor and some of the deputies about a vote, upon a motion to
have the fine of £200 imposed upon Mr. Robert Keaine to be
abated.  Some would have had it at £100,—others at 100
marks, others at 50, and because the governor put the lowest
to the vote first, whereas divers called for the highest, they
charged the governor with breach of order, whereupon he
grew into some heat, professing that he would not suffer such
things, etc.  The deputies took this as a menacing, and much
offence they took at it; but the next day he cleared his intention to them, and all was quiet.

Mo. 4 (*June*).]  Divers of the inhabitants of Linne, finding
themselves straitened, looked out for a new plantation, and
going to Long Island, they agreed with the Lord Sterling's
agent there, one Mr. Forrett,[2] for a parcel of the isle near the
west end, and agreed with the Indians for their right.  The
Dutch, hearing of this, and making claim to that part of the
island by a former purchase of the Indians, sent men to take
possession of the place, and set up the arms of the Prince of
Orange upon a tree.  The Linne men sent ten or twelve men

[1] This liberality to Winthrop, suffering thus heavily through his devotion to
the public service, is the best possible evidence of the esteem in which he was
held.  The large gift of Richard Dummer, in particular, who had been disciplined in the antinomian excitement, (see Vol. I., p. 215), is a sign, from a
magnanimous sufferer, of appreciation of substantial worth in a persecutor.

[2] Read Farrett.  James Farrett, a Scotsman, was from 1637 to 1641 the
agent of Lord Stirling for selling lands on Long Island.  See Slafter, *Sir William Alexander*, pp. 87–90.

with provisions, etc., who began to build, and took down the prince's arms, and, in place thereof, an Indian had drawn an unhandsome face. The Dutch took this in high displeasure, and sent soldiers and fetched away their men, and imprisoned them a few days, and then took an oath of them [*blank*] and so discharged them. Upon this the Linne men (finding themselves too weak, and having no encouragement to expect aid from the English) deserted that place, and took another at the east end of the same island; and, being now about forty families, they proceeded in their plantation, and called one Mr. Pierson, a godly learned man, and a member of the church of Boston, to go with them, who with some seven or eight more of the company gathered (9)[1] into a church body at Linne, (before they went,) and the whole company entered into a civil combination (with the advice of some of our magistrates) to become a corporation.

Upon this occasion, the Dutch governor, one William Kyfte, (a discreet man,) wrote to our governor complaint of the English usurpations, both at Connecticut, and now also at Long Island, and of the abuse offered to the Prince's arms, etc., and thereupon excused his imprisoning our men. To which the governor returned answer, (in Latin, his letter being in the same,) that our desire had always been to hold peace and good correspondency with all our neighbors; and though we would not maintain any of our countrymen in any unjust action, yet we might not suffer them to be injured, etc. As for our neighbors of Connecticut, etc., he knew they were not under our government, and for those at Long Island, they went voluntarily from us, etc.[2]

[1] *I. e.*, probably in November.
[2] From another authority, we learn that the arms of the Prince of Orange were pulled down by Lieutenant Daniel Howe, who was at times deputy for Lynn in the General Court. The growth of the plantations, now causing encroachment east and west, involved the English in disputes with Dutch and French neighbors. The occupation of Long Island (near Oyster Bay) was a menace to Manhattan

This year there came over great store of provisions, both out of England and Ireland, and but few passengers, (and those orought very little money,) which was occasioned by the store of money and quick markets, which the merchants found here the two or three years before, so as now all our money was drained from us, and cattle and all commodities grew very cheap, which enforced us at the next general court, in the 8th month, to make an order, that corn should pass in payments of new debts; Indian at 4s. the bushel; rye at 5s., and wheat at 6s.; and that, upon all executions for former debts, the creditor might take what goods he pleased, (or, if he had no goods, then his lands,) to be appraised by three men, one chosen by the creditor, one by the debtor, and the third by the marshal.

One of the ships, which came this summer, struck upon a whale with a full gale, which put the ship a stays; the whale struck the ship on her bow, with her tail a little above water, and brake the planks and six timbers and a beam, and staved two hogsheads of vinegar.

(7.) (*September.*)] There was some rumor of the Indians plotting mischief against the English; and, to strengthen this, the governor of Plymouth, a Mr. Bradford, wrote a letter to this effect: that he was informed, (and did believe it,) that the Naragansett sachem, Miantunnomoh, had sent a great present of wampum to the Mohawks, to aid him against the English, and that it was accepted, and aid promised. The like news was brought by Mr. Haynes, one of the magistrates upon Connecticut, and many words were taken up from some Indians among us, which our fears interpreted the same way.[1] The governor and council gave no great credit to these suspicions, yet they thought fit to take order, strengthening the watches in all towns, and causing them to be ordered by the military officers, (being before committed to the constables' charge,)

[1] Rumors thus accredited as to danger from this powerful tribe were certainly disquieting. We shall have occasion to note certain very harsh measures taken by the colonists, who felt they were environed by great perils.

and withal sent Capt. Jenyson with three men and an Indian interpreter to the Naragansett sachems, to know the truth of their intentions, etc. They were verv kindly entertained, but they would not speak with him in the presence of his Indian interpreter, because he was a Pequod, and a servant, and their enemy, and might discover their councils. So he made use of another interpreter. They denied all confederations with the Mohawks, etc., and professed their purpose to continue friendship with us, and not to use any hostility towards the English, except they began, etc., and promised to come to Boston (as he was desired) if Mr. Williams might come with him, (but that we had denied). Only Janemoh, the Niantick sachem, carried himself proudly, and refused to come to us, or to yield to any thing, only he said he would not harm us, except we invaded him.

The governor and council took from Cutshamekin the powder and shot they had bought of our people, with promise to pay for it, or restore it, etc.

This summer there came divers godly men, as they pretended, from Christophers with their families. The occasion was, one Mr. Collins, a young scholar, full of zeal, etc., preaching in the island, it pleased God, divers were wrought upon by him, but he and they being persecuted, and their liberty restrained, they came away, and brought all their substance in tobacco, which came at so dead a market, as they could not get above two pence the pound (the freight came to one penny, observe,) nor could sell half at that rate. They arrived first at Quilipiack, (since called New Haven,) and so dispersed themselves here and there, and some returned to Ireland. Mr. Collins and one Mr. Hales (a young man very well conceited of himself and censorious of others) went to Aquiday, and so soon as Hales came acquainted with Mrs. Hutchinson, he was taken by her and became her disciple. Mr. Collins was entertained at Hartford to teach a school, and hearing of Mrs. Hutchinson's opinions, etc., wrote to Mr. Hales to beware of her.

Mr. Hales returned him answer, and the next morning he went away, without taking leave, and being come to Mrs. Hutchinson, he was also taken with her heresies, and in great admiration of her, so as these, and other the like before, when she dwelt in Boston, gave cause of suspicion of witchcraft, for it was certainly known, that Hawkins's wife (who continued with her, and was her bosom friend) had much familiarity with the devil in England, when she dwelt at St. Ives, where divers ministers and others resorted to her and found it true.

This summer here arrived one Mr. Thomas Gorge,[1] a young gentleman of the inns of court, a kinsman of Sir Ferdinand Gorge, and sent by him with commission for the government of his province of Somersetshire. He was sober and well disposed; he staid a few days at Boston, and was very careful to take advice of our magistrates how to manage his affairs, etc. When he came to Acomenticus, now called Bristol,[2] he found all out of order, for Mr. Burdett ruled all, and had let loose the reigns of liberty to his lusts, that he grew very notorious for his pride and adultery; and the neighbors now finding Mr. Gorge well inclined to reform things, they complained of him, and produced such foul matters against him, as he was laid hold on, and bound to appear at their court at Sacoe: but he dealt so with some other of the commissioners, that, when the court came, Mr. Vines and two more stood for him, but Mr. Gorge having the greater party on his side, and the jury finding him guilty of adultery and other crimes, with much labor and difficulty he was fined (under £30). He appealed unto England, but Mr. Gorge would not admit his appeal, but seized some of his cattle, etc. Upon this Mr. Burdett went

[1] Thomas Gorges, in spite of his connection with Sir Ferdinando, preserved friendly relations with his Puritan neighbors, and is remembered with honor by the historians of Maine. Richard Vines, too, a cavalier, seems to have been a respectable man. Perhaps the different bearing of the royalist agents to the Puritans may have been due in part to a recognition by them of the fact that the King was powerfully opposed, and that Massachusetts would have in Parliament an ally to be reckoned with.

[2] At present York, Maine.

into England, but when he came there he found the state so
changed, as his hopes were frustrated, and he, after taking part
with the cavaliers, was committed to prison.

One Baker, master's mate of the ship [blank,] being in drink,
used some reproachful words of the queen. The governor
and council were much in doubt what to do with him, but
having considered that he was distempered and sorry for
it, etc., and being a stranger and a chief officer in the ship, and
many ships were then in harbor, they thought it not fit to inflict
corporal punishment upon him, but after he had been two or
three days in prison, he was set an hour at the whipping post
with a paper on his head, and so dismissed.

Mo. 5. (*July*) 27.] Being the second day of the week, the
*Mary Rose*, a ship of Bristol, of about 200 tons, her master one
Capt. [blank,] lying before Charlton, was blown in pieces with
her own powder, being 21 barrels; wherein the judgment of
God appeared, for the master and company were many of them
profane scoffers at us, and at the ordinances of religion here;
so as, our churches keeping a fast for our native country, etc.,
they kept aboard, at their common service, when all the rest
of the masters came to our assemblies; likewise the Lord's day
following; and a friend of his going aboard next day and asking
him, why he came not on shore to our meetings, his answer
was, that he had a family of his own, etc., and they had as good
service aboard as we had on shore. Within two hours after
this (being about dinner time) the powder took fire (no man
knows how) and blew all up, viz. the captain and nine or ten of
his men, and some four or five strangers. There was a special
providence that there were no more, for many principal men
were going aboard at that time, and some were in a boat near
the ship, and others were diverted by a sudden shower of
rain, and others by other occasions. There was one man saved,
being carried up in the scuttle, and so let fall in the same into
the water, and being taken up by the ferry boat, near dead, he
came to himself the next morning, but could not tell any thing

of the blowing up of the ship, or how he came there. The rest of the dead bodies were after found, much bruised and broken. Some goods were saved, but the whole loss was estimated at £2,000. A 20s. piece was found sticking in a chip, for there was above £300 in money in her, and 15 tons of lead, and 10 pieces of ordnance, which a year after were taken up, and the hull of the ship drawn ashore.

This judgment of God upon these scorners of his ordinances and the ways of his servants (for they spake very evil of us, because they found not so good a market for their commodities as they expected, etc.) gives occasion to mention other examples of like kind, which fell out at this and other times, by which it will appear how the Lord hath owned this work, and preserved and prospered his people here beyond ordinary ways of providence.

One Capt. Mason of London,[1] a man in favor at court, and a professed enemy to us, had a plantation at Pascataquack; which he was at great charge about, and set up a sawmill, but nothing prospered. He provided a ship, which should have been employed to have brought a general governor, or in some other design to our prejudice, but in launching of it, her back was broken. He also employed Gardiner, and Morton, and others, to prosecute against us at council table, and by a quo warranto, etc., so as Morton wrote divers letters to his friends here, insulting against us, and assuring them of our speedy ruin, etc. But the Lord still disappointed them, and frustrated all their designs. As for this Mason, he fell sick and died soon after, and in his sickness he sent for the minister, and bewailed his enmity against us, and promised, if he recovered, to be as great a friend to New England as he had formerly been an enemy.

Sir Ferdinand Gorge also had sided with our adversaries against us, but underhand, pretending by his letters and

---

[1] John Mason, of the Piscataqua, must not be confounded with John Mason of Connecticut, captain in the Pequot war.

speeches to seek our welfare; but he never prospered. He attempted great matters, and was at large expenses about his province here, but he lost all.

One Austin (a man of good estate) came with his family in the year 1638 to Quinipiack, and not finding the country as he expected, he grew discontented, saying that he could not subsist here, and thereupon made off his estate, and with his family and £1000 in his purse, he returned for England in a ship bound for Spain, against the advice of the godly there, who told him he would be taken by the Turks; and it so fell out, for in Spain he embarked himself in a great ship bound for England which carried £200,000 in money, but the ship was taken by the Turks, and Austin and his wife and family were carried to Algiers, and sold there for slaves.[1]

The Lord showed his displeasure against others, though godly, who have spoken ill of this country, and so discouraged the hearts of his people; even the lords and others of Providence having spoken too much in that kind, thinking thereby to further their own plantation. They set out a ship the last year with passengers and goods for Providence, but it was taken by the Turks. Captain Newman, the same year, having taken good prizes in their service, returning home, when he was near Dover, was taken by a Dunkirker, and all lost. Mr. Humfrey, who was now for Providence with his company, raised an ill report of this country, were here kept, in spite of all their endeavors and means to have been gone this winter, and his corn and all his hay to the value of £160 were burnt by his own

---

[1] "Here," says Savage in a foot-note, "ends the perfect text of the second venerable MS. of the author, which began in my Vol. I., p. 197 [Vol. I., p. 191, of this edition]. On the morning of the 10th November [1825], the original was destroyed by fire, and my copy, on which the labor of collation, equally faithful and pleasant, had been bestowed by me, three times, in different years, was also lost. Another copy, designed for the printers, shared the same fate, except that the few pages foregoing, having been sent to the press, were preserved. From this place to the end of the second volume of the original MS. [ post, p. 207] the boast of a pure text, with correction of the grosser errors denoted in the margin, and supplying of omissions in the former edition, must be abandoned."

servants, who made a fire in his barn, and by gunpowder, which accidentally took fire, consumed all; himself having at the court before petitioned for some supply of his want, whereupon the court gave him £250. Soon after also Providence was taken by the Spaniards, and the lords lost all their care and cost to the value of above £60,000.[1]

Mo. 7. (*September*) 3.] Captain Underhill being brought, by the blessing of God in this church's censure of excommunication, to remorse for his foul sins, obtained, by means of the elders, and others of the church of Boston, a safe conduct under the hand of the governor and one of the council to repair to the church.  He came at the time of the court of assistants, and upon the lecture day, after sermon, the pastor called him forth and declared the occasion, and then gave him leave to speak: and indeed it was a spectacle which caused many weeping eyes, though it afforded matter of much rejoicing to behold the power of the Lord Jesus in his own ordinances, when they are dispensed in his own way, holding forth the authority of his regal sceptre in the simplicity of the gospel.  He came in his worst clothes (being accustomed to take great pride in his bravery and neatness) without a band, in a foul linen cap pulled close to his eyes; and standing upon a form, he did, with many deep sighs and abundance of tears, lay open his wicked course, his adultery, his hypocrisy, his persecution of God's people here, and especially his pride (as the root of all, which caused God to give him over to his other sinful courses) and contempt of the magistrates.  He justified God and the church and the court in all that had been inflicted on him.  He declared what power Satan had of him since the casting out of the church; how his presumptuous laying hold of mercy and pardon, before God gave it, did then fail him when the terrors of God came

---

[1] So ended in disaster the scheme which had threatened the uprooting of New England, the hand of God in Winthrop's eyes being clearly visible in the misfortunes of the disaffected.  The Providence referred to is the island Providence, or Catalina, off the Nicaraguan coast.

upon him, so as he could have no rest, nor could see any issue but utter despair, which had put him divers times upon resolutions of destroying himself, had not the Lord in mercy prevented him, even when his sword was ready to have done the execution. Many fearful temptations he met with beside, and in all these his heart shut up in hardness and impenitency as the bondslave of Satan, till the Lord, after a long time and great afflictions, had broken his heart, and brought him to humble himself before him night and day with prayers and tears till his strength was wasted; and indeed he appeared as a man worn out with sorrow, and yet he could find no peace, therefore he was now come to seek it in this ordinance of God. He spake well, save that his blubbering, etc., interrupted him, and all along he discovered a broken and melting heart, and gave good exhortations to take heed of such vanities and beginnings of evil as had occasioned his fall; and in the end he earnestly and humbly besought the church to have compassion of him, and to deliver him out of the hands of Satan. So accordingly he was received into the church again; and after he came into the court (for the general court began soon after) and made confession of his sin against them, etc., and desired pardon, which the court freely granted him, so far as concerned their private judgment. But for his adultery they would not pardon that for example's sake, nor would restore him to freedom, though they released his banishment, and declared the former law against adultery to be of no force; so as there was no law now to touch his life, for the new law against adultery was made since his fact committed. He confessed also in the congregation, that though he was very familiar with that woman, and had gained her affection, etc., yet she withstood him six months against all his solicitations (which he thought no woman could have resisted) before he could overcome her chastity, but being once overcome, she was wholly at his will. And to make his peace the more sound, he went to her husband (being a cooper) and fell upon his knees before him in the presence of

some of the elders and others, and confessed the wrong he had
done him, and besought him to forgive him, which he did very
freely, and in testimony thereof he sent the captain's wife a
token.[1]

4. 5. 6.] It rained three days and nights together, and the
tides were extraordinary high.

Mo. 9 (*November*).] It is before declared how the church
of Boston sent messengers and a letter to their members at
Aquiday, and how they refused to hear them, pretending themselves to be no members, being now so far removed. Whereupon the elders and most of the church intended to have cast
them out, as refusers to hear the church; but some others desired that the church would write to them once again, which
accordingly was done, and the letter drawn by Mr. Cotton,
wherein he fully repeated all former proceedings, both of the
church and of the court, and justified both, and condemned
their errors and disturbance of the peace here, and their remonstrance, and Mr. Wheelwright's sermon, (which formerly,
among other his failings, being misled by their subtilty, etc.,
he had justified and commended,) and showed how the church
had been wronged by them.

Miantunnomoh, the sachem of Naragansett, came, and was
met at Dorchester by Captain Gibbons and a guard of twelve
musketeers, and well entertained at Roxbury by the governor;
but when we came to parley, he refused to treat with us by our
Pequod interpreter, as he had done before to Captain Jenyson,
and the governor being as resolute as he, refused to use any
other interpreter, thinking it a dishonor to us to give so much
way to them. Whereupon he came from Roxbury to Boston,
departing in a rude manner, without showing any respect or
sign of thankfulness to the governor for his entertainment,

---

[1] This curious passage, held by Savage to be one of Winthrop's "best delinea-
tions of manners," is not conclusive as to the sincerity of Underhill's repentance.
Underhill is supposed to have lived until 1672, his later career being in Connecticut,
on Long Island, and among the Dutch. He held offices of importance, and
found opportunity to increase his fame as an Indian fighter.

whereof the governor informed the general court, and would show him no countenance, nor admit him to dine at our table, as formerly he had done, till he had acknowledged his failing, etc., which he readily did, so soon as he could be made to understand it, and did speak with our committees and us by a Pequod maid who could speak English perfectly. But it was conceived by some of the court that he kept back such things as he accounted secrets of state, and that he would carry home in his breast, as an injury, the strict terms he was put to both in this, and the satisfaction he was urged to for not observing our custom in matter of manners, for he told us that when our men came to him, they were permitted to use their own fashions, and so he expected the same liberty with us. So as he departed and nothing agreed, only the former articles of peace were read to him and allowed by him with this addition, that if any of his men did set traps in our jurisdiction, etc., they should be liable to satisfy all damages, etc.

Mo. 8 (*October*).] The elders had moved at a general court before, that the distinction between the two jurisdictions might be set down, that the churches might know their power, and the civil magistrate his. The same had been moved by the magistrates formerly, and now at this court they presented a writing to that effect, to be considered by the court, wherein they declared that the civil magistrate should not proceed against a church member before the church had dealt with him, with some other restraints which the court did not allow of. So the matter was referred to further consideration, and it appeared, indeed, that divers of the elders did not agree in those points.[1]

At this court Mr. Ezekiel Rogers, pastor of the church in Rowley, being not kindly dealt with, nor justly, as he alleged,

[1] The passage illustrates the growth of ecclesiastical power at the expense of the civil authority, the theocratic feature of the polity becoming now pronounced.

concerning the limits of their town, moved for further enlargement for taking in a neck of land upon Merrimack near Cochitawit,[1] for which end they desired their line might run square
from Ipswich line. This line was granted, and he said it should
satisfy, but within an hour after it was discovered that he was
mistaken, and that such a line would not reach the neck,
whereupon he came again and confessed his mistake, and still
demanded the neck. The court was very doubtful what to do
in it, having formerly granted a plantation at Cochitawit, and
did not yield his request. Whereupon he pleaded justice, upon
some promises of large accommodations, etc., when we desired
his sitting down with us, and grew into some passion, so as in
departing from the court, he said he would acquaint the elders
with it. This behavior, being menacing, as it was taken,
gave just cause of offence to the court, so as he was sent for,
not by the officer, but by one of Rowley deputies. Before he
came, he wrote to the governor, wherein he confessed his passionate distemper, declared his meaning in those offensive
speeches, as that his meaning was that he would propound the
case to the elders for advice only about the equity of it, which
he still defended. This would not be accepted, but the court
would have him appear and answer: only they left him to take
his own time, so the next day he came, not accompanied with
any other of the elders, though many were then in town, and
did freely and humbly blame himself for his passionate distemper; and the court knowing that he would not yield from the
justice of his cause, (as he apprehended it,) they would not put
him upon any temptation, but accepted his satisfaction, and
freely granted what he formerly desired.

A commission had formerly been granted to Mr. Endecott
and Mr. Stoughton for joining with the commissioners of
Plymouth, who met the second time at Scituate, and there came
to a full agreement, which was certified this court, and recorded
to this effect: That the bounds should be that branch of

[1] Later Andover.

Conyhassett creek nearest to Scituate, with 60 acres of marsh in the south side.[1] The scarcity of money made a great change in all commerce. Merchants would sell no wares but for ready money, men could not pay their debts though they had enough, prices of lands and cattle fell soon to the one half and less, yea to a third, and after one fourth part.

Mo. 10. (*December*) 9.] The church of Watertown ordained Mr. Knolles,[2] a godly man and a prime scholar, pastor, and so they had now two pastors and no teacher, differing from the practice of the other churches, as also they did in their privacy, not giving notice thereof to the neighboring churches, nor to the magistrates, as the common practice was.

At the court of assistants one Hugh Bewett was banished for holding publicly and maintaining that he was free from original sin and from actual also for half a year before, and that all true christians after [*blank*] are enabled to live without committing actual sin.

15.] A pinnace called the *Coach*, being in her voyage to New Haven (late Quinipiack) between Salem and Cape Cod, sprang a leak, so as in the morning they found her hold half filled with water; whereupon the seamen and passengers betook themselves to their skiff, being a very small one, and the wind then growing very high at S. W.   Only one Jackson, a godly man and an experienced seaman, would not leave the vessel before he had tried the utmost, so getting them in again, and laying the bark upon the contrary side, they fell to getting out the water, which, it pleased God, they overcame, and having a fine fresh gale, they got safe back to Salem.

[1] The full text of the agreement is given by Bradford, *History of Plymouth Plantation*, p. 351, of the edition in this series.
[2] Rev. John Knowles, not to be confounded with Hanserd Knollys before mentioned. His ordination after this fashion, as colleague of the respected Phillips, is an extreme assertion of the spirit of Congregationalism; in this we may see the hand of Phillips, whose radical temper was manifest from the first. Savage finds here a confirmation of his belief that no essential difference separated the offices of preacher and pastor.

Mr. Pelham's house in Cambridge took fire in the dead of the night by the chimney. A neighbor's wife hearing some noise among her hens, persuaded her husband to arise, which, being very cold, he was loth to do, yet through her great importunity he did, and so espied the fire, and came running in his shirt, and had much to do to awake any body, but he got them up at last, and so saved all. The fire being ready to lay hold upon the stairs, they had all been burnt in their chambers, if God had not by his special providence sent help at that very instant.

About this time a pinnace called the *Make Shift*, (so called because she was built of the wreck of a greater vessel at the Isle of Sable, and by that means the men saved,) being on a voyage to the southward, was cast away upon a ledge of rocks near Long Island, the goods were all lost, but the men were saved. No winter but some vessels have been cast away in that voyage.

About this time there fell out a thing worthy of observation. Mr. Winthrop the younger, one of the magistrates, having many books in a chamber where there was corn of divers sorts, had among them one wherein the Greek testament, the psalms and the common prayer were bound together. He found the common prayer eaten with mice, every leaf of it, and not any of the two other touched, nor any other of his books, though there were above a thousand.[1]

Quere, of the child at Cambridge killed by a cat.

Mo. 8 (*October*).] We received a letter at the general court from the magistrates of Connecticut and New Haven and of Aquiday, wherein they declared their dislike of such as would have the Indians rooted out, as being of the cursed race of Ham,

[1] The mice, like the men, in New England, Winthrop thinks were characterized by most aggressive dissent; but Savage suggests that the mice, perhaps, "not liking psalmody and not understanding Greek, took their food from another part of the volume. . . . If the cat [mentioned in the next line of text] had been in Winthrop's library, she might have prevented the stigma on the Common Prayer."

and their desire of our mutual accord in seeking to gain them by justice and kindness, and withal to watch over them to prevent any danger by them, etc. We returned answer of our consent with them in all things propounded, only we refused to include those of Aquiday in our answer, or to have any treaty with them.

Mo. 10 (*December*).] About the end of this month, a fishing ship arrived at Isle of Shoals, and another soon after, and there came no more this season for fishing. They brought us news of the Scots entering into England, and the calling of a parliament, and the hope of a thorough reformation, etc., whereupon some among us began to think of returning back to England. Others despairing of any more supply from thence, and yet not knowing how to live there, if they should return, bent their minds wholly to removal to the south parts, supposing they should find better means of subsistence there, and for this end put off their estates here at very low rates. These things, together with the scarcity of money, caused a sudden and very great abatement of the prices of all our own commodities. Corn (Indian) was sold ordinarily at three shillings the bushel, a good cow at seven or eight pounds, and some at £5,—and other things answerable (see the order of court in 8ber. (*October*) about these things) whereby it came to pass that men could not pay their debts, for no money nor beaver were to be had, and he who last year, or but three months before, was worth £1000, could not now, if he should sell his whole estate, raise £200, whereby God taught us the vanity of all outward things, etc.[1]

[1] The Parliament whose opening is referred to in this paragraph was the famous Long Parliament; the convening of this body was an event epoch-making for New as well as Old England. Since persecution no longer came from court and church, the main incentive to emigration was removed. The additions to the colony were henceforth not numerous: the body of twenty-thousand that were already established, a compact, homogeneous population, during the coming century and a half multiplied from within itself almost undisturbed. These are the people who have given character to the six north-eastern states of America, and influenced so widely the character and fortunes of our country in general. See Palfrey, *History of New England*, preface. Though king and bishop ceased

One Taylor, of Linne, having a milch cow in the ship as he came over, sold the milk to the passengers for 2d the quart, and being after at a sermon wherein oppression was complained of, etc., he fell distracted. Quere, of the price, for 2d the quart was not dear at sea.

This evil was very notorious among all sorts of people, it being the common rule that most men walked by in all their commerce, to buy as cheap as they could, and to sell as dear.

A great ship called the *Charles*, of above 300 tons, brought passengers hither this year. The master was a plain, quiet man, but his company were very wicked, and did wrong the passengers much, and being at Pascataquack to take in clapboards with another ship wherein Mr. Peter by occasion preached one Lord's day, the company of the *Charles* did use all the means they could to disturb the exercise, by hooting and hollooing, but in their return they were set upon by the Turks and divers of them killed.

A wicked fellow, given up to bestiality, fearing to be taken by the hand of justice, fled to Long Island, and there was drowned. He had confessed to some, that he was so given up to that abomination, that he never saw any beast go before him but he lusted after it.

Mr. Nathaniel Eaton, of whom mention is made before, being come to Virginia, took upon him to be a minister, but was given up of God to extreme pride and sensuality, being usually

to trouble, the colonies were still beset by embarrassments from over sea. The victory of Parliament at length was a victory which they welcomed; but the Presbyterians who now came into power were no friends to Congregationalism. In 1648, the Independents triumphed over the Presbyterians: these indeed the colonists might feel were brothers of their own household. They had followed the "New England way" in setting up the Commonwealth. See Thornton, *Historical Relation of New England to the English Commonwealth*; also Borgeaud, *The Rise of Modern Democracy in Old and New England*. But Independency during the Commonwealth took on through Roger Williams, Vane, Cromwell and the rest, a tolerant temper not congenial to John Endicott and Nathaniel Ward, nor even to the more moderate minds of Winthrop and Cotton. Now, for twenty years, New England wrought out its own problems, but at last, at the Restoration, the hand of the Stuart was again felt.

drunken, as the custom is there.[1] He sent for his wife and children. Her friends here persuaded her to stay awhile, but she went notwithstanding, and the vessel was never heard of after.

[1] Virginia stands low in Winthrop's esteem; though, as Savage suggests, the charge of drunkenness is to be referred only to the clergy. The passage may be another illustration of the depth of the estrangement from the Church of England. The previous passage respecting Eaton is in Vol. I., pp. 310–315.

## 1641

Mo. 12. (*February*) 2.] The church of Dorchester being furnished with a very godly and able pastor, one Mr. Mather, and having invited to them one Mr. Burr, who had been a minister in England, and of very good report there for piety and learning, with intent to call him also to office, after he was received a member in their church, and had given good proofs of his gifts and godliness to the satisfaction of the church, they gave him a call to office, which he deferring to accept, in the mean time he delivered some points savoring of familism, wherein the church desiring satisfaction, and he not so free to give it as was meet, it was agreed that Mr. Mather and he should confer together, and so the church should be informed wherein the difference lay. Accordingly Mr. Burr wrote his judgment in the points in difference, in such manner and terms as from some of his propositions there could no other be gathered but that he was erroneous; but this was again so qualified in other parts as might admit of a charitable construction. Mr. Mather reports to the church the errors which might be collected, without mentioning the qualification, or acquainting Mr. Burr with it before. When this was published, Mr. Burr disclaimed the errors, and Mr. Mather maintained them from his writings; whereupon the church was divided, some joining with the one, and some with the other, so as it grew to some heat and alienation, and many days were spent for reconciliation, but all in vain. In the end they agreed to call in help from other churches, so this day there was a meeting at Dorchester of the governor and another of the magistrates, and about ten of the elders of the neighboring churches, wherein four days were spent in opening the cause, and such offences as had fallen out in the prosecution; and in conclusion the magistrates and

22

elders declared their judgment and advice in the case to this effect; that both sides had cause to be humbled for their failings, more particularly Mr. Burr for his doubtful and unsafe expressions, and backwardness to give clear satisfaction, etc., and Mr. Mather for his inconsideration, both in not acquainting Mr. Burr with his collections before he had published them to the church, and in not certifying the qualifications of those errors which were in his writings: for which they were advised to set a day apart for reconciliation. Upon this Mr. Mather and Mr. Burr took the blame of their failings upon themselves, and freely submitted to the judgment and advice given, to which the rest of the church yielded a silent assent, and God was much glorified in the close thereof; and Mr. Burr did again fully renounce those erroneous opinions of which he had been suspected, confessing that he was in the dark about these points, till God, by occasion of this agitation, had cleared them to him, which he did with much meekness and many tears.[1]

The church of Boston were necessitated to build a new meeting house. and a great difference arose about the place of situation, which had much troubled other churches on the like occasion, but after some debate it was referred to a committee, and was quietly determined. It cost about £1000, which was raised out of the weekly voluntary contribution without any noise or complaint, when in some other churches which did it by way of rates, there was much difficulty and compulsion by levies to raise a far less sum.

The general fear of want of foreign commodities, now our money was gone, and that things were like to go well in England, set us on work to provide shipping of our own, for which end Mr. Peter,[2] being a man of a very public spirit and singular activity for all occasions, procured some to join for building a ship at Salem of 300 tons, and the inhabitants of Boston, stirred

[1] Burr, of good education and ability, gave promise of eminence, but died the year following this.
[2] Rev. Hugh Peter.

up by his example, set upon the building another at Boston of 150 tons. The work was hard to accomplish for want of money, etc., but our shipwrights were content to take such pay as the country could make. The shipwright at Salem, through want of care of his tackle, etc., occasioned the death of one Baker, who was desired with five or six more to help hale up a piece of timber, which, the rope breaking, fell down upon them. The rest by special providence were saved. This Baker, going forth in the morning very well, after he had prayed, told his wife he should see her no more, though he could not forsee any danger towards him.

The court having found by experience, that it would not avail by any law to redress the excessive rates of laborers' and workmen's wages, etc. (for being restrained, they would either remove to other places where they might have more, or else being able to live by planting and other employments of their own, they would not be hired at all,) it was therefore referred to the several towns to set down rates among themselves. This took better effect, so that in a voluntary way, by the counsel and persuasion of the elders, and example of some who led the way, they were brought to more moderation than they could be by compulsion. But it held not long.

Upon the great liberty which the king had left the parliament to in England, some of our friends there wrote to us advice to send over some to solicit for us in the parliament, giving us hope that we might obtain much, etc. But consulting about it, we declined the motion for this consideration, that if we should put ourselves under the protection of the parliament, we must then be subject to all such laws as they should make, or at least such as they might impose upon us; in which course though they should intend our good, yet it might prove very prejudicial to us.[1] But upon this occasion the court of assist-

[1] Jonathan Trumbull, revolutionary governor of Connecticut, noted this passage as characterized by the same independence of Parliament, that marked the men of his own time.

ants being assembled, and advising with some of the elders
about some course to serve the providence of God, in making
use of present opportunity of a ship of our own being ready
bound for England, it was thought fit to send some chosen men
in her with commission to negotiate for us, as occasion should
be offered, both in furthering the work of reformation of the
churches there which was now like to be attempted, and to
satisfy our countrymen of the true cause why our engagements
there have not been satisfied this year, as they were wont to be
in all former time since we were here planted; and also to seek
out some way, by procuring cotton from the West Indies, or
other means that might be lawful, and not dishonorable to the
gospel for our present supply of clothing, etc., for the country
was like to afford enough for food, etc. The persons designed
hereto were Mr. Peter, pastor of the church of Salem,[1] Mr.
Welde, the pastor of the church of Roxbury, and Mr. Hibbins
of Boston. For this end the governor and near all the rest of
the magistrates and some of the elders wrote a letter to the
church of Salem, acquainting them with our intentions, and
desiring them to spare their pastor for that service. The
governor also moved the church of Roxbury for Mr. Welde,
whom, after some time of consideration, they freely yielded.
But when it was propounded to the church of Salem, Mr.
Endecott, being a member thereof, and having formerly opposed it, did now again the like in the church. Some reasons
were there alleged, as that officers should not be taken from their
churches for civil occasions, that the voyage would be long and
dangerous, that it would be reported that we were in such want
as we had sent to England to beg relief, which would be very
dishonorable to religion, and that we ought to trust God who
had never failed us hitherto, etc. But the main reason, indeed,
which was privately intimated, was their fear lest he should be

[1] Evidences abound of the great usefulness of Hugh Peter, who figures less
in the dreary controversies than as the promoter of works of practical advantage.
The reluctance of Salem to part with him can easily be understood.

kept there, or diverted to the West Indies, for Mr. Humfrey intended to go with him, who was already engaged that way by the lord Say, etc., and therefore it was feared he should fall under strong temptations that way, being once in England; and Mr. Humfrey discovered his intentions the more by falling foul upon Mr. Endecott in the open assembly at Salem for opposing this motion, and with that bitterness as gave great offence, and was like to have grown to a professed breach between them, but being both godly, and hearkening to seasonable counsel they were soon reconciled, upon a free and public acknowledgment of such failings as had passed. But the church, not willing to let their pastor go, nor yet to give a plain denial to the magistrates' request, wrote an answer by way of excuse, tendering some reasons of their unsatisfiedness about his going, etc. The agitation of this business was soon about the country, whereby we perceived there would be sinister interpretations made of it, and the ship being suddenly to depart, we gave it over for that season.

Mo. 2. (*April*) 13.] A negro maid, servant to Mr. Stoughton of Dorchester, being well approved by divers years' experience, for sound knowledge and true godliness, was received into the church and baptized.

Some agitation fell out between us and Plymouth about Seacunk. Some of our people finding it fit for plantations, and thinking it out of our patent, which Plymouth men understanding, forbad them, and sent to us to signify that it was within their grant, and that we would therefore forbid ours to proceed. But the planters having acquainted us with their title, and offering to yield it to our jurisdiction, and assuring us that it could not be in the Plymouth patent, we made answer to Plymouth accordingly, and encouraged our neighbors to go on, so as divers letters passing between us, and they sending some to take possession for them, at length we sent some to Plymouth to see their patent, who bringing us a copy of so much as concerned the thing in question, though we were not fully satisfied thereby, yet not being willing to strive for land, we sat still.

There fell out much trouble about this time at Pascataquack. Mr. Knolles had gathered a church of such as he could get, men very raw for the most part, etc. Afterwards there came amongst them one Mr. Larkham, who had been a minister at Northam near Barnstable in England, a man not savoring the right way of church discipline, but being a man of good parts and wealthy, the people were soon taken with him, and the greater part were forward to cast off Mr. Knolles their pastor and to choose him, for they were not willing nor able to maintain two officers, so Mr. Knolles gave place to him, and he being thus chosen, did soon discover himself. He received into the church all that offered themselves, though men notoriously scandalous and ignorant, so they would promise amendment, and fell into contention with the people, and would take upon him to rule all, even the magistrates (such as they were;) so as there soon grew sharp contention between him and Mr. Knolles, to whom the more religious still adhered, whereupon they were divided into two churches. Mr. Knolles and his company excommunicated Mr. Larkham, and he again laid violent hands upon Mr. Knolles. In this heat it began to grow to a tumult, some of their magistrates joined with Mr. Larkham and assembled a company to fetch Capt. Underhill (another of their magistrates and their captain) to their court, and he also gathered some of the neighbors to defend himself, and to see the peace kept; so they marched forth towards Mr. Larkham's, one carrying a Bible upon a staff for an ensign, and Mr. Knolles with them armed with a pistol. When Mr. Larkham and his company saw them thus provided, they proceeded no further, but sent to Mr. Williams, who was governor of those in the lower part of the river, who came up with a company of armed men and beset Mr. Knolles' house, where Capt. Underhill then was, and there they kept a guard upon them night and day, and in the mean time they called a court, and Mr. Williams sitting as judge, they found Capt. Underhill and his company guilty of a riot, and set great fines upon them, and ordered him and some others to depart the plantation. The cause of this eager prosecution of Capt. Underhill was, because he had procured a good part of the inhabitants there to offer themselves again to the government of the Massachusetts, who being thus prosecuted, they sent a petition to us for aid.[1]

The governor and council considered of their petition,and gave commission to Mr. Bradstreet, one of our magistrates, Mr. Peter and Mr. Dalton, two of our elders, to go thither and to endeavor to reconcile them, and if they could not effect that, then to inquire how things stood, and to certify us, etc.   They went accordingly, and finding both sides to be in fault, at length they brought matters to a peaceable end.   Mr. Larkham was released of his excommunication and Capt. Underhill and the rest from their censures, and by occasion of these agitations Mr. Knolles was discovered to be an unclean person, and to have solicited the chastity of two maids, his servants, and to have used filthy dalliance with them, which he acknowledged before the church there, and so was dismissed, and removed from Pascataquack.   This sin of his was the more notorious, because the fact, which was first discovered, was the same night after he had been exhorting the people by reasons and from scripture, to proceed against Capt, Underhill for his adultery.   And it is very observable how God gave up these two, and some others who had held with Mrs. Hutchinson, in crying down all evidence from sanctification, etc., to fall into these unclean courses, whereby themselves and their erroneous opinions were laid open to the world.

Mr. Peter and Mr. Dalton, with one of Acomenticus, went

[1] Knollys, who in this small religious war bore as ensign a Bible upon a pole, was Hanserd Knollys, several times mentioned heretofore, and later conspicuous in England.  The reprobate and combative Underhill appears again, while Francis Williams had been appointed by Mason and Gorges as governor at Portsmouth and Dover.  Winthrop's portrayal of dissenters from the Massachusetts orthodoxy must be taken with some abatement.

from Pascataquack, with Mr. John Ward, who was to be entertained there for their minister; and though it be but six miles, yet they lost their way, and wandered two days and one night without food or fire, in the snow and wet. But God heard their prayers, wherein they earnestly pressed him for the honor of his great name, and when they were even quite spent, he brought them to the seaside, near the place they were to go to, blessed forever be his name.

Not long before a godly maid of the church of Linne, going in a deep snow from Meadford homeward, was lost, and some of her clothes found after among the rocks.

One John Baker, a member of the church of Boston, removing from thence to Newbury for enlargement of his outward accommodation, being grown wealthy from nothing, grew there very disordered, fell into drunkenness and such violent contention with another brother, maintaining the same by lying, and other evil courses, that the magistrates sent to have him apprehended. But he rescued himself out of the officer's hands and removed to Acomenticus, where he continued near two years, and now at this time he came to Boston, and humbled himself before the church, confessing all his wickedness, with many tears, and showing how he had been followed with Satan, and how he had labored to pacify his conscience by secret confessions to God, etc., but could have no peace; yet could not bring his heart to return and make public acknowledgment, until the hand of God fell upon one Swain his neighbor, who fell into despair, and would often utter dreadful speeches against himself, and cry out that he was all on fire under the wrath of God, but would never discover any other heinous sin, but that having gotten about £40 by his labor, he went into England and there spent it in wicked company, and so continued, and after a small time hanged himself. This Baker coming in, and seeing him thus dead, was so struck with it as he could have no rest, till he came and made his peace with the church and court. Upon his confession, the church was doubtful whether they ought not to cast him out, his offences being so scandalous, notwithstanding they were well persuaded of the truth of his repentance; but the judgment of the church was, that, seeing he had excommunicated himself by deserting the church, and Christ had ratified it by giving him up to Satan, whereby the ordinance had had its proper effect, therefore he ought now to be received and pardoned, whereto the church agreed. Yet this man fell into gross distempers soon after.

Mr. Cotton out of that in Revelations 15. none could enter into the temple until, etc., delivered, that neither Jews nor any more of the Gentiles should be called until Antichrist were destroyed, viz. to a church estate, though here and there a proselyte.

Upon the Lord's day at Concord two children were left at home alone, one lying in a cradle, the other having burned a cloth, and fearing its mother should see it, thrust it into a hay stack by the door (the fire not being quite out) whereby the hay and house were burned and the child in the cradle before they came from the meeting. About the same time two houses were burned at Sudbury.

By occasion of these fires I may add another of a different kind, but of much observation. A godly woman of the church of Boston, dwelling sometimes in London, brought with her a parcel of very fine linen of great value, which she set her heart too much upon, and had been at charge to have it all newly washed, and curiously folded and pressed, and so left it in press in her parlor over night. She had a negro maid went into the room very late, and let fall some snuff of the candle upon the linen, so as by the morning all the linen was burned to tinder, and the boards underneath, and some stools and a part of the wainscot burned, and never perceived by any in the house, though some lodged in the chamber over head, and no ceiling between. But it pleased God that the loss of this linen did her much good, both in taking off her heart from worldly comforts, and in preparing her for a far greater affliction by the untimely death of her husband, who was slain not long after at Isle of Providence.

Mo. 4. (*June*) 2.] The court of elections, Richard Belling-ham, Esq., chosen governor. See more a few leaves after.

This year the two ships were finished, one at Salem of 300 tons, and another at Boston of 160 tons.

The parliament of England setting upon a general reforma-tion both of church and state, the Earl of Strafford being be-headed, and the archbishop[1] (our great enemy) and many others of the great officers and judges, bishops and others, imprisoned and called to account, this caused all men to stay in England in expectation of a new world, so as few coming to us, all foreign commodities grew scarce, and our own of no price. Corn would buy nothing: a cow which cost last year £20 might now be bought for 4 or £5, etc., and many gone out of the country, so as no man could pay his debts, nor the merchants make return into England for their commodities, which occasioned many there to speak evil of us. These straits set our people on work to provide fish, clapboards, plank, etc., and to sow hemp and flax (which prospered very well) and to look out to the West Indies for a trade for cotton. The general court also made orders about payment of debts, setting corn at the wonted price, and payable for all debts which should arise after a time pre-fixed. They thought fit also to send some chosen men into England, to congratulate the happy success there, and to satisfy our creditors of the true cause why we could not make so current payment now as in former years we had done, and to be ready to make use of any opportunity God should offer for the good of the country here, as also to give any advice, as it should be required, for the settling the right form of church discipline there, but with this caution, that they should not seek supply of our wants in any dishonorable way, as by begging or the like, for we were resolved to wait upon the Lord in the use of all means which were lawful and honorable. The men

[1] Laud.

chosen were Mr. Hugh Peter, pastor of the church in Salem Mr. Thos. Welde, pastor of the church in Roxbury, and Mr William Hibbins of Boston.[1] There being no ship which was to return right for England, they went to Newfoundland, in tending to get a passage from thence in the fishing fleet. They departed hence the 3d of the 6th month, and with them went one of the magistrates, Mr. John Winthrop, jun. This act of the court did not satisfy all the elders, and many others disliked it, supposing that it would be conceived we had sent them on begging; and the church of Salem was unwillingly drawn to give leave to their pastor to go, for the court was not minded to use their power in taking an officer from the church without their consent, but in the end they and the other churches submitted to the desire of the court. These with other passengers to the number of forty went to Newfoundland, expecting to go from thence in some fishing ships. They arrived there in 14 days, but could not go altogether, so were forced to divide themselves and go from several parts of the island, as they could get shipping. The ministers preached to the seamen, etc., at the island, who were much affected with the word taught, and entertained them with all courtesy, as we understood by letters from them which came by a fishing ship to the Isles of Shoales about the beginning of October.

21.] A young man, a tanner in Boston, going to wash himself in a creek, said, jestingly, I will go and drown myself now, which fell out accordingly; for by the slipperiness of the earth, he was carried beyond his depth, and having no skill to swim, was drowned, though company were at hand, and one in the water with him.

Letters came from the governor, etc., of Connecticut for advice about the difference between them and the Dutch. The

---

[1] Here we take farewell of Hugh Peter. Thomas Welde acted in England with the Presbyterians, becoming estranged from Independency on account of its tolerance. His connection with Winthrop's *Short Story* of the Hutchinsonian troubles has been noted before.

Dutch governor had pressed them hard for his interest in all Hartford, etc., as far as one might see from their house, alleging he had purchased so much of the Pequods, and threatened force of arms. They of the river alleged their purchase of other Indians, the true owners of the place, etc., with other arguments from our patent and that of Saybrook. We re- turned answer without determining of either side, but advising to a moderate way, as the yielding some more land to the Dutch house (for they had left them but 30 acres). But the Dutch would not be thus pacified, but prepared to send soldiers to be billeted at their house. But it pleased the Lord to disappoint their purpose, for the Indians falling out with them, killed four of their men at their fort Orange,[1] whereof three were English, who had gone to dwell among them, whereby they were forced to keep their soldiers at home to defend themselves; and Mr. Peter going for England, and being well acquainted with the chief merchants in Holland, undertook to pacify the West India company, but for want of commission from those of Hartford, the company there would not treat with him.

About this time three boys of Summer's Islands[2] stole away in an open boat or skiff, and having been eight weeks at sea, their boat was cast away upon a strand without Long Island, and themselves were saved by the Indians.

A church being gathered at Providence in the West Indies, and their pastor, Mr. Sherwood, and another minister being sent prisoners into England by one Carter, the deputy governor, the rest of the church, being but five, wrote to our churches complaining of the persecution of their magistrates and others, and desiring our prayers and help from us, which moved the churches and magistrates more willingly to further those who were already resolved and preparing for that Island. Where- upon two small vessels, each of about 30 tons, with divers families and goods, so many as they could bestow, 30 men, 5

---

[1] Now Albany.
[2] The Summer, or Somers, Islands were the Bermudas.

women, and 8 children, set sail for the Island, and touching at Christophers, they heard that a great fleet of Spanish ships was abroad, and that it was feared they had taken Providence, so as the master, Mr. Peirce, a godly man and most expert mariner, advised them to return, and offered to bear part of the loss. But they not hearkening to him, he replied, Then am I a dead man. And coming to the Island, they marvelled they saw no colors upon the fort, nor any boat coming towards them, whereupon he was counselled to drop an anchor. He liked the advice, but yet stood on into the harbor, and after a second advice, he still went on; but being come within pistol shot of one fort and hailing, and no answer made, he put his bark a stays, and being upon the deck, which was also full of passengers, women and children, and hearing one cry out, they are traversing a piece at us, he threw himself in at the door of the cuddy, and one Samuel Wakeman, a member of the church of Hartford, who was sent with goods to buy cotton, cast himself down by him, and presently a great shot took them both. Mr. Peirce[1] died within an hour; the other, having only his thighs tore, lived ten days. Mr. Peirce had read to the company that morning (as it fell in course) that in Genesis the last, Lo I die, but God will surely visit you and bring you back; out of which words he used godly exhortations to them. Then they shot from all parts about thirty great shot, besides small, and tore the sails and shrouds, but hurt not the bark, nor any person more in it. The other vessel was then a league behind, which was marvelled at, for she was the better sailer, and could fetch up the other at pleasure; but that morning they could not by any means keep company with her. After this the passengers, being ashamed to return, would have been set on shore at Cape Grace de Dios, or Florida, or Virginia, but the seamen would not, and through the wonderful providence of God they came all safe home the 3d of 7ber following. This

[1] Apparently William Peirce, earlier master of the *Lyon*, the boldest and most trusted of the sea captains who at that time frequented the New England harbors.

brought some of them to see their error, and acknowledge it in the open congregation, but others were hardened.  There was a special providence in that the ministers were sent prisoners into England before the Island was taken, for otherwise it is most probable they had been all put to the sword, because some Spaniards had been slain there a little before by the deputy governor his command, after the lieutenant had received them upon quarter, in an attempt they had made upon the Island, wherein they were repulsed with the loss of two or three hundred men.  They took it after, and gave the people quarter and sent them home.

A like providence there was, though not so safe, in that divers godly people, in their voyage to the Island the year before, were taken prisoners by the Turks, and so their lives saved, paying their ransom.

This year divers families in Linne and Ipswich having sent to view Long Island, and finding a very commodious place for plantations, but challenged by the Dutch, they treated with the Dutch governor to take it from them.   He offered them very fair terms, as that they should have the very same liberties, both civil and ecclesiastical, which they enjoyed in the Massachusetts, only liberty for appeal to the Dutch, and after ten years to pay the 10th of their corn.   The court were offended at this, and sought to stay them, not for going from us, but for strengthening the Dutch, our doubtful neighbors, and taking that from them which our king challenged and had granted a patent of, with Martha's Vineyard and other islands thereby, to the earl of Sterling, especially for binding themselves by an oath of fealty; whereupon divers of the chief being called before the general court in 8ber, and reasons laid down to dissuade them, they were convinced, and promised to desist.

This summer the merchants of Boston set out a vessel again to the Isle of Sable, with 12 men, to stay there a year.   They sent again in the 8th month, and in three weeks the vessel returned and brought home 400 pair of sea horse teeth, which were esteemed worth £300, and left all the men well, and 12 ton of oil and many skins, which they could not bring away, being put from the island in a storm.

I must here return to supply what was omitted concerning the proceedings of the last court of elections. There had been much laboring to have Mr. Bellingham chosen, and when the votes were numbered he had six more than the others; but there were divers who had not given in their votes, who now came into the court and desired their liberty, which was denied by some of the magistrates, because they had not given them in at the doors. But others thought it was an injury, yet were silent, because it concerned themselves, for the order of giving in their votes at the door was no order of court, but only direction of some of the magistrates; and without question, if any freeman tender his vote before the election be passed and published, it ought to be received.

Some of the freemen, without the consent of the magistrates or governor, had chosen Mr. Nathaniel Ward[1] to preach at this court, pretending that it was a part of their liberty. The governor (whose right indeed it is, for till the court be assembled the freemen are but private persons) would not strive about it, for though it did not belong to them, yet if they would have it, there was reason to yield it to them. Yet they had no great reason to choose him, though otherwise very able, seeing he had cast off his pastor's place at Ipswich, and was now no minister by the received determination of our churches. In his sermon he delivered many useful things, but in a moral and political discourse, grounding his propositions much upon the old Roman and Grecian governments, which sure is an error, for if religion and the word of God makes men wiser than their neighbors, and these times have the advantage of all

---

[1] Nathaniel Ward, author of the *Simple Cobler of Aggawam*, and credited with the main work in compiling the *Body of Liberties*, was the raciest and most entertaining, if the narrowest and most intolerant, of the writers and speakers of New England. Naturally, the freemen desired much to hear him, and his counsels as to political and constitutional matters made impression.

that have gone before us in experience and observation, it is probable that by all these helps, we may better frame rules of government for ourselves than to receive others upon the bare authority of the wisdom, justice, etc. of those heathen commonwealths. Among other things, he advised the people to keep all their magistrates in an equal rank, and not give more honor or power to one than to another, which is easier to advise than to prove, seeing it is against the practice of Israel (where some were rulers of thousands, and some but of tens) and of all nations known or recorded. Another advice he gave, that magistrates should not give private advice, and take knowledge of any man's cause before it came to public hearing. This was debated after in the general court, where some of the deputies moved to have it ordered. But it was opposed by some of the magistrates upon these reasons: 1. Because we must then provide lawyers to direct men in their causes. 2. The magistrates must not grant out original process, as now they do, for to what end are they betrusted with this, but that they should take notice of the cause of the action, that they might either divert the suit, if the cause be unjust, or direct it in a right course, if it be good. 3. By this occasion the magistrate hath opportunity to end many differences in a friendly way, without charge to the parties, or trouble to the court. 4. It prevents many difficulties and tediousness to the court to understand the cause aright (no advocate being allowed, and the parties being not able, for the most part, to open the cause fully and clearly, especially in public). 5. It is allowed in criminal causes, and why not in civil. 6. Whereas it is objected that such magistrate is in danger to be prejudiced, answer, if the thing be lawful and useful, it must not be laid aside for the temptations which are incident to it, for in the least duties men are exposed to great temptations.

At this court it was ordered, that the elders should be desired to agree upon a form of catechism which might be put forth in print.

Offence being taken by many of the people that the court had given Mr. Humfrey £250, the deputies moved it might be ordered, that the court should not have power to grant any benevolences; but it was considered that the court could not deprive itself of its honor, and that hereby we should lay a blemish upon the court, which might do more hurt to the country by weakening the reputation of the wisdom and faithfulness of the court in the hearts of the people, than the money saved would recompense. Therefore it was thought better to order it by way of declaration, as if it were to deter importunity of suitors in this kind, that the court would give no more benevolences till our debts were paid, and stock in the treasury, except upon foreign occasions, etc.

There arose a question in the court about the punishment of single fornication, because, by the law of God, the man was only to marry the maid, or pay a sum of money to her father; but the case falling out between two servants, they were whipped for the wrong offered to the master in abusing his house, and were not able to make him other satisfaction. The like difficulty arose about a rape, which was not death by the law of God, but because it was committed by a boy upon a child of 7 or 8 years old, he was severely whipped. Yet it may seem by the equity of the law against sodomy, that it should be death for a man to have carnal copulation with a girl so young, as there cán be no possibility of generation, for it is against nature as well as sodomy and buggery.

At this court the gentlemen, who had the two patents of Dover and Strawberry bank at Pascataquack in the name of the lords and themselves, granted all their interest of jurisdiction, etc., to our court, reserving the most of the land to themselves.[1] Whereupon a commission was granted to Mr.

[1] Lords Saye and Brooke, and their associates, gave up to Massachusetts their rights of jurisdiction under the Hilton and Squamscot patents.

Bradstreet and Mr. Simonds,[1] with two or three of Pascataquack, to call a court there and assemble the people to take
their submission, etc., but Mr. Humfrey, Mr. Peter, and Mr.
Dalton had been sent before to understand the minds of the
people, to reconcile some differences between them, and to prepare them. See more.

Mrs. Hutchinson and those of Aquiday island broached new
heresies every year. Divers of them turned professed anabaptists, and would not wear any arms, and denied all magistracy
among Christians, and maintained that there were no churches
since those founded by the apostles and evangelists, nor could
any be, nor any pastors ordained, nor seals administered but by
such, and that the church was to want these all the time she
continued in the wilderness, as yet she was. Her son Francis
and her son-in-law Mr. Collins (who was driven from Barbadoes
where he had preached a time and done some good, but so soon
as he came to her was infected with her heresies) came to Boston, and were there sent for to come before the governor and
council. But they refused to come, except they were brought;
so the officer led him, and being come (there were divers of the
elders present) he was charged with a letter he had written to
some in our jurisdiction, wherein he charged all our churches
and ministers to be antichristian, and many other reproachful
speeches, terming our king, king of Babylon, and sought to
possess the people's hearts with evil thoughts of our government
and of our churches, etc. He acknowledged the letter, and
maintained what he had written, yet sought to evade by confessing there was a true magistracy in the world, and that
Christians must be subject to it. He maintained also that
there were no gentile churches (as he termed them) since the
apostles' times, and that none now could ordain ministers, etc.
Francis Hutchinson did agree with him in some of these, but

[1] Simon Bradstreet and Samuel Symonds, younger men now coming forward
into prominent position, at a later time reached the highest positions, as governor
and deputy-governor.

not resolutely in all; but he had reviled the church of Boston (being then a member of it) calling her a strumpet.  They were both committed to prison; and it fell out that one Stoddard, being then one of the constables of Boston, was required to take Francis Hutchinson into his custody till the afternoon, and said withal to the governor, Sir, I came to observe what you did, that if you should proceed with a brother otherwise than you ought, I might deal with you in a church way.  For this insolent behavior he was committed, but being dealt with by the elders and others, he came to see his error, which was that he did conceive that the magistrate ought not to deal with a member of the church before the church had proceeded with him.  So the next Lord's day in the open assembly, he did freely and very affectionately confess his error and his contempt of authority, and being bound to appear at the next court, he did the like there to the satisfaction of all.  Yet for example's sake he was fined 20s., which though some of the magistrates would have had it much less, or rather remitted, seeing his clear repentance and satisfaction in public left no poison or danger in his example, nor had the commonwealth or any person sustained danger by it.  At the same court Mr. Collins was fined £100 and Francis Hutchinson £50, and to remain in prison till they gave security for it.  We assessed the fines the higher, partly that by occasion thereof they might be the longer kept in from doing harm, (for they were kept close prisoners,) and also because that family had put the country to so much charge in the synod and other occasions to the value of £500 at least: but after, because the winter drew on, and the prison was inconvenient, we abated them to £40 and £20.  But they seemed not willing to pay any thing.  They refused to come to the church assemblies except they were led, and so they came duly.  At last we took their own bonds for their fine, and so dismissed them.[1]

[1] From the Colony Records it appears that Collins and Francis Hutchinson were forbidden to return to the colony on pain of death.

Other troubles arose in the island by reason of one Nicholas Easton, a tanner, a man very bold, though ignorant. He using to teach at Newport, where Mr. Coddington their governor lived, maintained that man hath no power or will in himself, but as he is acted by God, and that seeing God filled all things, nothing could be or move but by him, and so he must needs be the author of sin, etc., and that a Christian is united to the essence of God. Being showed what blasphemous consequences would follow hereupon, they professed to abhor the consequences, but still defended the propositions, which discovered their ignorance, not apprehending how God could make a creature as it were in himself, and yet no part of his essence, as we see by familiar instances; the light is in the air, and in every part of it, yet it is not air, but a distinct thing from it. There joined with Nicholas Easton Mr. Coddington, Mr. Coggeshall,[1] and some others, but their minister, Mr. Clark, and Mr. Lenthall, and Mr. Harding, and some others dissented and publicly opposed, whereby it grew to such heat of contention, that it made a schism among them.

Mo. 7 (*September*).] Captain Underhill, coming to Boston, was presently apprehended by the governor's warrant to appear at the next court, and bound for his good behavior in the mean time, which was ill taken by many, seeing he did not stand presented by any man, and had been reconciled to the church and to the court, who had remitted his sentence of banishment, and showed their willingness to have pardoned him fully, but for fear of offence. And it was held by some of the magistrates, that the court, having reversed the sentence against him for former misdemeanors, had implicitly pardoned all other misdemeanors before that time, and his adultery was no more then but a misdemeanor; but to bind a man to his good behavior, when he stands reconciled to the church and commonwealth, was certainly an error, as it was also to commit such an one,

[1] All three of the men were of high repute in civil life, each serving his colony as governor.

being not presented nor accused. So easily may a magistrate be misled on the right hand by the secret whisperings of such as pretend a zeal of justice and the punishment of sin. The governor caused him to be indicted at the next court, but he was acquitted by proclamation.

Mo. 7. (*September*) 11.] It being court time, about 7 or 8 in the evening there appeared to the southward a great light, about 30 or 40 feet in length; it went very swift, and continued about a minute. It was observed by many in the bay and at Plymouth and New Haven, etc., and it seemed to all to be in the same position.

15.] A great training at Boston two days. About 1200 men were exercised in most sorts of land service; yet it was observed that there was no man drunk, though there was plenty of wine and strong beer in the town, not an oath sworn, no quarrel, nor any hurt done.

The parliament in England falling so readily to reform all public grievances, some of our people being then in London preferred a petition to the Lords' house for redress of that restraint which had been put upon ships and passengers to New England, whereupon an order was made, that we should enjoy all our liberties, etc., according to our patent, whereby our patent, which had been condemned and called in upon an erroneous judgment in a quo warranto, was now implicitly revived and confirmed. This petition was preferred without warrant from our court.

7. (*September*) 2.] A day of thanksgiving was kept in all our churches for the good success of the parliament in England.

This year men followed the fishing so well, that there was about 300,000 dry fish sent to the market.

The lords and gentlemen that had two patents at Pascata-quack, finding no means to govern the people there, nor to restrain them from spoiling their timber, etc., agreed to assign their interest to us (reserving the greatest part of the propriety cf their lands). So commissioners being sent thither, the whole

river agreed to come under our jurisdiction under two propositions. 1. If we took them in upon a voluntary submission,
then they would have liberty to choose their own magistrates,
etc. 2. If we took them in as being within the line of our
patent, they would then submit to be as Ipswich and Salem,
etc., and would have such liberties for felling timber, etc., as
they had enjoyed. etc., and so referred it to the next general
court; and to have courts there as Ipswich and Salem had.
And accordingly at the general court in the 3d month next,
they sent two deputies, who, being members of the church
there, were sworn freemen, and order made for giving the oath
to others at their own court, the like liberty to other courts for
ease of the people.[1]

Mo. 9. (*November*) 8.] Monsieur Rochett, a Rocheller and
a Protestant, came from Monsieur La Tour, planted upon St.
John's River up the great bay on this side Cape Sable. He
brought no letters with him, but only letters from Mr. Shurt of
Pemaquid, where he left his men and boat. He propounded
to us, 1. Liberty of free commerce. This was granted. 2.
Assistance against D'Aulnay of Penobscott, whom he had war
with. 3. That he might make return of goods out of England
by our merchants. In these two we excused any treaty
with him, as having no letters or commission from La Tour.
He was courteously entertained here, and after a few days
departed.[2]

9.] Query, whether the following be fit to be published.

The governor, Mr. Bellingham, was married, (I would not
mention such ordinary matters in our history, but by occasion
of some remarkable accidents). The young gentlewoman was
ready to be contracted to a friend of his, who lodged in his
house, and by his consent had proceeded so far with her, when
on the sudden the governor treated with her, and obtained her

---

[1] An important crisis both for Massachusetts and the New Hampshire settle-
ments.

[2] On Latour and D'Aulnay, see Vol. I., p. 163, note 1.

for himself. He excused it by the strength of his affection, and that she was not absolutely promised to the other gentleman. Two errors more he committed upon it. 1. That he would not have his contract published where he dwelt, contrary to an order of court. 2. That he married himself contrary to the constant practice of the country. The great inquest presented him for breach of the order of court, and at the court following, in the 4th month, the secretary called him to answer the prosecution. But he not going off the bench, as the manner was, and but few of the magistrates present, he put it off to another time, intending to speak with him privately, and with the rest of the magistrates about the case, and accordingly he told him the reason why he did not proceed, viz., being unwilling to command him publicly to go off the bench, and yet not thinking it fit he should sit as a judge, when he was by law to answer as an offender. This he took ill, and said he would not go off the bench, except he were commanded.[1]

Archibald Tomson, of Marblehead, carrying dung to his ground in a canoe upon the Lord's day, in fair weather and still water, it sunk under him in the harbor near the shores and he was never seen after.

One Knore, of Charlestown, coming down Mistick in a small boat laden with wood, was found dead in it: a good caveat for men not to go single in boats in such a season of the year, for it was very stormy weather.

9. (*November*) 12.] A great tempest of wind and rain from the S. E. all the night, as fierce as an hurricane. It continued very violent at N. W. all the day after. Divers boats and one bark were cast away in the harbor, but (which was a wonder to all) no dwelling house blown down, nor any person killed; and the day after it came to S. E. again, and continued all the night with much wind and rain; and thereupon (it being about the

[1] After such an experience of Bellingham, it is not strange that the colony should restore its chief dignity to Winthrop once more in May, 1642.

new moon) followed the highest tide which we had seen since
our arrival here.

The summer past was very cool and wet, so as much Indian
corn never ripened, though some stood till the 20th of this
month. It was observed, that people who fed upon that corn
were extraordinarily infected with worms in their bodies all the
year following, which in some was well prevented by leaving
their bread and feeding upon salt fish.

The *Charles* of Dartmouth, of 400 tons, lying at Pascataquack to take in pipe staves, was forced from her anchors in
the last tempest and driven upon the rocks; yet all her masts
were before taken down to be new masted. There rode by her
a small ship which was safe. This small ship was before despised by the men of the greater, and they would needs unrig
their ship upon the Lord's day, though they were admonished
not to do it. In the same great tempest a shallop of 3 tons
rode it out all night at the head of Cape Anne, and came in
safe after.

Mr. Stephen Batchellor, the pastor of the church at Hampton, who had suffered much at the hands of the bishops in
England, being about 80 years of age, and having a lusty
comely woman to his wife, did solicit the chastity of his neighbor's wife, who acquainted her husband therewith; whereupon
he was dealt with, but denied it, as he had told the woman he
would do, and complained to the magistrates against the woman and her husband for slandering him. The church likewise dealing with him, he stiffly denied it, but soon after, when
the Lord's supper was to be administered, he did voluntarily
confess the attempt, and that he did intend to have defiled her,
if she would have consented. The church, being moved with
his free confession and tears, silently forgave him, and communicated with him: but after, finding how scandalous it was,
they took advice of other elders, and after long debate and
much pleading and standing upon the church's forgiving and
being reconciled to him in communicating with him after

he had confessed it, they proceeded to cast him out. After this he went on in a variable course, sometimes seeming very penitent, soon after again excusing himself, and casting blame upon others, especially his fellow elder Mr. Dalton, (who indeed had not carried himself in this cause so well as became him, and was brought to see his failing, and acknowledged it to the elders of the other churches who had taken much pains about this matter). So he behaved himself to the elders when they dealt with him. He was off and on for a long time, and when he had seemed most penitent, so as the church were ready to have received him in again, he would fall back again, and as it were repent of his repentance. In this time his house and near all his substance was consumed by fire. When he had continued excommunicated near two years, and much agitation had been about the matter, and the church being divided, so as he could not be received in, at length the matter was referred to some magistrates and elders, and by their mediation he was released of his excommunication, but not received to his pastor's office. Upon occasion of this meeting for mediation, Mr. Wilson, pastor of Boston, wrote this letter to him, (the letter is worthy inserting).[1] . . .

The general court held in the 10th month past was full of uncomfortable agitations and contentions. The principal occasion (for history must tell the whole truth) was from the governor, who being a gentleman of good repute in England for wisdom and godliness, finding now that some other of the magistrates bare more sway with the people than himself, and that they were called to be of the standing council for life, and himself passed by, was so taken with an evil spirit of emulation and jealousy (through his melancholic disposition) as he set himself in an opposite frame to them in all proceedings, which did much retard all business, and was occasion of grief to many godly minds, and matter of reproach to the whole court in the mouths of others, and brought himself low in the

[1] It is not preserved. Several pages of Winthrop's text are here omitted.

eyes of those with whom formerly he had been in honor. Some instances I will give.

There fell out a case between Mr. Dudley, one of the council, and Mr. Howe, a ruling elder of the church of Watertown, about a title to a mill. The case is too long here to report, but it was so clear on Mr. Dudley's part, both in law and equity, (most of the magistrates also and deputies concurring therein,) as the elders, being desired to be present at the hearing of the case, they also consented with the judgment of the court, before the case was put to vote, and some of them humbly advised the court that it would be greatly to their dishonor, and an apparent injustice, if they should otherwise determine. Notwithstanding, he still labored to have the cause carried against Mr. Dudley, reproved some of the elders for their faithful advice, took upon him to answer all the arguments, but so weakly as many were ashamed at it, and in reading an order of court whereupon the issue of the case chiefly depended, he sought to help himself by such unworthy shifts, as interpreting some things against the very letter and common sense, wholly omitting the most material part, etc., refusing to put things to the vote that made against his purpose, etc., that all might see by what spirit he was led.

Another case fell out about Mr. Maverick of Nottles Island, who had been formerly fined £100 for giving entertainment to Mr. Owen and one Hale's wife, who had escaped out of prison, where they had been put for notorious suspicion of adultery,[1] as shall after be showed. The court upon his petition had referred it to the usual committee, who made return that their opinion was, the court might do well to remit it to £60, which he knew would please some of the council well, who had often declared their judgment that fines should be so imposed as they might upon occasion be moderated. So when

---

[1] Maverick, it must be supposed, believed the parties innocent. He was of a bold as well as humane spirit, and ready to suffer while sheltering those whom he thought persecuted.

the petition was returned to him, he takes it and alters the sum
from £60 to £80, without acquainting the court therewith,
nor would say that he had done it, when the committee informed the court of the alteration, before the secretary charged
him with it.  Then he said, he did it in jest, and when the
secretary said he had reformed it, and the court called to have
it put to the vote, he refused, and stirred up much heat and
contention about it, so in the end the court required the deputy
to put it to the vote.

Upon these and other miscarriages the deputies consulted
together, and sent up their speaker,[1] with some others, to give
him a solemn admonition, which was never done to any governor before, nor was it in their power without the magistrates
had joined.

These continual oppositions and delays, tending to the
hindrance and perverting of justice, afforded much occasion
of grief to all the magistrates, especially to Mr. Dudley, who
being a very wise and just man, and one that would not
be trodden under foot of any man, took occasion (alleging his
age, etc.) to tell the court that he was resolved to leave his
place, and therefore desired them against the next court of
elections to think of some other.  The court was much affected
with it, and entreated him, with manifestation of much affection and respect towards him, to leave off these thoughts, and
offered him any ease and liberty that his age and infirmities
might stand in need of, but he continued resolute.  Thereupon
the governor also made a speech, as if he desired to leave his
place of magistracy also, but he was fain to make his own
answer, for no man desired him to keep, or to consider better
of it.[2]

This session continued three weeks, and established 100

[1] At this period, magistrates and deputies sat together in the General Court,
the governor or deputy-governor presiding: the division into two bodies had not
yet taken place.  Savage understands by "speaker" here a temporary spokes-
man.

[2] Bellingham's unpopularity was plainly well-deserved.

laws, which were called the *Body of Liberties*.[1] They had been composed by Mr. Nathaniel Ward, (sometime pastor of the church of Ipswich: he had been a minister in England, and formerly a student and practiser in the course of the common law,) and had been revised and altered by the court, and sent forth into every town to be further considered of, and now again in this court, they were revised, amended, and presented, and so established for three years, by that experience to have them fully amended and established to be perpetual.

At this session Mr. Hathorn, one of the deputies, and usually one of their speakers, made a motion to some other of the deputies of leaving out two of their ancientest magistrates, because they were grown poor, and spake reproachfully of them under that motion. This coming to Mr. Cotton his knowledge, he took occasion from his text, the next lecture day, to confute, and sharply (in his mild manner) to reprove such miscarriage, which he termed a slighting or dishonoring of parents, and told the country, that such as were decayed in their estates by attending the service of the country ought to be maintained by the country, and not set aside for their poverty, being otherwise so well gifted, and approved by long experience to be faithful. This public reproof gave such a check to the former motion as it was never revived after. Yet by what followed it appeared, that the fire, from which it brake out, was only raked up, not quenched, as will be showed anon.

Mr. Hathorn[2] and some others were very earnest to have some certain penalty set upon lying, swearing, etc., which the deputy and some other of the magistrates opposed, (not dislik-

[1] For the *Body of Liberties*, prefaced by a learned and copious introduction by Francis C. Gray, see *Collections of Massachusetts Historical Society*, third series, VIII. 191; also Whitmore, *The Colonial Laws of Massachusetts* (Boston, 1889); *Old South Leaflets*, No. 164; and *American History Leaflets*, No. 25.

[2] William Hathorne, or Hawthorne, a leader in Salem till near the end of the century, was first speaker of the deputies, after the separation of the General Court into two bodies, presently to be described. He was the ancestor of Nathaniel Hawthorne. The deputy-governor mentioned was John Endicott.

ing to have laws made against these or any other offences, but in respect of the certain punishment,) whereupon Mr. Hathorn charged him with seeking to have the government arbitrary, etc., and the matter grew to some heat, for the deputy was a wise and a stout gentleman, and knew Mr. Hathorn his neighbor well, but the strife soon fell, and there was no more spoken of it that court. Yet this gave occasion to some of the magistrates to prepare some arguments against the course intended, of bringing all punishments to a certainty. The scope of these reasons was to make good this proposition, viz. All punishments, except such as are made certain in the law of God, or are not subject to variation by merit of circumstances, ought to be left arbitrary to the wisdom of the judges.

Reason 1. God hath left a pattern hereof in his word, where so few penalties are prescribed, and so many referred to the judges; and God himself varieth the punishments of the same offences, as the offences vary in their circumstances; as in manslaughter, in the case of a riotous son proving incorrigible, in the same sin aggravated by presumption, theft, etc., which are not only rules in these particular cases, but to guide the judges by proportion in all other cases: as upon the law of adultery, it may be a question whether Bathsheba ought to die by that law, in regard to the great temptation, and the command and power of the kings of Israel. So that which was capital in the men of Jabesh Gilead, Judges [xxi. 10] in not coming up to the princes upon proclamation, was but confiscation of goods, etc., in Ezra 10. 8. See 2d Sam. 14. 6. 11.

Reason 2. All punishments ought to be just, and, offences varying so much in their merit by occasion of circumstances, it would be unjust to inflict the same punishment upon the least as upon the greatest.

3. Justice requireth that every cause should be heard before it be judged, which cannot be when the sentence and punishment is determined before hand.

4. Such parts and gifts, as the word of God requires in a judge, were not so necessary, if all punishments were determined beforehand.

5. God hath not confined all wisdom, etc., to any one generation, that they should set rules for all others to walk by.

6. It is against reason that some men should better judge of the merit of a cause in the bare theory thereof, than others (as wise and godly) should be able to discern of it pro re nata.

7. Difference of times, places, etc., may aggravate or extenuate some offences.

8. We must trust God, who can and will provide as wise and righteous judgment for his people in time to come, as in the present or forepassed times; and we should not attempt the limiting of his providence, and frustrating the gifts of others by determining all punishments, etc.

Objection. In theft and some other cases, as cases capital, God hath prescribed a certain punishment.

Ans. 1. In theft, etc., the law respects the damage and injury of the party, which is still one and the same, though circumstances may aggravate or extenuate the sin. 2. In capital cases death is appointed as the highest degree of punishment which man's justice can reach.

Objection. Then we might as well leave all laws arbitrary at the discretion of the judge.

Ans. 1. The reason is not like. 1. God gave a certain law where he left the punishment arbitrary, so as we have a clear rule to guide the law where the punishment may be uncertain. The varying of the offence in the circumstances doth not vary the ground or equity of the law, nor the nature of the guilt, as it doth the measure of the reward. He is as fully guilty of theft who steals a loaf of bread for his hunger, as he that steals an horse for his pleasure.

Objection. The statutes in England set down a certain penalty for most offences.

Ans. 1. We are not bound to make such examples ourselves. 2. The penalty, commonly, is not so much as the least degree of that offence deserves: 12*d*. for an oath, 5*s*. for drunkenness, etc.

# 1642

Mo. 11 (*January*)]. Those of Providence, being all ana-baptists, were divided in judgment; some were only against baptizing of infants; others denied all magistracy and churches, etc., of which Gorton, who had lately been whipped at Aquiday, as is before mentioned, was their instructer and captain.[1] These, being too strong for the other party, provoked them by injuries, so as they came armed into the field, each against other, but Mr. Williams pacified them for the present. This occasioned the weaker party to write a letter, under all their hands, to our governor and magistrates, complaining of the wrongs they suffered, and desiring aid, or, if not that, counsel from us. We answered them that we could not levy any war, etc. without a general court. For counsel we told them, that except they did submit themselves to some jurisdiction, either Plymouth or ours, we had no calling or warrant to interpose in their contentions, but if they were once subject to any, then

---

[1] Here enters upon the stage Samuel Gorton, an enthusiast of somewhat better birth and education than many of his fellow-fanatics. He was scarcely less of an embarrassment to the come-outers about Narragansett Bay, than to the men of Plymouth and Massachusetts. Gorton underwent severe persecution, which he endured heroically, the severities being among the least excusable of those inflicted by Puritan intolerance. A good account of Gorton, who reached considerable influence, is contained in the *Dictionary of National Biography.* See also Richman, *Rhode Island,* especially I. 144–148. No account of Gorton's whipping at Aquiday is to be found on any previous page of Winthrop; but Lechford, in his *Plain Dealing,* says of this Rhode Island experience, "there lately they whipt one Mr. Gorton, a grave man, for denying their power, and abusing some of their magistrates with uncivil terms; the governour, Mr. Coddington, saying, in court, you that are for the king lay hold on Gorton, and he again on the other side called forth, all you that are for the king lay hold on Coddington, whereupon Gorton was banished the island. So with his wife and children he went to Providence. They began about a small trespass of swine, but it is thought some other matter was ingredient." The case of Gorton makes it plain that even in and about Narragansett Bay there were bounds to the exercise of tolerance.

they had a calling to protect them.    After this answer we heard
no more from them for a time.

The frost was so great and continual this winter, that all
the bay was frozen over, so much and so long, as the like,
by the Indians' relation, had not been these 40 years, and it
continued from the 18th of this month to the 21st of the 12th
month (*February*); so as horses and carts went over in many
places where ships have sailed.    Capt. Gibbons and his wife,
with divers on foot by them, came riding from his farm at
Pullen point, right over to Boston, the 17th of the 12th month,
when it had thawed so much as the water was above the ice
half a foot in some places; and they passed with loads of wood
and six oxen from Muddy river to Boston, and when it thawed
it removed great rocks of above a ton or more weight, and
brought them on shore.    The snow likewise was very deep,
especially northward about Acomenticus, above three feet, and
much more beyond.    It was frozen also to sea so far as one
could well discern.

To the southward also the frost was as great and the snow
as deep, and at Virginia itself the great bay was much of it
frozen over, and all their great rivers, so as they lost much cattle
for want of hay, and most of their swine.

There was a shallop with eight men to go from Pascataquack
to Pemaquid about the beginning of the frost, they would needs
set forth upon the Lord's day, though forewarned, etc.    They
were taken with a N. W. tempest and put to sea about 14 days:
at length they recovered Monhigen.    Four of them died with
cold, the rest were discovered by a fisherman a good time after,
and so brought off the Island.

There was great fear lest much hurt might have been done
upon the breaking up of the frost, (men and beasts were grown
so bold,) but, by the good providence of God, not one person
miscarried, save one Warde of Salem, an honest young man,
who going to show a traveller the safest passage over the river,
as he thought, by the salthouse, fell in, and, though he had a

pitchfork in his hand, yet was presently carried under the ice by the tide. The traveller fell in with one leg while he went to help the other, but God preserved him. He had about him all the letters from England which were brought in a ship newly arrived at the Isle of Shoals, which sure were the occasion of God's preserving him, more than any goodness of the man. Most of the bridges were broken down and divers mills.

About this time one Turner of Charlestown, a man of about 50 years of age, having led a loose and disorderly life, and being wounded in conscience at a sermon of Mr. Shepherd's, he kept it in and did not discover his distress to such as might have offered him help, etc., nor did attend upon the public means as he ought to have done, and after a good space he went out from his wife on the Lord's day at night, having kept at home all that day, and drowned himself in a little pit where was not above two feet water. . . .

Three men coming in a shallop from Braintree, the wind taking them short at Castle Island, one of them stepping forward to hand the sail, caused a fowling piece with a French lock, which lay in the boat, to go off. The whole charge went through the thigh of one man within one inch of his belly, yet missed the bone, then the shot (being goose shot) scattered a little and struck the second man under his right side upon his breast, so as above 40 shot entered his body, many into the capacity of his breast. The third man being now only able to steer, but not to get home the boat, it pleased God the wind favored him so as he did fetch the governor's garden,[1] and there being a small boat and men at that time, they brought them to Boston before they were too far spent with cold and pain, and beyond all expectation, they were both soon perfectly recovered, yet he who was shot in the breast fell into a fever and spit blood.

One John Turner, a merchant's factor of London, had gone from hence to the West Indies the year before in a small pin-

[1] Governor's Island.

nace of 15 tons, and returned with great advantage in indigo, pieces of 8,[1] etc. He said he got them by trade, but it was suspected he got them by prize. He prepared a bigger vessel and well manned in the beginning of winter, and putting to sea was forced in again three times. 1. By a leak. 2. By a contrary wind; and 3. he spent his mast in fair weather, and having gotten a new at Cape Anne, and towing it towards the bay, he lost it by the way, and so by these occasions and by the frost, he was kept in all winter. Thereupon he gave over his voyage and went to Virginia, and there sold his vessel and shipped himself and his commodities in a Dutch ship for the West Indies.

Mo. 1. (*March*) 27.] Mr. William Aspenwall, who had been banished, as is before declared, for joining with Mr. Wheelwright, being licensed by the general court to come and tender his submission, etc., was this day reconciled to the church of Boston. He made a very free and full acknowledgment of his error and seducement, and that with much detestation of his sin. The like he did after, before the magistrates, who were appointed by the court to take his submission, and upon their certificate thereof at the next general court, his sentence of banishment was released.

It is observable how the Lord doth honor his people and justify their ways, even before the heathen, when their proceedings are true and just, as appears by this instance. Those at New Haven, intending a plantation at Delaware, sent some men to purchase a large portion of land of the Indians there, but they refused to deal with them. It so fell out that a Pequod sachem (being fled his country in our war with them, and having seated himself with his company upon that river ever since) was accidentally there at that time. He, taking notice of the English and their desire, persuaded the other sachem to deal with them, and told him that howsoever they had killed his countrymen and driven him out, yet they were honest men,

---

[1] Pieces of eight reals, *i. e.*, dollars.

and had just cause to do as they did, for the Pequods had done them wrong, and refused to give such reasonable satisfaction as was demanded of them. Whereupon the sachem entertained them, and let them have what land they desired.

2. (*April*) 14.] A general fast was kept for our native country and Ireland and our own occasions.

The spring began very early, and the weather was very mild, but the third and fourth month proved very wet and cold, so that the low meadows were much spoiled, and at Connecticut they had such a flood as brake their bridges, and killed all their winter corn, and forced them to plant much of their Indian over.

The last winter divers vessels were cast away to the southward, one at Long Island, where 8 or 9 persons were drowned. These were loose people, who lived by trucking with the Indians.

Mo. 3. (*May*) 9.] The ship *Eleanor* of London, one Mr. Inglee master, arrived at Boston. She was laden with tobacco from Virginia, and having been about 14 days at sea, she was taken with such a tempest, as though all her sails were down and made up, yet they were blown from the yards, and she was laid over on one side two and a half hours, so low as the water stood upon her deck, and the sea over-raking her continually, and the day was as dark as if it had been night, and though they had cut her masts, yet she righted not till the tempest assuaged. She staid here till the 4th of the (4) (*June*) and was well fitted with masts, sails, rigging, and victuals at such reasonable rates as the master was much affected with his entertainment, and professed that he never found the like usage in Virginia where he had traded these ten years.

Captain Underhill, finding no employment here that would maintain him and his family, and having good offers made him by the Dutch governor, (he speaking the Dutch tongue and his wife a Dutch woman,) had been with the governor, and being returned desired the church's leave to depart. The church, understanding that the English, at Stamford near the Dutch, had offered him employment and maintenance, (after their ability,) advised him rather to go thither, seeing they were our country-men and in a church estate. He accepted this advice. His wife, being more forward to this, consented, and the church furnished him out, and provided a pinnace to transport him; but when he came there he changed his mind, or at least his course, and went to the Dutch.[1]

18.] The court of elections was. Mr. Winthrop was again chosen governor, and Mr. Endecott deputy governor. This being done, Mr. Dudley went away, and though he were chosen an assistant, yet he would not accept it. Some of the elders went to his house to deal with him. His answer was, that he had sufficient reasons to excuse and warrant his refusal, which he did not think fit to publish, but he would impart to any one or two of them whom they should appoint, which he did accordingly. The elders acquainted the court with what they had done, but not with the reasons of his refusal, only that they thought them not sufficient. The court sent a magistrate and two deputies to desire him to come to the court, for as a counsellor he was to assist in the general court. The next day he came, and after some excuse he consented to accept the place, so that the court would declare that if at any time he should depart out of the jurisdiction, (which he protested he did not intend,) no oath, either of officer, counsellor, or assistant should hold him in any bond where he stood. This he desired, not for his own satisfaction, but that it might be a satisfaction to others who might scruple his liberty herein. After much debate the court made a general order which gave him satisfaction.

One Mr. Blinman, a minister in Wales, a godly and able man, came over with some friends of his, and being invited to Green's Harbor,[2] near Plymouth, they went thither, but ere the

---

[1] John Underhill thus disappears from the stage to dwell with the Dutch, his former associates no doubt gladly bidding him farewell.

[2] Now Marshfield.

year was expired there fell out some difference among them, which by no means could be reconciled, so as they agreed to part, and he came with his company and sat down at Cape Anne, which at this court was established to be a plantation, and called Gloucester.

A book was brought into the court, wherein the institution of the standing council was pretended to be a sinful innovation. The governor moved to have the contents of the book examined, and then, if there appeared cause, to inquire after the author. But the greatest part of the court, having some intimation of the author, of whose honest intentions they were well persuaded, would not consent, only they permitted it to be read, but not to be spoken unto, but would have inquiry first made how it came into the court. Whereupon it was found to have been made by Mr. Saltonstall, one of the assistants, and by him sent to Mr. Hathorn (then a deputy of the court) to be tendered to the court, if he should approve of it. Mr. Hathorn did not acquaint the court with it, but delivered it to one of the freemen to consider of, with whom it remained about half a year, till he delivered it to Mr. Dudley. This discovery being made, the governor moved again that the matter of the book might be considered, but the court could not agree to it except Mr. Saltonstall were first acquit from any censure concerning the said book. This was thought to be a course out of all order, and upon that some passages very offensive and unwarrantable were mentioned, about which also the court being divided, the governor moved to take the advice of the elders concerning the soundness of the propositions and arguments. This the court would not allow neither, except the whole cause were referred also, which he thought sure they would have accepted, for the cause being of a civil nature, it belonged to the court, and not to the elders, to judge of the merit thereof. In the end, a day or two after, when no further proceeding was otherwise like to be had, it was agreed, that in regard the court was not jealous of any evil intention in Mr.

Saltonstall, etc., and that when he did write and deliver it, (as was supposed,) there was an order in force, which gave liberty to every freeman to consider and deliver their judgments to the next court about such fundamental laws as were then to be established, (whereof one did concern the institution and power of the council,) therefore he should be discharged from any censure or further inquiry about the same, which was voted accordingly, although there were some expressions in the book which would not be warranted by that order, as that the council was instituted unwarily to satisfy Mr. Vane's desire, etc., whereas it was well known to many in the court, as themselves affirmed, that it was upon the advice and solicitation of the elders, and after much deliberation from court to court. Other passages there were also, which were very unsound, reproachful and dangerous, and was manifested by an answer made thereunto by Mr. Dudley, and received at the next session of the court, and by some observations made by Mr. Norris, a grave and judicious elder, teacher of the church in Salem, (and with some difficulty read also in court,) who, not suspecting the author, handled him somewhat sharply according to the merit of the matter.

This summer five ships more were built, three at Boston, and one at Dorchester, and one at Salem.

A cooper's wife of Hingham, having been long in a sad melancholic distemper near to phrensy, and having formerly attempted to drown her child, but prevented by God's gracious providence, did now again take an opportunity, being alone, to carry her child, aged three years, to a creek near her house, and stripping it of the clothes, threw it into the water and mud. But, the tide being low, the little child scrambled out, and taking up its clothes, came to its mother who was set down not far off. She carried the child again, and threw it in so far as it could not get out; but then it pleased God, that a young man, coming that way, saved it. She would give no other reason for it, but that she did it to save it from misery, and withal that she was assured, she had sinned against the Holy Ghost, and that she could not repent of any sin. Thus doth Satan work by the advantage of our infirmities, which should stir us up to cleave the more fast to Christ Jesus, and to walk the more humbly and watchfully in all our conversation.

At this general court appeared one Richard Gibson a scholar, sent some three or four years since to Richman's Island[1] to be a minister to a fishing plantation there belonging to one Mr. Trelawney of Plymouth in England. He removed from thence to Pascataquack, and this year was entertained by the fishermen at the Isle of Shoals to preach to them. He, being wholly addicted to the hierarchy and discipline of England, did exercise a ministerial function in the same way, and did marry and baptize at the Isle of Shoals which was now found to be within our jurisdiction. This man being incensed against Mr. Larkham, pastor of the church at Northam, (late Dover,) for some speeches he delivered in his sermon against such hirelings, etc., he sent an open letter to him, wherein he did scandalize our government, oppose our title to those parts, and provoke the people, by way of arguments, to revolt from us (this letter being showed to many before it came to Mr. Larkham). Mr. Gibson being now showed this letter, and charged with his offence, he could not deny the thing, whereupon he was committed to the marshall. In a day or two after he preferred a petition, which gave not satisfaction, but the next day he made a full acknowledgment of all he was charged with, and the evil thereof, submitting himself to the favor of the court. Whereupon, in regard he was a stranger, and was to depart the country within a few days, he was discharged without any fine or other punishment.

Mo. 4. (*June*) 8.] One Nathaniel Briscoe, a godly young man, newly admitted a member of the church of Boston, being single, he kept with his father, a godly poor man, but minded

[1] Near Scarborough, Maine. Robert Trelawney and Moses Goodyear had here a grant, of disputed bounds, from the Council for New England, 1631.

his own advantage more than his father's necessity, so as that his father, desiring in the evening to have his help the next day, he neglected his father's request, and rose very early next morning to go help another man for wages, and being loading a boat in a small creek, he fell into the water and was drowned.

About this time the adventurers to the Isle of Sable fetched off their men and goods all safe. The oil, teeth, seal and horse hides, and some black fox skins, came to near £1500.

One Darby Field, an Irishman, living about Pascataquack, being accompanied with two Indians, went to the top of the white hill.[1] He made his journey in 18 days. His relation at his return was, that it was about one hundred miles from Saco, that after 40 miles travel he did, for the most part, ascend, and within 12 miles of the top was neither tree nor grass, but low savins, which they went upon the top of sometimes, but a continual ascent upon rocks, on a ridge between two valleys filled with snow, out of which came two branches of Saco river, which met at the foot of the hill where was an Indian town of some 200 people. Some of them accompanied him within 8 miles of the top, but durst go no further, telling him that no Indian ever dared to go higher, and that he would die if he went. So they staid there till his return, and his two Indians took courage by his example and went with him. They went divers times through the thick clouds for a good space, and within 4 miles of the top they had no clouds, but very cold. By the way, among the rocks, there were two ponds, one a blackish water and the other reddish. The top of all was plain about 60 feet square. On the north side there was such a precipice, as they could scarce discern to the bottom. They had neither cloud nor wind on the top, and moderate heat. All the country about him seemed a level, except here and there a hill rising above the rest, but far beneath them. He saw to the north a great water which he judged to be about

[1] The first ascent of the White Mountains by a European.

100 miles broad, but could see no land beyond it.  The sea by
Saco seemed as if it had been within 20 miles.  He saw also a
sea to the eastward, which he judged to be the gulf of Canada:
he saw some great waters in parts to the westward, which he
judged to be the great lake which Canada river comes out of.
He found there much muscovy glass,[1] they could rive out pieces
of 40 feet long and 7 or 8 broad.  When he came back to the
Indians, he found them drying themselves by the fire, for they
had a great tempest of wind and rain.  About a month after
he went again with five or six in his company, then they had
some wind on the top, and some clouds above them which hid
the sun.  They brought some stones which they supposed had
been diamonds, but they were most crystal.  See after, another
relation more true and exact.

Mo. 4 (*June*) 22.]  In the time of the general court, in a
great tempest of thunder and lightning, in the evening, the
lightning struck the upper sail of the windmill in Boston by the
ferry,[2] and shattered it in many pieces, and, missing the stones,
struck into the standard, rived it down in three parts to the
bottom, and one of the spars; and the main standard being
bound about with a great iron hoop, fastened with many long
spikes, it was plucked off, broken in the middle, and thrown
upon the floor, and the boards upon the sides of the mill rived
off, the sacks, etc., in the mill set on fire, and the miller being
under the mill, upon the ground, chopping a piece of board, was
struck dead, but company coming in, found him to breathe, so
they carried him to an house, and within an hour or two he
began to stir, and strove with such force, as six men could
scarce hold him down.  The next day he came to his senses,
but knew nothing of what had befallen him, but found himself
very sore on divers parts of his body.  His hair on one side of
his head and beard was singed, one of his shoes torn off his
foot, but his foot not hurt.

[1] Strictly, Muscovy glass was isinglass.  Here mica is meant.
[2] The wind-mill was on Copp's Hill, opposite Charlestown.

The Indians at Kennebeck, hearing of the general conspiracy against the English, determined to begin there, and one of them knowing that Mr. Edward Winslow did use to walk within the palisadoes, prepared his piece to shoot him, but as he was about it, Mr. Winslow not seeing him nor suspecting any thing, but thinking he had walked enough, went suddenly into the house, and so God preserved him.

At the same general court there fell out a great business upon a very small occasion. Anno 1636, there was a stray sow in Boston, which was brought to Captain Keayne: he had it cried divers times, and divers came to see it, but none made claim to it for near a year. He kept it in his yard with a sow of his own. Afterwards one Sherman's wife, having lost such a sow, laid claim to it, but came not to see it, till Captain Keayne had killed his own sow. After being showed the stray sow, and finding it to have other marks than she had claimed her sow by, she gave out that he had killed her sow. The noise hereof being spread about the town, the matter was brought before the elders of the church as a case of offence; many witnesses were examined, and Captain Keayne was cleared. She not being satisfied with this, by the instigation of one George Story, a young merchant of London, who kept in her house, (her husband being then in England,) and had been brought before the governor upon complaint of Captain Keayne as living under suspicion, she brought the cause to the inferior court at Boston, where, upon a full hearing, Capt. Keayne was again cleared, and the jury gave him £3 for his cost, and he bringing his action against Story and her for reporting about that he had stolen her sow, recovered £20 damages of either of them. Story upon this searcheth town and country to find matter against Captain Keayne about this stray sow, and got one of his witnesses to come into Salem court and to confess there that he had forsworn himself; and upon this he petitions in Sherman's name, to this general court, to have the cause heard again. which was granted, and the best part of

seven days were spent in examining of witnesses and debating
of the cause; and yet it was not determined, for there being
nine magistrates and thirty deputies, nc sentence could by law
pass without the greater number of both, which neither plaintiff
nor defendant had, for there were for the plaintiff two magistrates and fifteen deputies, and for the defendant seven magistrates and eight deputies, the other seven deputies stood
doubtful.   Much contention and earnestness there was, which
indeed did mostly arise from the difficulty of the case, in regard
of cross witnesses, and some prejudices (as one professed) against
the person, which blinded some men's judgments that they
could not attend the true nature and course of the evidence.
For all the plaintiff's witnesses amounted to no more but an
evidence of probability, so as they might all swear true, and
yet the sow in question might not be the plaintiff's.   But the
defendant's witnesses gave a certain evidence, upon their
certain knowledge, and that upon certain grounds, (and these
as many and more and of as good credit as the others,) so as if
this testimony were true, it was not possible the sow should be
the plaintiff's.   Besides, whereas the plaintiff's wife was admitted to take her oath for the marks of her sow, the defendant
and his wife (being a very godly sober woman) was denied the
like, although propounded in the court by Mr. Cotton, upon
that rule in the law        he shall swear he hath not put his
hands to his neighbor's goods.   Yet they both in the open court
solemnly, as in the presence of God, declared their innocency,
etc.   Further, if the case had been doubtful, yet the defendant's
lawful possession ought to have been preferred to the plaintiff's
doubtful title, for in equali jure melior est conditio possidentis.
But the defendant being of ill report in the country for a hard
dealer in his course of trading, and having been formerly censured in the court and in the church also, by admonition for
such offences, carried many weak minds strongly against him.
And the truth is, he was very worthy of blame in that kind,
as divers others in the country were also in those times, though

they were not detected as he was; yet to give every man his due, he was very useful to the country both by his hospitality and otherwise. But one dead fly spoils much good ointment.

There was great expectation in the country, by occasion of Story's clamors against him, that the cause would have passed against the captain, but falling out otherwise, gave occasion to many to speak unreverently of the court, especially of the magistrates, and the report went, that their negative voice had hindered the course of justice, and that these magistrates must be put out, that the power of the negative voice might be taken away. Thereupon it was thought fit by the governor and other of the magistrates to publish a declaration of the true state of the cause, that truth might not be condemned unknown. This was framed before the court brake up; for prevention whereof, the governor tendered a declaration in nature of a pacification, whereby it might have appeared, that, howsoever the members of the court dissented in judgment, yet they were the same in affection, and had a charitable opinion of each other; but this was opposed by some of the plaintiff's part, so it was laid by. And because there was much laboring in the country upon a false supposition, that the magistrate's negative voice stopped the plaintiff in the case of the sow, one of the magistrates published a declaration of the necessity of upholding the same. It may be here inserted, being but brief.[1]

---

[1] The account here of a dispute over a very trivial matter must not be overlooked, since from the small occasion proceeded a memorable constitutional change. Captain Robert Keayne, a well-to-do and highly connected man, interested in many important events, often was the object of popular ill-will, at this time being under suspicion of extortion. The charge made against him by Mistress Sherman seemed to many well-based, and being pushed with vigor by her and her friend Story, brought about at last nothing less than a constitutional crisis. Among the magistrates Bellingham and Saltonstall sided with the people; but the magistrates in general opposing, much agitation arose as to the "negative vote," which ended in the establishment for the colony of the bicameral system, the magistrates to sit by themselves as a senate, and the deputies to constitute an independent house. This change, whose consummation Winthrop notes on a later page, has profoundly affected political development. *Records of Massachusetts Bay*, under date.

**Mo. 5.** (*July*) 7.] From Maryland came one Mr. Neale
with two pinnaces and commission from Mr. Calvert, the governor there, to buy mares and sheep, but having nothing to pay
for them but bills charged upon the Lord Baltimore in England,
no man would deal with him.   One of his vessels was so eaten
with worms that he was forced to leave her.

Mr. Chancey of Scituate persevered in his opinion of dipping
in baptism, and practised accordingly, first upon two of his
own, which being in very cold weather, one of them swooned
away.   Another, having a child about three years old, feared
it would be frightened, (as others had been, and one caught
hold of Mr. Chancey and had near pulled him into the water,)
she brought her child to Boston, with letters testimonial from
Mr. Chancey, and had it baptized there.

21.]   A general fast was kept by order of the general court
and advice of some of the elders.   The occasion was princi-
pally for the danger we conceived our native country was in,
and the foul sins which had broken out among ourselves, etc.

23.]   Osamaken, the great sachem of Pakanocott in Plymouth jurisdiction, came, attended with many men and some
other sagamores accompanying him, to visit the governor, who
entertained him kindly, etc.

The *Mary Rose*, which had been blown up and sunk with all
her ordnance, ballast, much lead, and other goods, was now
weighed and brought to shore by the industry and diligence of
one Edward Bendall of Boston.   The court gave the owners
above a year's time to recover her and free the harbor, which
was much damnified by her; and they having given her over
and never attempting to weigh her, Edward Bendall undertook
it upon these terms, viz., if he freed the harbor, he should have
the whole, otherwise he should have half of all he recovered.
He made two great tubs, bigger than a butt, very tight, and
open at one end, upon which were hanged so many weights as
would sink it to the ground (600wt).   It was let down, the
diver sitting in it, a cord in his hand to give notice when they

should draw him up, and another cord to show when they should remove it from place to place, so he could continue in his tub near half an hour, and fasten ropes to the ordnance, and put the lead, etc., into a net or tub.   And when the tub was drawn up, one knocked upon the head of it, and thrust a long pole under water, which the diver laid hold of, and so was drawn up by it; for they might not draw the open end out of water for endangering him, etc.[1]   The case of the money, shot out of one of the guns, which came to a trial in the court at Boston, (8) (*October*) 27, see in the next leaf.

5. (*July*) 28.]   A Dutch ship of 300 tons arrived here, laden with salt from the West Indies, which she sold here for plank and pipe staves.   She brought two Spanish merchants, who being taken at sea, while they went in a frigate from Domingo to find an English ship which they had freighted there, and was by their agreement stolen out of the harbor, where she had been long embarred, they hired this Dutchman to bring them hither where they had appointed their ship to come, not daring to go into Spain or England.   They staid here about a month, but their ship came not, so they went away again.   We heard after that their ship had been 14 days beating upon our coast, and being put back, still, by N. W. winds, she bare up, and went for England, and arriving at Southampton, the parliament made use of the treasure.

God would not suffer her to come to us, lest our hearts should have been taken with her wealth, and so have caused the Spaniard to have an evil eye upon us.

Some of the elders went to Concord, being sent for by the church there, to advise with them about the maintenance of their elders, etc.   They found them wavering about removal, not finding their plantation answerable to their expectation, and the maintenance of two elders too heavy a burden for them. The elders' advice was, that they should continue and wait

[1] A very early instance, perhaps the earliest on record, of the use of the diving-bell.

upon God, and be helpful to their elders in labor and what they could, and all to be ordered by the deacons, (whose office had not formerly been improved this way amongst them,) and that the elders should be content with what means the church was able at present to afford them, and if either of them should be called to some other place, then to advise with other churches about removal.

One Wequash Cook, an Indian, living about Connecticut river's mouth, and keeping much at Saybrook with Mr. Fenwick, attained to good knowledge of the things of God and salvation by Christ, so as he became a preacher to other Indians, and labored much to convert them, but without any effect, for within a short time he fell sick, not without suspicion of poison from them, and died very comfortably.

There was about £30 put into one of the guns of the *Mary Rose*, which was known all abroad. The guns being taken up and searched, they pulled out of one of them a wad of rope yarn. They handled it and found it very heavy, and began to undo it, but being very wet and foul they threw it down; and about 8 or 9 days after, coming to try one of the guns, and finding this wad lying there, they thrust it in after the powder, and shot it off into the channel, but perceived part of it to break and fall short, and the rest fell into the middle of the channel. But the next low water there was taken up several pieces of gold and some silver. This was in a place where people passed daily, and never any found there before that time. Those who found the money refused to restore it to him who had bought and taken up the wreck. Whereupon he brought his action, and the money was adjudged to him.

Two ships arrived from England, but brought not above five or six passengers, save our own people, and very few goods, except rigging, etc., for some ships which were building here.

Now came over a book of Mr. Cotton's sermons upon

the seven vials. Mr. Humfrey had gotten the notes from some who had took them by characters,[1] and printed them in London, he had 300 copies for it, which was a great wrong to Mr. Cotton, and he was much grieved at it, for it had been fit he should have perused and corrected the copy before it had been printed.

Mo. 6 (*August*).] Mr. Welde, Mr. Peter, and Mr. Hibbins, who were sent the last year into England, had procured £500 which they sent over in linen, woollen, and other useful commodities for the country, which, because the stock might be preserved and returned this year for a further supply, were put off together, for about eighty pounds profit, and the principal returned by Mr. Stoughton in the next ship.

By their means also, Mr. Richard Andrews, an haberdasher in Cheapside, London, a godly man, and who had been a former benefactor to this country, having 500 pounds due to him from the governor and company of Plymouth, gave it to this colony to be laid out in cattle, and other course of trade, for the poor.

Two fishermen drowned in a shallop, which was overset near Pascataquack.

24.] The ship *Trial*, about 200 tons, built at Boston by the merchants there, being now ready to set sail, (Mr. Thomas Coytmore[2] master, and divers godly seamen in her,) Mr. Cotton was desired to preach aboard her, etc., but upon consideration that the audience would be too great for the ship, the sermon was at the meeting house.

A plantation was begun the last year at Delaware Bay by those of New Haven, and some 20 families were transported thither, but this summer there fell such sickness and mortality among them as dissolved the plantation. The same sickness and mortality befell the Swedes also, who were planted upon

---

[1] *I. e.*, in shorthand.

[2] Thomas Coytmore, a worthy freeman whose widow became in 1647 the fourth wife of Winthrop.

the same river. The English were after driven out by the Swedes.

Mo. 7 (*September*).] Mr. William Hibbins, who was one of those who were sent over into England the year before, arrived now in safety, with divers others who went over then also. He made a public declaration to the church in Boston, of all the good providences of the Lord towards him in his voyage to and fro, etc., wherein it was very observable what care the Lord had of them, and what desperate dangers they were delivered from upon the seas, such as the eldest seamen were amazed; and indeed such preservations and deliverances have been so frequent, to such ships as have carried those of the Lord's family between the two Englands, as would fill a perfect volume to report them all.

6.] There came letters from divers Lords of the upper house, and some 30 of the house of commons, and others from the ministers there, who stood for the independency of churches, to Mr. Cotton of Boston, Mr. Hooker of Hartford, and Mr. Davenport of New Haven, to call them, or some of them, if all could not, to England, to assist in the synod there appointed, to consider and advise about the settling of church government. Upon this such of the magistrates and elders as were at hand met together, and were most of them of opinion that it was a call of God, yet took respite of concluding, till they might hear from the rest. Whereupon a messenger was presently despatched to Connecticut, and New Haven, with the letters, etc. Upon return, it was found that Mr. Hooker liked not the business, nor thought it any sufficient call for them to go 3,000 miles to agree with three men, (meaning those three ministers who were for independency, and did solicit in the parliament, etc.). Mr. Davenport thought otherwise of it, so as the church there set apart a day to seek the Lord in it, and thereupon came to this conclusion, that seeing the church had no other officer but himself, therefore they might not spare him.

Mr. Cotton apprehended strongly a call of God in it, though

he were very averse to a sea voyage, and the more because his ordinary topic in Acts 13, led him to deliver that doctrine of the interest all churches have in each other's members for mutual helpfulness, etc. But soon after came other letters out of England, upon the breach between the king and parliament, from one of the former Lords, and from Mr. Welde and Mr. Peter, to advise them to stay till they heard further; so this care came to an end.[1]

There arrived another ship with salt, which was put off for pipe staves, etc., so by an unexpected providence we were supplied of salt to go on with our fishing, and of ships to take off our pipe staves, which lay upon men's hands.

There fell out a very sad accident at Weymouth. One Richard Sylvester, having three small children, he and his wife going to the assembly, upon the Lord's day, left their children at home. The eldest was without doors looking to some cattle; the middle-most, being a son about five years old, seeing his father's fowling piece, (being a very great one,) stand in the chimney, took it and laid it upon a stool, as he had seen his father do, and pulled up the cock, (the spring being weak,) and put down the hammer, then went to the other end and blowed in the mouth of the piece, as he had seen his father also do, and with that stirring the piece, being charged, it went off, and shot the child into the mouth and through his head. When the father came home he found his child lie dead, and could not have imagined how he should have been so killed, but the youngest child, (being but three years old, and could scarce speak,) showed him the whole manner of it.

---

[1] This invitation, extended by Owen, Goodwin and Nye, the three chief ministers of the Independents in England, to the three lights of the New England Congregationalism, to take part in the Westminster Assembly, is very significant. From the three, especially Cotton, had gone back to England a powerful influence, so much so that Independency in England was called "the New England way." At this period Independency was just rising into consequence, but afterwards it became dominant. It would have been a calamity to New England had Cotton, Hooker and Davenport at this time departed, and their presence in England could scarcely have affected the general result.

There arrived in a small pinnace one Mr. Bennet, a gentleman of Virginia, with letters from many well disposed people of the upper new farms[1] in Virginia to the elders here, bewailing their sad condition for want of the means of salvation, and earnestly entreating a supply of faithful ministers, whom, upon experience of their gifts and godliness, they might call to office, etc.   Upon these letters, (which were openly read in Boston upon a lecture day,) the elders met, and set a day apart to seek God in it, and agreed upon three who might most likely be spared, viz., Mr. Phillips of Watertown, Mr. Tompson of Braintree, and Mr. Miller of Rowley, for these churches had each of them two.   Having designed these men, they acquainted the general court herewith, who did approve thereof, and ordered that the governor should commend them to the governor and council of Virginia, which was done accordingly.   But Mr. Phillips being not willing to go, Mr. Knolles, his fellow elder, and Mr. Tompson, with the consent of their churches, were sent away, and departed on their way 8ber (*October*) 7. to Taunton, to meet the bark at Narragansett. Mr. Miller did not accept the call.   The main argument, which prevailed with the churches to dismiss them to that work, and with the court to allow and further it, was the advancement of the kingdom of Christ in those parts, and the confidence they had in the promise, that whosoever shall part with father, etc., for my sake and the gospel's, shall receive an hundred fold. We were so far from fearing any loss by parting with such desirable men, as we looked at them as seed sown, which would bring us in a plentiful harvest, and we accounted it no small honor that God had put upon his poor churches here, that other parts of the world should seek to us for help in this kind.   For about the same time, two of our vessels which had been gone near a year, and were much feared to be lost, returned home with a good supply of cotton, and brought home letters with

[1] Perhaps the reading should be "of upper Norfolke." At any rate the chief signers of the letter were magistrates of that county.

them from Barbadoes and other islands in those parts, intreating us to supply them with ministers. But, understanding that these people were much infected with familism, etc., the elders did nothing about it, intending to inquire further by another vessel, which was preparing for those parts.

Mo. 7. (*September*) 1.] There came letters from the court at Connecticut, and from two of the magistrates there, and from Mr. Ludlow, near the Dutch, certifying us that the Indians all over the country had combined themselves to cut off all the English, that the time was appointed after harvest, the manner also, they should go by small companies to the chief men's houses by way of trading, etc., and should kill them in the houses and seize their weapons, and then others should be at hand to prosecute the massacre; and that this was discovered by three several Indians, near about the same time and in the same manner; one to Mr. Eaton of New Haven, another to Mr. Ludlow, and the third to Mr. Haynes. This last being hurt near to death by a cart, etc., sent after Mr. Haynes, and told him that Englishman's God was angry with him, and had set Englishman's cow to kill him, because he had concealed such a conspiracy against the English, and so told him of it, as the other two had done. Upon this their advice to us was, that it was better to enter into war presently, and begin with them, and if we would send 100 men to the river's mouth of Connecticut, they would meet us with a proportionable number.

Upon these letters, the governor called so many of the magistrates as were near, and being met, they sent out summons for a general court, to be kept six days after, and in the mean time, it was thought fit, for our safety, and to strike some terror into the Indians, to disarm such as were within our jurisdiction. Accordingly we sent men to Cutshamekin, at Braintree, to fetch him and his guns, bows, etc., which was done, and he came willingly, and being late in the night when they came to Boston, he was put in the prison; but the next morning, finding upon examination of him and divers of his men, no ground of suspicion of his partaking in any such conspiracy, he was dismissed.

Upon the warrant which went to Ipswich, Rowley, and Newbury, to disarm Passaconamy, who lived by Merrimack, they sent forth 40 men armed the next day, being the Lord's day. But it rained all the day, as it had done divers days before, and also after, so as they could not go to his wigwam, but they came to his son's and took him, which they had warrant for, and a squaw and her child, which they had no warrant for, and therefore order was given so soon as we heard of it, to send them home again. They, fearing his son's escape, led him in a line, but he taking an opportunity, slipped his line and escaped from them, but one very indiscreetly made a shot at him, and missed him narrowly. Upon the intelligence of these unwarranted proceedings, and considering that Passaconamy would look at it as a manifest injury, (as indeed we conceived it to be, and had always shunned to give them any just occasion against us,) the court being now assembled, we sent Cutshamekin to him to let him know that what was done to his son and squaw was without order, and to show him the occasion whereupon we had sent to disarm all the Indians, and that when we should find that they were innocent of any such conspiracy, we would restore all their arms again, and to will him also to come speak with us. He returned answer that he knew not what was become of his son and his squaw, (for one of them was run into the woods and came not again for ten days after, and the other was still in custody,) if he had them safe again, then he would come to us. Accordingly about a fortnight after he sent his eldest son to us, who delivered up his guns, etc.

Mo. 7. (*September*) 8.] The general court being assembled, we considered of the letters and other intelligence from Connecticut, and although the thing seemed very probable, yet we thought it not sufficient ground for us to begin a war, for it was possible it might be otherwise, and that all this might

come out of the enmity which had been between Miantunnomoh
and Onkus, who continually sought to discredit each other with
the English.  We considered also of the like reports which had
formerly been raised almost every year since we came, and how
they proved to be but reports raised up by the opposite factions
among the Indians.  Besides we found ourselves in very ill
case for war, and if we should begin, we must then be forced
to stand continually upon our guard, and to desert our farms
and business abroad, and all our trade with the Indians, which
things would bring us very low; and besides, if upon this intelligence we should kill any of them, or lose any of our own,
and it should be found after to have been a false report, we
might provoke God's displeasure, and blemish our wisdom and
integrity before the heathen.  Further it was considered that
our beginning with them could not secure us against them: we
might destroy some part of their corn and wigwams, and force
them to fly into the woods, etc., but the men would be still
remaining to do us mischief, for they will never fight us in the
open field.  Lastly, it was considered that such as were to be
sent out in such an expedition were, for the most part, godly,
and would be as well assured of the justice of the cause as the
warrant of their call, and then we would not fear their forwardness and courage, but if they should be sent out, not well
resolved, we might fear the success.

According to these considerations, we returned answer to
Connecticut, and withal we sent two men with two interpreters,
an Englishman and an Indian, to Miantunnomoh, to let him
know what intelligence we had of his drawing the rest of the
Indians into a confederation against us, and of his purpose
to make his son sachem of Pequod, and of other things which
were breaches of the league he made with us, and to desire
him to come by such a time to give us satisfaction about them.
If he refused to come, and gave them no satisfactory answer,
then to let him know that if he regarded not our friendship,
he would give us occasion to right ourselves.   And instruction

was given them, that if he gave them occasion, they should tell him the reason of our disarming the Indians, and excuse the injury done to Passaconamy, to be a mistake and without our order. The messengers coming to him, he carried them apart into the woods, taking only one of his chief men with him, and gave them very rational answers to all their propositions, and promised also to come over to us, which he did within the time prefixed.

When he came, the court was assembled, and before his admission, we considered how to treat with him, (for we knew him to be a very subtile man,) and agreed upon the points and order, and that none should propound any thing to him but the governor, and if any other of the court had any thing material to suggest, he should impart it to the governor.

Being called in, and mutual salutations passed, he was set down at the lower end of the table, over against the governor, and had only two or three of his counsellors, and two or three of our neighboring Indians, such as he desired, but would not speak of any business at any time, before some of his counsellors were present, alleging, that he would have them present, that they might bear witness with him, at his return home, of all his sayings.

In all his answers he was very deliberate and showed good understanding in the principles of justice and equity, and ingenuity withal. He demanded that his accusers might be brought forth, to the end, that if they could not make good what they had charged him with, they might suffer what he was worthy of, and must have expected, if he had been found guilty, viz., death. We answered, we knew them not, nor were they within our power, nor would we give credit to them, before we had given him knowledge of it, according to our agreement with him. He replied, if you did not give credit to it, why then did you disarm the Indians. We answered, for our security, and because we had been credibly informed that some of the eastern Indians had lately robbed divers Englishmen's houses at Saco, and taken away their powder and guns. This answer satisfied him. He gave divers reasons, why we should hold him free of any such conspiracy, and why we should conceive it was a report raised by Onkus, etc., and therefore offered to meet Onkus at Connecticut, or rather at Boston, and would prove to his face his treachery against the English, etc., and told us he would come to us at any time; for though some had dissuaded him, assuring him, that the English would put him to death, or keep him in prison, yet he being innocent of any ill intention against the English, he knew them to be so just, as they would do him no wrong, and told us, that if we sent but any Indian to him that he liked, he would come to us, and we should not need to send any of our own men. He urged much, that those might be punished, who had raised this slander, and put it to our consideration what damage it had been to him, in that he was forced to keep his men at home, and not suffer them to go forth on hunting, etc., till he had given the English satisfaction, and the charge and trouble it had put the English unto, etc. We spent the better part of two days in treating with him, and in conclusion he did accommodate himself to us to our satisfaction; only some difficulty we had, to bring him to desert the Nianticks, if we had just cause of war with them. They were, he said, as his own flesh, being allied by continual intermarriages, etc. But at last he condescended,[1] that if they should do us wrong, as he could not draw them to give us satisfaction for, nor himself could satisfy, as if it were for blood, etc., then he would leave them to us.

When we should go to dinner, there was a table provided for the Indians, to dine by themselves, and Miantunnomoh was left to sit with them. This he was discontented at, and would eat nothing, till the governor sent him meat from his table. So at night, and all the time he staid, he sat at the lower end of the magistrate's table. When he departed, we gave him

[1] Agreed.

and his counsellors coats and tobacco, and when he came to take his leave of the governor, and such of the magistrates as were present, he returned, and gave his hand to the governor again, saying, that was for the rest of the magistrates who were absent.

The court being adjourned for a few days, till we might hear from Miantunnomoh, (it was assembled again at such time as he came to Boston,) there came letters from Connecticut, certifying us of divers insolencies of the Indians, which so confirmed their minds in believing the former report, as they were now resolved to make war upon the Indians, and earnestly pressing us to delay no longer to send forth our men to join with them, and that they thought they should be forced to begin before they could hear from us again.

Upon receipt of these letters, the governor assembled such of the magistrates and deputies as were at hand, and divers of the elders also, (for they were then met at Boston upon other occasions,) and imparted the letters to them, with other letters sent from the governor of Plymouth, intimating some observations they had, which made them very much to suspect, that there was such a plot in hand, etc.   We all sat in consultation hereabout all the day, and in the end concluded, 1. That all these informations might arise from a false ground, and out of the enmity which was between the Naragansett and Monhigen. 2. Being thus doubtful, it was not a sufficient ground for us to war upon them.   3. That all these particular insolencies and wrongs ought to be revenged and repaired by course of justice, if it might be obtained, otherwise we should never be free from war.   And accordingly, letters were sent back to our brethren at Connecticut, to acquaint them with our opinions, and to dissuade them from going forth, alleging how dishonorable it would be to us all, that, while we were upon treaty with the Indians, they should make war upon them, for they would account their act as our own, seeing we had formerly professed to the Indians, that we were all as one, and in our late message to Miantunnomoh, had remembered him again of the same, and he had answered that he did so account us. Upon receipt of this our answer, they forbare to enter into war, but (it seemed) unwillingly, and as not well pleased with us.

Although we apprehended no danger, yet we continued our military watches, till near the end of 8ber (*October*), and restored the Indians all their arms we had taken from them: for although we saw it was very dangerous to us, that they should have guns, etc., yet we saw not in justice how we could take them away, seeing they came lawfully by them, (by trade with the French and Dutch for the most part,) and used them only for killing of fowl and deer, etc., except they brought themselves into the state of an enemy, therefore we thought it better to trust God with our safety than to save ourselves by unrighteousness.[1]

At this court we were informed of some English to the eastward, who ordinarily traded powder to the Indians, and lived alone under no government; whereupon we granted warrant to a gentleman, that upon due proof, etc., he should take away their powder, leaving them sufficient for their own occasions.

This court also took order, that every town should be furnished with powder out of the common store, paying for it in country commodities; likewise for muskets, and for military watches, and alarms, etc. Presently upon this, there arose an alarm in the night upon this occasion. (7.) (*September*) 19. A man, travelling late from Dorchester to Watertown, lost his way, and being benighted and in a swamp about 10 of the clock, hearing some wolves howl, and fearing to be devoured of them, he cried out help, help. One that dwelt within hearing, over

[1] It is not known what reasons the Connecticut men had at this time for fearing an Indian outbreak. Uncas and Miantonomo, sachems respectively of the Mohegans and Narragansetts, were unfriendly and intrigued against each other. Massachusetts had good reason to be anxious, and no blame can attach to the magistrates for watching Miantonomo, who had managed to quiet the suspicions of his white neighbors.

against Cambridge, hallooed to him. The other still cried out, which caused the man to fear that the Indians had gotten some English man and were torturing him, but not daring to go to him, he discharged a piece two or three times. This gave the alarm to Watertown, and so it went as far as Salem and Dorchester, but about one or two of the clock no enemy appearing, etc., all retired but the watch.

At this court also, four of Providence, who could not consort with Gorton and that company, and therefore were continually injured and molested by them, came and offered themselves and their lands, etc., to us, and were accepted under our government and protection. This we did partly to rescue these men from unjust violence, and partly to draw in the rest in those parts, either under ourselves or Plymouth, who now lived under no government, but grew very offensive, and the place was likely to be of use to us, especially if we should have occasion of sending out against any Indians of Naragansett and likewise for an outlet into the Naragansett Bay, and seeing it came without our seeking, and would be no charge to us, we thought it not wisdom to let it slip.[1]

The English of Southampton, on Long Island, having certain intelligence of one of those Indians who murdered Hammond, who was put ashore there with others, when their pinnace was wrecked, sent Captain Howe, and eight or ten men to take him. He being in the wigwam, ran out, and with his knife wounded one of the English in the breast, and so behaved himself as they were forced to kill him.

22.] The court, with advice of the elders, ordered a general fast. The occasions were, 1. The ill news we had out of England concerning the breach between the king and parliament. 2. The danger of the Indians. 3. The unseasonable weather,

---

[1] The settlement at Providence was anything but a happy family. The more moderate spirits were sometimes outraged; it was soon found that there must be limits to tolerance. The action of the four Providence men, which gave Massachusetts pretext for a protectorate, was taken in accordance with the advice recorded on p. 53, *ante*.

the rain having continued so long, viz. near a fortnight together, scarce one fair day, and much corn and hay spoiled, though indeed it proved a blessing to us, for it being with warm easterly winds, it brought the Indian corn to maturity, which otherwise would not have been ripe, and it pleased God, that so soon as the fast was agreed upon, the weather changed, and proved fair after.

At this court, the propositions sent from Connecticut, about a combination, etc., were read, and referred to a committee to consider of after the court, who meeting, added some few cautions and new articles, and for the taking in of Plymouth, (who were now willing,) and Sir Ferdinando Gorges' province, and so returned them back to Connecticut, to be considered upon against the spring, for winter was now approaching, and there could be no meeting before, etc.

The sudden fall of land and cattle, and the scarcity of foreign commodities, and money, etc., with the thin access of people from England, put many into an unsettled frame of spirit, so as they concluded there would be no subsisting here, and accordingly they began to hasten away, some to the West Indies, others to the Dutch, at Long Island, etc., (for the governor there invited them by fair offers,) and others back for England. Among others who returned thither, there was one of the magistrates, Mr. Humfrey, and four ministers, and a schoolmaster. These would needs go against all advice, and had a fair and speedy voyage, till they came near England, all which time, three of the ministers, with the schoolmaster, spake reproachfully of the people and of the country, but the wind coming up against them, they were tossed up and down, being in 10ber (*December*), so long till their provisions and other necessaries were near spent, and they were forced to strait allowance, yet at length the wind coming fair again, they got into the Sleeve,[1] but then there arose so great a tempest at S. E. as they could bear no sail, and so were out of hope of

[1] The English Channel, Fr. *La Manche*.

being saved (being in the night also). Then they humbled themselves before the Lord, and acknowledged God's hand to be justly out against them for speaking evil of this good land and the Lord's people here, etc. Only one of them, Mr. Phillips of Wrentham, in England, had not joined with the rest, but spake well of the people, and of the country; upon this it pleased the Lord to spare their lives, and when they expected every moment to have been dashed upon the rocks, (for they were hard by the Needles,) he turned the wind so as they were carried safe to the Isle of Wight by St. Helen's: yet the Lord followed them on shore. Some were exposed to great straits and found no entertainment, their friends forsaking them. One had a daughter that presently ran mad, and two other of his daughters, being under ten years of age, were discovered to have been often abused by divers lewd persons, and filthiness in his family. The schoolmaster had no sooner hired an house, and gotten in some scholars, but the plague set in, and took away two of his own children.

Others who went to other places, upon like grounds, succeeded no better. They fled for fear of want, and many of them fell into it, even to extremity, as if they had hastened into the misery which they feared and fled from, besides the depriving themselves of the ordinances and church fellowship, and those civil liberties which they enjoyed here; whereas, such as staid in their places, kept their peace and ease, and enjoyed still the blessing of the ordinances, and never tasted of those troubles and miseries, which they heard to have befallen those who departed. Much disputation there was about liberty of removing for outward advantages, and all ways were sought for an open door to get out at; but it is to be feared many crept out at a broken wall. For such as come together into a wilderness, where are nothing but wild beasts and beastlike men, and there confederate together in civil and church estate, whereby they do, implicitly at least, bind themselves to support each other, and all of them that society, whether civil or sacred, whereof they are members, how they can break from this without free consent, is hard to find, so as may satisfy a tender or good conscience in time of trial.  Ask thy conscience, if thou wouldst have plucked up thy stakes, and brought thy family 3000 miles, if thou hadst expected that all, or most, would have forsaken thee there.  Ask again, what liberty thou hast towards others, which thou likest not to allow others towards thyself; for if one may go, another may, and so the greater part, and so church and commonwealth may be left destitute in a wilderness, exposed to misery and reproach, and all for thy ease and pleasure, whereas these all, being now thy brethren, as near to thee as the Israelites were to Moses, it were much safer for thee, after his example, to choose rather to suffer affliction with thy brethren, than to enlarge thy ease and pleasure by furthering the occasion of their ruin.[1]

Nine bachelors commenced at Cambridge; they were young men of good hope, and performed their acts, so as gave good proof of their proficiency in the tongues and arts.  (8.) (*October*) 5.  The general court had settled a government or superintendency over the college, viz., all the magistrates and elders over the six nearest churches and the president, or the greatest part of these.  Most of them were now present at this first commencement, and dined at the college with the scholars' ordinary commons, which was done of purpose for the students' encouragement, etc., and it gave good content to all.[2]

At this commencement, complaint was made to the governors of two young men, of good quality, lately come out of England, for foul misbehavior, in swearing and ribaldry

---

[1] A pathetic outpouring from the fatherly heart of Winthrop over his straitened and apparently disintegrating colony.

[2] This entry relates to the first commencement at Cambridge.  The college was founded in 1636.  Nowhere in the *Journal* is there mention of the benefaction of John Harvard.  The act of 1642 vested the government in all the magistrates of *the jurisdiction* (*i. e.*, of Massachusetts), the teaching elders of the six nearest towns, and the president.  One of the nine who were graduated was the celebrated George Downing.

speeches, etc., for which, though they were adulti, they were corrected in the college, and sequestered, etc., for a time.

6.] Here came in a French shallop with some 14 men, whereof one was La Tour his lieutenant. They brought letters from La Tour to the governor, full of compliments, and desire of assistance from us against Monsieur D'Aulnay. They staid here about a week, and were kindly entertained, and though they were papists, yet they came to our church meeting; and the lieutenant seemed to be much affected to find things as he did, and professed he never saw so good order in any place. One of the elders gave him a French testament with Marlorat's notes, which he kindly accepted, and promised to read it.[1]

13.] Six ships went hence, laden with pipe staves and other commodities of this country; four went a little before. Of these, four were built in the country this year. Thus God provided for us beyond expectation.

6.] Mention is made before of the white hills, discovered by one Darby Field. The report he brought of shining stones, etc., caused divers others to travel thither, but they found nothing worth their pains. Amongst others, Mr. Gorge and Mr. Vines, two of the magistrates of Sir Ferdinand Gorge his province, went thither about the end of this month. They went up Saco river in birch canoes, and that way, they found it 90 miles to Pegwagget, an Indian town,[2] but by land it is but 60. Upon Saco river, they found many thousand acres of rich meadow, but there are ten falls, which hinder boats, etc. From the Indian town, they went up hill (for the most part) about 30 miles in woody lands, then they went about 7 or 8 miles

---

[1] La Tour and d'Aulnay, already mentioned as agents under the Chevalier Rasilly, for superintending the French claim to the eastward. They had quarrelled, and their English neighbors, as we shall see, were for years much embarrassed by them. The Huguenot commentator, Augustin Marlorat (1506-1563), is the writer alluded to.

[2] Pigwacket, or Pequawket, is now Fryeburg, Maine.

upon shattered rocks, without tree or grass, very steep all the way. At the top is a plain about 3 or 4 miles over, all shattered stones, and upon that is another rock or spire, about a mile in height, and about an acre of ground at the top. At the top of the plain arise four great rivers, each of them so much water, at the first issue, as would drive a mill; Connecticut river from two heads, at the N. W. and S. W. which join in one about 60 miles off, Saco river on the S. E., Amascoggen which runs into Casco Bay at the N. E., and Kennebeck, at the N. by E. The mountain runs E. and W. 30 or 40 miles, but the peak is above all the rest. They went and returned in 15 days.

8. (*October*) 18.] All the elders met at Ipswich; they took into consideration the book which was committed to them by the general court, and were much different in their judgments about it, but at length they agreed upon this answer in effect.[1]

Whereas in the book, there were three propositions laid down, and then the application of them to the standing council, and then the arguments enforcing the same: the propositions were these:—

1. In a commonwealth, rightly and religiously constituted, there is no power, office, administration, or authority, but such as are commanded and ordained of God.

2. The powers, offices, and administrations that are ordained of God, as aforesaid, being given, dispensed, and erected in a Christian commonwealth by his good providence, proportioned by his rule to their state and condition, established by his power against all opposition, carried on and accompanied with his presence and blessing, ought not to be by them either changed or altered, but upon such grounds, for such ends, in that manner, and only so far as the mind of God may be manifested therein.

3. The mind of God is never manifested concerning the change or alteration of any civil ordinance, erected or estab-

---

[1] The Body of Lawes now comes in to give form and definiteness to the theocracy.

lished by him as aforesaid in a Christian commonwealth, so long as all the cases, counsels, services, and occasions thereof may be duly and fully ended, ordered, executed, and performed without any change or alteration of government.

In their answer they allowed the said propositions to be sound, with this distinction in the 1st. viz. That all lawful powers are ordained, etc., either expressly or by consequence, by particular examples or by general rules.

In the applications they distinguished between a standing council invested with a kind of transcendent authority beyond other magistrates, or else any kind of standing council distinct from magistrates; the former they seem implicitly to disallow; the latter they approve as necessary for us, not disproportionable to our estate, nor of any dangerous consequence for disunion among the magistrates, or factions among the people, which were the arguments used by the author against our council. Some passages they wish had been spared, and other things omitted, which, if supplied, might have cleared some passages, which may seem to reflect upon the present councils, which they do think not to be of that moment, but that the uprightness of his intentions considered, and the liberty given for advice, according to the rules of religion, peace, and prudence, they would be passed by.

Lastly, they declare their present thoughts about the moulding and perfecting of a council, in four rules.

1. That all the magistrates, by their calling and office, together with the care of judicature, are to consult for the provision, protection, and universal welfare of the commonwealth.

2. Some select men taken out from the assistants, or other freemen, being called thereunto, be in especial, to attend by way of council, for the provision, protection, and welfare of the commonwealth.

3. This council, as counsellors, have no power of judicature.

4. In cases of instant danger to the commonwealth, in the interim, before a general court can be called, (which were meet

to be done with all speed,) what shall be consented unto and concluded by this council, or the major part of them, together with the consent of the magistrates, or the major part of them, may stand good and firm till the general court.

9. (*November*) 7.]  Some of our merchants sent a pinnace to trade with La Tour in St. John's river.  He welcomed them very kindly, and wrote to our governor letters very gratulatory for his lieutenant's entertainment, etc., and withal a relation of the state of the controversy between himself and Monsieur D'Aulnay.  In their return they met with D'Aulnay at Pema-quid, who wrote also to our governor, and sent him a printed copy of the arrest[1] against La Tour, and threatened us, that if any of our vessels came to La Tour, he would make prize of them.

22.]  The village at the end of Charlestown bounds was called Woburn, where they had gathered a church, and this day Mr. Carter was ordained their pastor, with the assistance of the elders of other churches.  Some difference there was about his ordination; some advised, in regard they had no elder of their own, nor any members very fit to solemnize such an ordinance, they would desire some of the elders of the other churches to have performed it; but others supposing it might be an occasion of introducing a dependency of churches, etc., and so a presbytery, would not allow it.  So it was performed by one of their own members, but not so well and orderly as it ought.[2]

Divers houses were burnt this year, by drying flax.  Among others, one Briscoe, of Watertown, a rich man, a tanner, who had refused to let his neighbor have leather for corn, saying he had corn enough, had his barn, and corn, and leather, etc., burnt, to the value of 200 pounds.

Mr. Larkam of Northam, alias Dover, suddenly discovering

---

[1] *Arrêt*, decree.

[2] The ceremony is described with much fulness in a noted passage, book II., ch. 22, of *The Wonder-Working Providence of Sion's Saviour in New England*, by Captain Edward Johnson of Woburn, one of the chief participants.

a purpose to go to England, and fearing to be dissuaded by his people, gave them his faithful promise not to go, but yet soon after he got on ship board, and so departed. It was time for him to be gone, for not long after a widow which kept in his house, being a very handsome woman, and about 50 years of age, proved to be with child, and being examined, at first refused to confess the father, but in the end she laid it to Mr. Larkam. Upon this the church of Dover looked out for another elder, and wrote to the elders to desire their help.

There arrived at Boston a small ship from the Madeiras with wine and sugar, etc., which were presently sold for pipe staves, and other commodities of the country, which were returned to the Madeiras: but the merchant himself, one Mr. Parish, staid divers months after. He had lived at the Madeiras many years among the priests and jesuits, who told him, when he was to come hither, that those of New England were the worst of all heretics, and that they were the cause of the troubles in England, and of the pulling down the bishops there.[1] When he went away, he blessed God for bringing him hither, professing that he would not lose what he had gotten in New England for all the wealth in the world. He went away in a pinnace built here intending a speedy return. By the way his pinnace (being calked in the winter) proved very leaky, so as all the seamen, being tired out with pumping, gave her over, but Mr. Parish continued the pump, and so kept her up, till it pleased God they espied land, and so they came safe to Fayal.

10 (*December*).] Those of the lower part of the river Pascataquack invited one Mr. James Parker of Weymouth, a godly man and a scholar, one who had been many years a deputy for the public court, to be their minister. He, by advice of divers of the magistrates and elders, accepted the call, and went and taught among them this winter, and it pleased God to give

---

[1] A testimony from foreign parts as to the prevalence in Old England of the "New England way," during the Civil War.

great success to his labors, so as above 40 of them, whereof
the most had been very profane, and some of them professed
enemies to the way of our churches, wrote to the magistrates
and elders, acknowledging the sinful course they had lived in,
and bewailing the same, and blessing God for calling them out
of it, and earnestly desiring that Mr. Parker might be settled
amongst them.  Most of them fell back again in time, embracing this present world.

This winter was the greatest snow we had, since we came
into the country, but it lay not long, and the frost was more
moderate than in some other winters.

# 1643

12 (*February*).] News came out of England, by two fishing ships, of the civil wars there between the king and the parliament, whereupon the churches kept divers days of humiliation. But some of the magistrates were not satisfied about the often reiteration of them for the same cause, but they would not contend with the elders about it, but left the churches to their liberty.

1. (*March*) 5.] At 7 in the morning, being the Lord's day, there was a great earthquake. It came with a rumbling noise like the former, but through the Lord's mercy it did no harm.

The churches held a different course in raising the ministers' maintenance. Some did it by way of taxation, which was very offensive to some. Amongst others, one Briscoe of Watertown, who had his barn burnt, as before mentioned, being grieved with that course in their town, the rather because himself and others, who were no members, were taxed, wrote a book against it, wherein, besides his arguments, which were naught, he cast reproach upon the elders and officers. This book he published underhand, which occasioned much stir in the town. At length, he and two more were convented before the court, where he acknowledged his fault in those reproachful speeches, and in publishing it, whereas it had been his duty to have acquainted the court or magistrates with his grievance, etc., (but for the arguments in the point, there was nothing required of him,) and was fined 10 pounds for that, and some slighting of the court, and one of the publishers, 40 shillings.

Corn was very scarce all over the country, so as by the end of the 2d month, many families in most towns had none to eat, but were forced to live of clams, muscles, cataos, dry fish, etc., and sure this came by the just hand of the Lord, to punish our ingratitude and covetousness.  For corn being plenty divers years before, it was so undervalued, as it would not pass for any commodity: if one offered a shop keeper corn for any thing, his answer would be, he knew not what to do with it. So for laborers and artificers; but now they would have done any work, or parted with any commodity, for corn.  And the husbandman, he now made his advantage, for he would part with no corn, for the most part, but for ready money or for cattle, at such a price as should be 12d. in the bushel more to him than ready money.  And indeed it was a very sad thing to see how little of a public spirit appeared in the country, but of self-love too much.  Yet there were some here and there, who were men of another spirit, and were willing to abridge themselves, that others might be supplied.  The immediate causes of this scarcity were the cold and wet summer, especially in the time of the first harvest; also, the pigeons came in such flocks, (above 10,000 in one flock,) that beat down, and eat up a very great quantity of all sorts of English grain; much corn spent in setting out the ships, ketches, etc.; lastly, there were such abundance of mice in the barns, that devoured much there.  The mice also did much spoil in orchards, eating off the bark at the bottom of the fruit trees in the time of the snow, so as never had been known the like spoil in any former winter.  So many enemies doth the Lord arm against our daily bread, that we might know we are to eat it in the sweat of our brows.

1. (*March*) 30.]  The *Trial*, Mr. Coytmore master, arrived, and a week after one of the ketches.  He sailed first to Fayal, where he found an extraordinary good market for his pipe staves and fish.  He took wine and sugar, etc., and sailed thence to Christophers in the West Indies, where he put off some of his wine for cotton and tobacco, etc., and for iron, which the islanders had saved of the ships which were there cast away. He obtained license, also, of the governor, Sir Thomas Warner, to take up what ordnance, anchors, etc., he could, and was to

have the one half; and by the help of a diving tub, he took up 50 guns, and anchors, and cables, which he brought home, and some gold and silver also, which he got by trade, and so, through the Lord's blessing, they made a good voyage, which did much encourage the merchants, and made wine and sugar and cotton very plentiful, and cheap, in the country.

Two ketches also, which were gone to the West Indies for cotton, etc., arrived safe not long after, and made return with profit. Another ship also, called the *Increase*, sent to the Madeiras, returned safe, and two other ships, after, though they went among the Turks.

There was a piece of justice executed at New Haven, which, being the first in that kind, is not unworthy to be recorded. Mr. Malbon, one of the magistrates there, had a daughter about [*blank*] years of age, which was openly whipped, her father joining in the sentence. The cause was thus.[1]

The wife of one Onion of Roxbury died in great despair: she had been a servant there, and was very stubborn and self-willed. After she was married, she proved very worldly, aiming at great matters. Her first child was still-born, through her unruliness and falling into a fever. She fell withal into great horror and trembling, so as it shook the room, etc., and crying out of her torment, and of her stubbornness and unprofitableness under the means, and her lying to her dame in denying somewhat that in liquorishness she had taken away, and of her worldliness, saying that she neglected her spiritual good for a little worldly trash, and now she must go to everlasting torments, and exhorted others to take heed of such evils, etc., and still crying out O! ten thousand worlds for one drop of Christ, etc. After she had then been silent a few hours, she began to speak again, and being exhorted to consider of God's infinite mercy, etc., she gave still this answer, "I cannot for my life," and so died.

[1] Winthrop has left a blank space in the manuscript, in which to insert the explanation, but does not give it.

The three ministers which were sent to Virginia, viz., Mr. Tompson, Mr. Knolles, and Mr. James from New Haven, departed (8) (*October*) 7. and were eleven weeks before they arrived. They lay windbound sometime at Aquiday: then, as they passed Hellgate between Long Island and the Dutch, their pinnace was bilged upon the rocks, so as she was near foundered before they could run on the next shore. The Dutch governor gave them slender entertainment; but Mr. Allerton of New Haven,[1] being there, took great pains and care for them, and procured them a very good pinnace and all things necessary. So they set sail in the dead of winter, and had much foul weather, so as with great difficulty and danger they arrived safe in Virginia. Here they found very loving and liberal entertainment, and were bestowed in several places, not by the governor, but by some well disposed people who desired their company. In their way the difficulties and dangers, which they were continually exercised with, put them to some question whether their call were of God or not; but so soon as they arrived there and had been somewhat refreshed, Mr. Tompson wrote back, that being a very melancholic man and of a crazy body, he found his health so repaired, and his spirit so enlarged, etc., as he had not been in the like condition since he came to New England. But this was to strengthen him for a greater trial, for his wife, a godly young woman, and a comfortable help to him, being left behind with a company of small children, was taken away by death, and all his children scattered, but well disposed of among his godly friends.

4. (*June*) 20.] Mr. Knolles returned from Virginia, and brought letters from his congregation and others there to our elders, which were openly read in Boston at a lecture, whereby it appeared that God had greatly blessed their ministry there, so as the people's hearts were much inflamed with desire after the ordinances, and though the state did silence the ministers, because they would not conform to the order of

[1] Isaac Allerton, formerly of Plymouth.

England,[1] yet the people resorted to them in private houses to hear them as before.

There fell out hot wars between the Dutch and the Indians thereabout. The occasion was this. An Indian, being drunk, had slain an old Dutchman. The Dutch required the murderer, but he could not be had. The people called often upon the governor to take revenge, but he still put it off, either for that he thought it not just, or not safe, etc. It fell out that the Mowhawks, a people that live upon or near Hudson's river, either upon their own quarrel, or rather, as the report went, being set on by the Dutch, came suddenly upon the Indians near the Dutch and killed about 30 of them, the rest fled for shelter to the Dutch. One Marine, a Dutch captain, hearing of it, goeth to the governor,[2] and obtains commission of him to kill so many as he could of them, and accordingly went with a company of armed men, and setting upon them, fearing no ill from the Dutch, he slew about 70 or 80 men, women and children. Upon this the Indians burnt divers of their farm houses and their cattle in them, and slew all they could meet with, to the number of 20 or more, of men, women and children, and pressed so hard upon the Dutch, even home to their fort, that they were forced to call in the English to their aid, and entertained Captain Underhill, etc., which Marine, the Dutch captain, took so ill, seeing the governor to prefer him before himself, that he presented his pistol at the governor, but was staid by a stander-by. Then a tenant of Marine discharged his musket at the governor, but missed him narrowly, whereupon the sentinel, by the governor's command, shot that fellow presently dead. His head was set upon the gallows, and the captain was sent prisoner into Holland. The people, also, were so offended at the governor for the damage they now sustained by the Indians, though they were all for war before, that the governor durst not trust himself among them,

---

[1] By act of assembly, forbidding non-conformist worship.
[2] William Kieft.

but entertained a guard of 50 English about his person, and the Indians did so annoy them by sudden assaults out of the swamps, etc., that he was forced to keep a running army to be ready to oppose them upon all occasions.

The Indians also of Long Island took part with their neighbors upon the main, and as the Dutch took away their corn, etc., so they fell to burning the Dutch houses. But these, by the mediation of Mr. Williams, who was then there to go in a Dutch ship for England, were pacified, and peace re-established between the Dutch and them.[1] At length they came to an accord of peace with the rest of the Indians also.

23.] One John Cook, an honest young man, being in his master's absence to salute a ship, etc., in the vanity of his mind thought to make the gun give a great report, and accordingly said to some, that he would make her speak. Overcharging her, she brake all into small pieces and scattered round about some men a flight shot off. Himself was killed, but no hurt found about him, but only one hand cut off and beaten a good distance from the place where he stood. And there appeared a special providence of God in it, for although there were many people up and down, yet none was hurt, nor was any near the gun when she was fired, whereas usually they gather thither on such occasions.

One of our ships, the *Seabridge*, arrived with 20 children and some other passengers out of England, and 300 pounds worth of goods purchased with the country's stock, given by some friends in England the year before; and those children, with many more to come after, were sent by money given one fast day in London, and allowed by the parliament and city for that purpose.

The house of commons also made an order in our favor, which was sent us under the hand of H. Elsynge, Cler. Parl. D. C.[2] to this effect, viz. Veneris[3] 10 Martii 1642.

---

[1] A characteristic service from Roger Williams.
[2] Clericus Parliamenti Domus Communis, *i. e.*, clerk of the House of Commons.
[3] *I. e.*, Die Veneris, or Friday, March 10. 1642/3.

Whereas the plantations in New England have, by the blessing of Almighty God, had good and prosperous success without any charge to this state, and are now likely to prove very happy for the propagation of the gospel in those parts, and very beneficial and commodious for this kingdom and nation, the commons now assembled in parliament do, for the better advancement of these plantations and encouragement of the planters, etc., ordain that all merchandizes, goods exported, etc., into New England to be spent, used or employed there, or being of the growth of that country, shall be imported hither, or put aboard to be spent, etc., in the voyage going or returning, and all and every the owners thereof, be free of all custom, etc., in England and New England, and all other ports, until this house shall take further order. This to be observed and allowed by all officers and persons whatsoever upon showing forth of this order, signed by the said clerk, without any other warrant.

Our general court, upon receipt of this order, caused the same, with our humble and thankful acknowledgment of so great a favor from that honorable assembly, to be entered verbatim among our records, in perpetuam rei memoriam.

One Richard [*blank*,] servant to one [*blank*] Williams of Dorchester, being come out of service, fell to work at his own hand and took great wages above others, and would not work but for ready money. By this means in a year, or little more, he had scraped together about 25 pounds, and then returned with his prey into England, speaking evil of the country by the way. He was not gone far, after his arrival, but the cavaliers met him and eased him of his money; so he knew no better way but to return to New England again, to repair his loss in that place which he had so much disparaged.

Mo. 3. (*May*) 10.] Our court of elections was held, when Mr. Ezekiel Rogers, pastor of the church in Rowley, preached. He was called to it by a company of freemen, whereof the most were deputies chosen for the court, appointed, by order of the last court, to meet at Salem about nomination of some to be put to the vote for the new magistrates. Mr. Rogers, hearing what exception was taken to this call, as unwarrantable, wrote to the governor for advice, etc., who returned him answer:

That he did account his calling not to be sufficient, yet the magistrates were not minded to strive with the deputies about it, but seeing it was noised in the country, and the people would expect him, and that he had advised with the magistrates about it, he wished him to go on.  In his sermon he described how the man ought to be qualified whom they should choose for their governor, yet dissuaded them earnestly from choosing the same man twice together, and expressed his dislike of that with such vehemency as gave offence.  But when it came to trial, the former governor, Mr. Winthrop, was chosen again, and two new magistrates, Mr. William Hibbins and Mr. Samuel Simons.

At this court came the commissioners from Plymouth, Connecticut and New Haven, viz., from Plymouth Mr. Edward Winslow and Mr. Collier, from Connecticut Mr. Haynes and Mr. Hopkins, with whom Mr. Fenwick of Saybrook joined, from New Haven Mr. Theophilus Eaton and Mr. Grigson. Our court chose a committee to treat with them, viz., the governor and Mr. Dudley, and Mr. Bradstreet, being of the magistrates; and of the deputies, Captain Gibbons, Mr. Tyng the treasurer, and Mr. Hathorn.[1]  These coming to consultation encountered some difficulties, but being all desirous of union and studious of peace, they readily yielded each to other in such things as tended to common utility, etc., so as in some two or three meetings they lovingly accorded upon these ensuing articles, which, being allowed by our court, and signed by all the commissioners, were sent to be also ratified by the general courts of other jurisdictions; only Plymouth commissioners, having power only to treat, but not to determine, de-

----

[1] The men mentioned in this entry were of the highest repute in their respective colonies, as was proper, since the business in hand was as grave as any in which New Englanders were ever concerned.  Thomas Grigson and William Tyng are the only ones not heretofore described.  The former was perhaps, next to Theophilus Eaton, the chief citizen of New Haven, where he was treasurer.  The latter filled the same office in Massachusetts, was one of the richest men in the community, and though not a magistrate, was for eight successive terms a deputy.

ferred the signing of them till they came home, but soon after
they were ratified by their general court also.[1]

Those of Sir Ferdinando Gorge his province, beyond
Pascataquack, were not received nor called into the confederation, because they ran a different course from us both
in their ministry and civil administration; for they had
lately made Acomenticus (a poor village) a corporation, and
had made a taylor their mayor, and had entertained one Hull,
an excommunicated person and very contentious, for their
minister.

At this court of elections there arose a scruple about the oath
which the governor and the rest of the magistrates were to
take, viz., about the first part of it: "You shall bear true faith
and allegiance to our sovereign Lord King Charles," seeing he
had violated the privileges of parliament, and made war upon
them, and thereby had lost much of his kingdom and many of
his subjects; whereupon it was thought fit to omit that part of
it for the present.

About this time two plantations began to be settled upon
Merrimack, Pentuckett called Haverill, and Cochichawick
called Andover.

---

[1] No event of our early history is more significant than the confederation of
the four colonies, Massachusetts, Plymouth, Connecticut and New Haven, a
distinct foreshadowing of the great American Union. Its importance has been
emphasized by all our historians. The league, a precedent for which was the
federation of the states of the Netherlands, was initiated by Connecticut and
New Haven, which, more exposed to pressure than their brethren farther east, the
Dutch on the Hudson elbowing sharply and the most formidable savages being
close at hand, sought support from their friends longer established. It must be
carefully noted that not all the English were included. The enterprises of Sir
Ferdinando Gorges were, as always, looked upon askance for reasons which
Winthrop assigns, as were also the undertakings at Providence and Aquidneck.
The independent spirit which breathes through the document is unmistakable, and
has been referred to by both liberal and tory historians, the one side approving,
the other condemning. About this time, says Palfrey (I. 633), the English
Parliament appoints a commission for colonial government, the terms used im-
plying an understanding quite different from that of the colonists: in fact the
Parliament of 1643 was disposed to be scarcely less arbitrary than the King, or
the later Parliament of George III.

*The articles of confederation between the plantations under the government of the Massachusetts, the plantations under the government of New Plymouth, the plantations under the government of Connecticut and the government of New Haven, with the plantations in combination therewith:*

WHEREAS we all came into these parts of America with one and the same end and aim, namely, to advance the kingdom of our Lord Jesus Christ, and to enjoy the liberties of the gospel in purity with peace: and whereas by our settling, by the wise providence of God, we are further dispersed upon the seacoasts and rivers than was at first intended, so that we cannot, according to our desire, with convenience communicate in one government and jurisdiction: and whereas we live encompassed with people of several nations and strange languages, which hereafter may prove injurious to us or our posterity; and for as much as the natives have formerly committed sundry insolences and outrages upon several plantations of the English, and have of late combined themselves against us, and seeing by reason of the sad distractions in England, (which they have heard of,) and by which they know we are hindered both from that humble way of seeking advice, and reaping those comfortable fruits of protection, which at other times we might well expect; we therefore do conceive it our bounden duty, without delay, to enter into a present consociation amongst ourselves for mutual help and strength in all future concernment, that, as in nation and religion, so in other respects, we be and continue one, according to the tenor and true meaning of the ensuing articles,—

1. Wherefore it is fully agreed and concluded between the parties above named, and they jointly and severally do, by these presents, agree and conclude that they all be, and henceforth be called by the name of the United Colonies of New England.

2. These united colonies, for themselves and their posterities, do jointly and severally hereby enter into a firm and perpetual league of friendship and amity, for offence and defence, mutual advice and succor upon all just occasions, both for preserving and propagating the truth and liberties of the gospel, and for their own mutual safety and welfare.

3. It is further agreed, that the plantations which at present are, or hereafter shall be settled within the limits of the Massachusetts, shall be forever under the government of the Massachusetts, and shall have peculiar jurisdiction amongst themselves in all cases as an entire body; and that Plymouth, Connecticut, and New Haven, shall each of them

in all respects have like peculiar jurisdiction and government within their limits, and in reference to the plantations which are already settled, or shall hereafter be erected, and shall settle within any of their limits respectively; provided that no other jurisdiction shall hereafter be taken in as a distinct head or member of this confederation, nor shall any other, either plantation or jurisdiction in present being, and not already in combination or under the jurisdiction of any of these confederates, be received by any of them: nor shall any two of these confederates join in one jurisdiction, without consent of the rest, which consent to be interpreted as in the 6th ensuing article is expressed.

4. It is also by these confederates agreed, that the charge of all just wars, whether offensive or defensive, upon what part or member of this confederation soever they shall fall, shall, both in men and provisions and all other disbursements, be borne by all the parts of this confederation in different proportions, according to their different abilities, in manner following, viz. That the commissioners for each jurisdiction, from time to time as there shall be occasion, bring account and number of all the males in each plantation, or any way belonging to or under their several jurisdictions, of what quality or condition soever they be, from sixteen years old to sixty, being inhabitants there, and that according to the different numbers which from time to time shall be found in each jurisdiction upon a true and just account, the service of men and all charges of the war be borne by the poll; each jurisdiction or plantation being left to their own just course or custom of rating themselves and people according to their different estates, with due respect to their qualities and exemptions among themselves, though the confederation take no notice of any such privilege; and that, according to the different charge of each jurisdiction and plantation, the whole advantage of the war, (if it please God so to bless their endeavors,) whether it be in lands, goods, or persons, shall be proportionably divided among the said confederates.

5. It is further agreed, that if any of these jurisdictions, or any plantation under or in combination with them, be invaded by any enemy whatsoever, upon notice and request of any three magistrates of that jurisdiction so invaded, the rest of the confederates, without any further notice or expostulation, shall forthwith send aid to the confederate in danger, but in different proportions, namely, the Massachusetts one hundred men sufficiently armed and provided for such a service and journey, and each of the rest 45 men so armed and provided; or any less number, if less be required, according to this proportion. But if such a confederate in danger may be supplied by their next confederate, not

exceeding the number hereby agreed, they may crave help thence, and seek no further for the present; the charge to be borne as in this article is expressed, and at their return to be victualled, and supplied with powder and shot, if there be need, for their journey, by that jurisdiction which employed or sent for them; but none of the jurisdictions to exceed these numbers till by a meeting of the commissioners for this confederation a greater aid appear necessary; and this proportion to continue till upon knowledge of the numbers in each jurisdiction, which shall be brought to the next meeting, some other proportion be ordered. But in any such case of sending men for present aid, whether before or after such order or alteration, it is agreed that at the meeting of the commissioners for this confederation, the cause of such war or invasion be duly considered, and if it appear that the fault lay in the party invaded, that then that jurisdiction or plantation make just satisfaction both to the invaders whom they have injured, and bear all the charge of the war themselves without requiring any allowance from the rest of the confederates towards the same. And further, that if any jurisdiction see any danger of an invasion approaching, and there be time for a meeting, that in such case three magistrates of that jurisdiction may summons a meeting at such convenient place as themselves shall think meet, to consider and provide against the threatened danger; provided when they are met, they may remove to what place they please: only while any of these four confederates have but three magistrates in their jurisdiction, a request or summons from any two of them shall be accounted of equal force with the three mentioned in both the clauses of this article, till there may be an increase of magistrates there.

6. It is also agreed, that for the managing and concluding of all affairs peculiar to and concerning the whole confederation, commissioners shall be chosen by and out of each of these four jurisdictions, viz., two for the Massachusetts, two for Plymouth, two for Connecticut, and two for New Haven, all in church fellowship with us, which shall bring full power from their several general courts respectively, to hear, examine, weigh, and determine all affairs of war or peace, leagues, aids, charges, and numbers of men for war, division of spoils, or whatever is gotten by conquest; receiving of more confederates or plantations into the combination with any of these confederates, and all things of like nature which are the proper concomitants or consequents of such a confederation for amity, offence and defence, not intermeddling with the government of any of the jurisdictions, which by the 3d article is preserved entirely to themselves. But if those eight commissioners, when they meet, shall not agree, yet it is concluded that any six of the eight, agreeing, shall have

power to settle and determine the business in question; but if six do not agree, that then such propositions, with their reasons, so far as they have been debated, be sent and referred to the four general courts, viz., the Massachusetts, Plymouth, Connecticut, and New Haven: and if at all the said general courts the business so referred be concluded, then to be prosecuted by the confederation and all their members. It is further agreed, that these eight commissioners shall meet once every year (besides extraordinary meetings according to the 5th article) to consider, treat, and conclude of all affairs belonging to this confederation, which meeting shall ever be the first Thursday in 7ber. (*September*), and that the next meeting after the date of these presents (which shall be accounted the second meeting) shall be at Boston in the Massachusetts, the third at Hartford, the fourth at New Haven, the fifth at Plymouth, the sixth and seventh at Boston, and so in course successively, if in the meantime some middle place be not found out and agreed upon, which may be commodious for all the jurisdictions.

7. It is further agreed, that at each meeting of these eight commissioners, whether ordinary or extraordinary, they all, or any six of them agreeing as before, may choose their president out of themselves, whose office and work shall be to take care and direct for order and a comely carrying on of all proceedings in their present meeting, but he shall be invested with no such power or respect, as by which he shall hinder the propounding or progress of any business, or any way cast the scales otherwise than in the preceding articles is agreed.

8. It is also agreed, that the commissioners for this confederation hereafter at their meetings, whether ordinary or extraordinary, as they may have commission or opportunity, do endeavor to frame and establish agreements and orders in general cases of a civil nature wherein all the plantations are interested for preserving peace amongst themselves, and preventing, as much as may be, all occasions of war or differences with others, as about free and speedy passage of justice in each jurisdiction to all the confederates equally, as to their own, receiving those that remove from one plantation to another without due certificates, how all the jurisdictions may carry it towards the Indians, that they neither grow insolent nor be injured without due satisfaction, lest war break in upon the confederates through miscarriages. It is also agreed, that if any servant run away from his master into any of these confederate jurisdictions, that in such case, upon certificate of one magistrate in the jurisdiction out of which the said servant fled, or upon other due proof, the said servant shall be delivered either to his master or any other that pursues and brings such certificate or proof: And that upon the escape

of any prisoner or fugitive for any criminal cause, whether breaking prison or getting from the officer, or otherwise escaping, upon the certificate of two magistrates of the jurisdiction out of which the escape is made, that he was a prisoner or such an offender at the time of the escape, the magistrate, or some of them of the jurisdiction where for the present the said prisoner or fugitive abideth, shall forthwith grant such a warrant as the case will bear, for the apprehending of any such person and the delivery of him into the hand of the officer or other person who pursueth him; and if there be help required for the safe returning of any such offender, then it shall be granted unto him that craves the same, he paying the charges thereof.[1]

9. And for that the justest wars may be of dangerous consequence, especially to the smaller plantations in these united colonies, it is agreed, that neither the Massachusetts, Plymouth, Connecticut, nor New Haven, nor any of the members of any of them, shall at any time hereafter begin, undertake, or engage themselves or this confederation, or any part thereof, in any war whatsoever, (sudden exigencies with the necessary consequences thereof excepted, which are also to be moderated as much as the case will permit,) without the consent and agreement of the aforenamed eight commissioners, or at least six of them, as in the 6th article is provided; and that no charge be required of any of the confederates, in case of a defensive war, till the said commissioners have met and approved the justice of the war, and have agreed upon the sum of money to be levied, which sum is then to be paid by the several confederates in proportion according to the 4th article.

10. That in extraordinary occasions, when meetings are summoned by three magistrates of any jurisdiction, or two, as in the 5th article, if any of the commissioners come not, due warning being given or sent, it is agreed that four of the commissioners shall have power to direct a war which cannot be delayed, and to send for due proportions of men out of each jurisdiction, as well as six might do if all met; but not less than six shall determine the justice of the war, or allow the demands or bills of charges, or cause any levies to be made for the same.

11. It is further agreed, that if any of the confederates shall hereafter break any of these present articles, or be otherway injurious to any one of the other jurisdictions, such breach of agreement or injury shall be duly considered and ordered by the commissioners for the other jurisdic-

---

[1] A rather curious forecast of the fugitive slave clause of the Constitution, the indentured servants, as often appears, being scarcely less in bondage than African slaves.

tions, that both peace, and this present confederation may be entirely preserved without violation.[1]

12. Lastly, this perpetual confederation, and the several articles and agreements thereof being read and seriously considered both by the general court for the Massachusetts and the commissioners for the other three, were subscribed presently by the commissioners, all save those of Plymouth, who, for want of sufficient commission from their general court, deferred their subscription till the next meeting, and then they subscribed also, and were to be allowed by the general courts of the several jurisdictions, which accordingly was done, and certified at the next meeting held at Boston, (7) (*September*) 7, 1643.

Boston, (3) 29,[2] 1643.

4. (*June*) 12.] Mr. La Tour arrived here in a ship of 140 tons, and 140 persons. The ship came from Rochelle, the master and his company were Protestants. There were two friars and two women sent to wait upon La Tour his lady. They came in with a fair wind, without any notice taken of them. They took a pilot out of one of our boats at sea, and left one of their men in his place. Capt. Gibbons' wife and children passed by the ship as they were going to their farm, but being discovered to La Tour by one of his gentlemen who knew her, La Tour manned out a shallop, which he towed after him to go speak with her. She seeing such a company of strangers making towards her, hastened to get from them, and landed at the governor's garden. La Tour landed presently after her, and there found the governor and his wife, and two of his sons, and his son's wife, and after mutual salutations he told the governor the cause of his coming, viz. that this ship being sent him out of France, D'Aulnay, his old

[1] Plainly in these articles no secession at will of any of the contracting parties was allowable.

[2] The date is clear in the manuscript, but Savage believes there is reason for making it May 19, as in the *Plymouth Records*, instead of 29. Three years later (1856) the publication of Bradford's *History* confirmed his view. The text, with some differences, especially in the ending, may be seen in Bradford, pp. 382–388, of the edition in the present series; also in the *Plymouth Records*, Vol. IX., *Colonial Records of Connecticut*, Vol. III., and *Old South Leaflets*, no. 169.

enemy, had so blocked up the river to his fort at St. John's, with two ships and a galliot, as his ship could not get in, whereupon he stole by in the night in his shallop, and was come to crave aid to convey him into his fort. The governor answered that he could say nothing to it till he had conferred with other of the magistrates; so after supper he went with him to Boston in La Tour's boat, having sent his own boat to Boston to carry home Mrs. Gibbons. Divers boats, having passed by him, had given notice hereof to Boston and Charles-town, his ship also arriving before Boston, the towns betook them to their arms, and three shallops with armed men came forth to meet the governor and to guard him home. But here the Lord gave us occasion to take notice of our weakness, etc., for if La Tour had been ill minded towards us, he had such an opportunity as we hope neither he nor any other shall ever have the like again; for coming by our castle and saluting it, there was none to answer him, for the last court had given order to have the castle-Island deserted, a great part of the work being fallen down, etc., so as he might have taken all the ordnance there. Then, having the governor and his family, and Captain Gibbons' wife, etc., in his power, he might have gone and spoiled Boston, and having so many men ready, they might have taken two ships in the harbor, and gone away without danger or resistance, but his neglecting this opportunity gave us assurance of his true meaning. So being landed at Boston, the governor, with a sufficient guard, brought him to his lodg-ing at Captain Gibbons'. This gave further assurance that he intended us no evil, because he voluntarily put his person in our power. The next day the governor called together such of the magistrates as were at hand, and some of the deputies, and propounding the cause to them, and La Tour being present, and the captain of his ship, etc., he showed his commission, which was fairly engrossed in parchment under the hand and seal of the Vice Admiral of France, and grand prior, etc., to bring supply to La Tour, whom he styled his majesty's lieu-

tenant general of L'Acadye, and also a letter from the agent of
the company of France to whom he hath reference, informing
him of the injurious practices of D'Aulnay against him, and
advising him to look to himself, etc., and superscribed to him
as lieutenant general, etc.   Upon this it appeared to us, (that
being dated in April last,) that notwithstanding the news
which D'Aulnay had sent to our governor the last year,
whereby La Tour was proclaimed a rebel, etc., yet he stood
in good terms with the state of France, and also with the
company.   Whereupon, though we could not grant him aid
without advice of the other commissioners of our confederacy,
yet we thought it not fit nor just to hinder any that would be
willing to be hired to aid him; and accordingly we answered
him that we would allow him a free mercate,[1] that he might
hire any ships which lay in our harbor, etc.   This answer he
was very well satisfied with and took very thankfully; he
also desired leave to land his men, that they might refresh
themselves, which was granted him, so they landed in small
companies, that our women, etc., might not be affrighted by
them.   This direction was duly observed.

But the training day at Boston falling out the next week,
and La Tour having requested that he might be permitted to
exercise his soldiers on shore, we expected him that day, so h~
landed 40 men in their arms, (they were all shot).[2]   They were
brought into the field by our train band, consisting of 150, and
in the forenoon they only beheld our men exercise.   When
they had dined, (La Tour and his officers with our officers, and
his soldiers invited home by the private soldiers,) in the afternoon they were permitted to exercise, (our governor and other
of the magistrates coming then into the field,) and all ours stood
and beheld them.   They were very expert in all their postures
and motions.

When it was near night, La Tour desired our governor
that his men might have leave to depart, which being granted,

[1] Market.                              [2] They were all muskets.

his captain acquainted our captain therewith, so he drew our men into a march, and the French fell into the middle.  When they were to depart, they gave a volley of shot and went to their boat, the French showing much admiration to see so many men of one town so well armed and disciplined, La Tour professing he could not have believed it, if he had not seen it. Our governor and others in the town entertained La Tour and his gentlemen with much courtesy, both in their houses and at table.  La Tour came duly to our church meetings, and always accompanied the governor to and from thence, who all the time of his abode here was attended with a good guard of halberts and musketeers.  Those who engrossed the ships, understanding his distress, and the justice of his cause, and the magistrates' permission, were willing to be entertained by him.[1]

But the rumor of these things soon spreading through the country, were diversely apprehended, not only by the common sort, but also by the elders, whereof some in their sermons spoke against their entertainment, and the aid permitted them; others

---

[1] The visit of La Tour to Boston is a picturesque episode.  At this moment France was on the brink of becoming involved in the English Civil War.  In the summer of 1643, the cause of Parliament, with which New England sympathized, was much depressed, while the King's party, most zealous in which was Queen Henrietta Maria, a French Catholic princess, seemed likely to triumph.  France was on the point of taking active part with the Cavaliers.  When therefore La Tour suddenly appeared in the harbor of the little town in a ship well armed and manned, great caution in dealing with him was necessary.  The fact that the ship's captain and part of the crew were Huguenots from Rochelle seemed to justify a policy of forbearance, as these were on good terms with La Tour.  It was a portentous sight indeed when a company of French soldiers, fully armed and drilled, manœuvred on the training field.  Dropping their muskets, and drawing their swords, they made a rapid charge, described, Savage says, in a note attached to the manuscript (burned in 1825). The more timorous feared this might be in earnest.  La Tour's audacious visit was a bold bid for support from the Puritans against his rival d'Aulnay.  He might easily have carried off the governor and burned the unprepared settlement, but his disposition was friendly, and he withdrew leaving Boston quite dazed over the transaction.  The controversy as to whether the heads had done wisely or foolishly is preserved in the prolix pages of labored argument fortified pro and con by far-fetched Biblical precedents, which follow the narrative of La Tour's visit.

spake in the justification of both.  One [*blank*,] a judicious minister, hearing that leave was granted them to exercise their men in Boston, out of his fear of popish leagues and care of our safety, spake as in way of prediction, that, before that day were ended, store of blood would be spilled in Boston.  Divers also wrote to the governor, laying before him great dangers, others charging sin upon the conscience in all these proceedings; so as he was forced to write and publish the true state of the cause, and the reasons of all their proceedings, which satisfied many, but not all.  Also, the masters and others, who were to go in the ships, desired advice about their proceedings, etc. whereupon the governor appointed another meeting, to which all the near magistrates and deputies, and the elders also were called, and there the matter was debated upon these heads.

1.  Whether it were lawful for Christians to aid idolaters, and how far we may hold communion with them?

2.  Whether it were safe for our state to suffer him to have aid from us against D'Aulnay?

To the first question, the arguments on the negative part were these.  1. Jehoshaphat is reproved for the like—wouldst thou help the wicked?  The answer to this was, first, this must be meant only in such case as that was, not simply according to the words of that one sentence taken apart from the rest, for otherwise it would be unlawful to help any wicked man, though a professed Protestant, and though our own countryman, father, brother, etc., and that in any case, though ready to be drowned, slain, famished, etc., second, Jehoshaphat aided him in a brotherly league of amity and affinity: I am as thou art, my people as thy people, etc.  2. Ahab was declared a wicked man by God, and denounced to destruction.  Answer. Ahab was in no distress, and so needed no aid.

2. Argument.  Jehoshaphat joining after with Ahazia in making ships, is reproved, etc.  Answer.  There is difference between helping a man in distress, which is a duty imposed,

and joining in a course of merchandise where the action is
voluntary: and it appears by this their joining, that the league
of amity continued between the two kingdoms.

3. Argument.    Josias did evil in aiding the king of Babylon
against Pharaoh Necho.    Answer 1. The king of Babylon
was in no distress, nor did desire his help, nor is it said he
intended his aid.    2. Josias, no doubt, did not break any known
general rule, being so strict an observer of all God's commandments; for it was not lawful for him to stop Pharaoh's army
from going through his country, but his sin was, that either he
did not believe the message of God by Pharaoh in that particular case, or did not inquire further about it from his own
prophets, and so it is expressed in that story.

4. Argument.    Amaziah, king of Judah, is reproved for
hiring an army out of Israel, because God was near with Israel.
Answer.    This is not to the question, which is of giving aid,
and not of hiring aid from others, nor was Amaziah in any
distress, but only sought to enlarge his dominion.

5. Argument.    By aiding papists, we advance and strengthen
popery.    Answer 1. We are not to omit things necessary and
lawful for a doubtful ill consequence, which is but accidental.
2. Such aid may as well work to the weakening of popery
by winning some of them to the love of the truth, as hath
sometimes fallen out, and sometimes by strengthening one
part of them against another, they may both be the more
weakened in the end.

For the 2d question, whether it be safe, etc., the arguments
on the negative part were these.

1. Papists are not to be trusted, seeing it is one of their
tenets that they are not to keep promise with heretics.    Answer. In this case we rely not upon their faith but their interest, it being for their advantage to hold in with us, we may
safely trust them; besides, we shall not need to hazard ourselves upon their fidelity, having sufficient strength to secure
ourselves.

**2.** We may provoke the state of France against us, or at least D'Aulnay, and so be brought into another war.   Answer. It appears by the commission and letter before-mentioned, that La Tour stands in good terms with the state of France and the company, etc.   It is usual in all states in Europe to suffer aid to be hired against their confederates, without any breach of the peace, as by the states of Holland against the Spaniards, and by both out of England, without any breach of the peace, or offence to either.   As for D'Aulnay, he hath carried himself so, as we could look for no other but ill measures from him, if he were able, though we should not permit La Tour to have help from us, for he hath taken Penobscott from us with our goods to a great value.   He made prize of our men and goods also at Isle Sable, and kept our men as slaves a good space, but never made satisfaction for our goods; likewise he entertained our servants which ran from us, and refuseth to return them, being demanded; he also furnisheth the Indians about us with guns and powder; and lastly, he wrote last year to our governor, forbidding our vessels to pass beyond his fort in the open sea, and threatening to make prize if he should meet, etc., and if the worst should happen that can be feared, yet if our way be lawful, and we innocent from wrong, etc., we may and must trust God with our safety so long as we serve his providence in the use of such means as he affords us.

3. Argument. Solomon tells us, that he that meddleth with a strife which belongs not to him, takes a dog by the ear, which is very dangerous.   Answer. This is a strife which doth belong to us, both in respect of La Tour seeking aid of us in his distress, and also in respect it so much concerns us to have D'Aulnay subdued or weakened: and it were not wisdom in us to stop the course of providence, which offers to do that for us without our charge, which we are like otherwise to be forced to undertake at our own charge.

4. It is not safe to permit this aid to go from us, especially without advice of the general court, lest it should miscarry,

and so prove a dishonor and weakening to us. Answer 1. For the general court, it could not have been assembled under fourteen days, and such delay, besides the necessary charge it would have put La Tour unto, and ourselves also by the strong watches we were forced to keep, it might have lost the opportunity of relieving him, or it might have put him upon some dangerous design of surprising our ships, etc. Besides, if the court had been assembled, we knew they would not have given him aid without consent of the commissioners of the other colonies, and for a bare permission, we might do it without the court; and to have deferred this needlessly, had been against that rule: say not to thy neighbor, go and come again, and to-morrow I will give thee, when there is power in thine hands to do it. As for the danger of miscarriage, it is not so much as in other our voyages to Spain or England, or, etc., and if the rule be safe that we walk by, the success cannot alter it.

5. We hear only one party, we should as well hear the other, otherwise we deal not judicially, and perhaps may aid a man in an unjust quarrel. Answer 1. We heard formerly D'Aulnay's allegations against La Tour, and notwithstanding all that, La Tour his cause appears just; for they being both the subjects of the same prince, the ship coming by permission from their prince's authority, D'Aulnay ought to permit him to enter peaceably. 2. Our men that go will first offer parley with D'Aulnay, and if La Tour his cause be unjust, they are not to offend the others. 3. La Tour being now in desperate distress, he is first to be succoured, before the cause be further inquired into, according to the example of Abraham, who, hearing of the distress of his kinsman Lot, staid not till he might send to Chedorlaomer to have his answer about the justice of his cause; yet there was strong presumption that his cause was just, and that Lot and all the rest were lawful prisoners, for they had been twelve years his subjects and were in rebellion at this time, but he stays not to inquire out the cause, the distress not

permitting it, but goes personally to rescue them: As put case—an Englishman or Spaniard should be driven into our harbor by a pirate, and should come and inform us so, and desire us to let him have aid to convey him safe to sea, might we not lawfully send out aid with him, before he had sent to the pirate to understand the cause; it would be time enough to demand that, when our aid came up with him. So if our neighboring Indians should send to us to desire aid against some other Indians who were coming to destroy them, should we first send to the other Indians to inquire the justice of the cause? No, but we should first send to save them, and after examine the cause.

The arguments on the affirmative part are many of them touched in the former answers to the arguments on the other part. The rest are these.

1. By the royal law, thou shalt love thy neighbor as thyself. If our neighbor be in distress, we ought to help him without any respect to religion or other quality; but an idolater in distress is our neighbor, as appears by that parable, Luke 10, where it is plainly concluded, that the Samaritan was neighbor to the distressed traveller, and our Saviour bids the lawyer, being a Jew, to do likewise, that is, even to a Samaritan, if in distress; and by the law of relations the distressed Jew was neighbor to the Samaritan, and the Samaritan in distress should have been so to him, though as opposite in religion as Protestants and papists. If such an one be not our neighbor, then we have no relation to him by any command of the second table, for that requires us to love our neighbor only, and then we may deceive, beat, and otherwise damnify him, and not sin, etc.

2. Argument out of Gal. 6. 10. Do good to all, but specially to the household of faith, by which it appears that under all, he includes such as were not believers, and those were heathen idolaters, and if we must do good to such, we must help them in distress.

3. We are exhorted to be like our Heavenly Father in doing good to the just and unjust, that is to all, as occasion is offered, even such as he causeth the sun to shine upon, and the rain to fall upon, though excommunicated persons, blasphemers, and persecutors, yet if they be in distress, we are to do them good, and therefore to relieve them.

4. We may hold some kind of communion with idolaters, as 1. We may have peace with them; 2. Commerce: Ezek. 27. 17. speaking of Tyrus, who were idolaters, he sayeth, Judah were thy merchants in wheat, etc., and the Jews were not forbidden to trade with the heathen in Nehemiah's time, so it were not on the Sabbath.   3. In eating and drinking and such like familiar converse: 1. Cor. 10. if an heathen invite a Christian to his table, he might go, etc., and so he might as well invite such to his table, as Solomon did the queen of Sheba, and the ambassadors of other princes round about him, who would not have resorted to him as they did, if he had not entertained them courteously; and he both received presents and gave presents to the queen of Sheba, and others who were then idolaters—and Neh. 5. 17. he sayeth, that with the Jews there were also at his table usually such of the heathen as came to him: so that it was not then (nor indeed at all by the law) unlawful for the Jews to eat with heathen, though the Pharisees made it unlawful by their tradition.

The fourth and last kind of communion is succor in distress.

To the second question, the arguments on the affirmative part were these, with others expressed before in the answers.

1. D'Aulnay is a dangerous neighbor to us; if he have none to oppose him, or to keep him employed at home, he will certainly be dealing with us, but if La Tour be not now helpen, he is undone, his fort, with his wife, children, and servants, will all be taken, he hath no place to go unto—this ship cannot carry back him and all his company to France, but will leave them on shore here, and how safe it will be for us to keep them is doubtful, but to let them go will be more dangerous, for they

must then go to D'Aulnay, and that will strengthen him greatly both by their number, and still also by their present knowledge of our state and place, which, in regard of our own safety, lays a necessity upon us of aiding La Tour, and aiding him so as he may subsist, and be able to make good his place against his enemy.

2. La Tour being in urgent distress, and therefore as our neighbor to be relieved, if it be well done of us, we may trust in God, and not be afraid of any terror, 1 Peter, 3. 6.

3. It will be no wisdom for D'Aulnay to begin with us, for he knows how much stronger we are than he, in men and shipping; and some experience we have had hereof, in that when our friends of Plymouth hired a ship in our harbor, and therewith went and battered his house at Penobscott, yet he took no occasion thereby against us, nor ever attempted any thing against them, though their trading house at Kennebeck be an hindrance to him, and easy for him to take at his pleasure.

There were other instances brought to the lawfulness, both in Joshua his aiding the Gibeonites, who were Canaanites, and had deluded him, and he might hereupon have left them to be spoiled by their neighbors. So when Jehoshaphat aided Jehorim against Moab, (for he had put away Baal,) Elisha speaks honorably to him and doth not reprove him, but for his presence sake saves their house by miracle, etc.

The like rumors and fears were raised upon our first expedition against the Pequods, 1636. The governor of Plymouth wrote to Mr. Winthrop, then deputy governor, in dislike of our attempt, and in apprehension of the great danger we had incurred, that we had provoked the Pequods, and no more, and had thereby occasioned a war, etc. But we found, through the Lord's special mercy, that that provocation and war proved a blessing to all the English. Our brethren of Connecticut wrote also to us, declaring their fears, and the danger we had cast them into by warring upon the Pequods, etc. And indeed we committed an error, in that we did not first give them

notice of our intention, that they might take the more care
of their own safety, but they could not be ignorant of our
preparations.

The governor by letters informed the rest of the commissioners of the united colonies of what had passed about La
Tour; but the reason why he did not defer him at first for his
answer, till some more of the magistrates and deputies might
have been assembled, and the elders likewise consulted with,
was this. Conceiving that he stood still under the same sentence of the arrest from the state of France, there would have
been no need of advice in the case, for we must have given
him the same answer we gave his lieutenant the last year, and
upon the same ground, viz. That however he might trade here
for such commodities as he stood in need of, yet he could expect no aid from us, for it would not be fit nor safe for us to
do that which might justly provoke the state of France against
us. But being met, and seeing the commission from the vice
admiral, etc., that occasion of danger being removed, we doubted not but we might safely give him such answer as we did,
without further trouble to the country or delay to him. See
more of this [blank] leaves after.

The sow business not being yet digested in the country,[1]
many of the elders being yet unsatisfied, and the more by reason of a new case stated by some of the plaintiff's side and
delivered to the elders, wherein they dealt very partially, for
they drew out all the evidence which made for the plaintiff, and
thereupon framed their conclusion without mentioning any of
the defendant's evidence. This being delivered to the elders,
and by them imparted to some of the other side, an answer
was presently drawn, which occasioned the elders to take a
view of all the evidence on both parties, and a meeting being
procured both of magistrates and elders (near all in the juris-

---

[1] For the "sow business," see p. 64. Palfrey well describes how through
this dispute over a trifling matter the bicameral feature became established in
the New England legislatures.

diction) and some of the deputies, the elders there declared, that notwithstanding their former opinions, yet, upon examination of all the testimonies, they found such contrariety and crossing of testimonies, as they did not see any ground for the court to proceed to judgment in the case, and therefore earnestly desired that the court might never be more troubled with it. To this all consented except Mr. Bellingham who still maintained his former opinion, and would have the magistrates lay down their negative voice, and so the cause to be heard again. This stiffness of his and singularity in opinion was very unpleasing to all the company, but they went on notwithstanding, and because a principal end of the meeting was to reconcile differences and take away offences, which were risen between some of the magistrates by occasion of this sow business and the treatise of Mr. Saltonstall against the council, so as Mr. Bellingham and he stood divided from the rest, which occasioned much opposition even in open court, and much partaking in the country, but by the wisdom and faithfulness of the elders Mr. Saltonstall was brought to see his failings in that treatise, which he did ingenuously acknowledge and bewail, and so he was reconciled with the rest of the magistrates. They labored also to make a perfect reconciliation between the governor and Mr. Bellingham. The governor offered himself ready to it, but the other was not forward, whereby it rested in a manner as it was. Mr. Dudley also had let fall a speech in the court to Mr. Rogers of Ipswich, which was grievous to him and other of the elders. The thing was this. Mr. Rogers being earnest in a cause between the town and Mr. Bradstreet, which also concerned his own interest, Mr. Dudley used this speech to him, "Do you think to come with your eldership here to carry matters," etc. Mr. Dudley was somewhat hard at first to be brought to see any evil in it, but at last he was convinced and did acknowledge it, and they were reconciled.

The deputies, also, who were present at this meeting and

had voted for the plaintiff in the case of the sow, seemed now
to be satisfied, and the elders agreed to deal with the deputies
of their several towns, to the end that that cause might never
trouble the court more. But all this notwithstanding, the
plaintiff, (or rather one G. Story her solicitor,) being of an unsatisfied spirit, and animated, or at least too much countenanced, by some of the court, preferred a petition at the court
of elections for a new hearing, and this being referred to the
committee for petitions, it was returned that the greater part of
them did conceive the cause should be heard again, and some
others in the court declared themselves of the same judgment,
which caused others to be much grieved to see such a spirit in
godly men, that neither the judgment of near all the magistrates, nor the concurrence of the elders and their mediation,
nor the loss of time and charge, nor the settling of peace in
court and country could prevail with them to let such a
cause fall, (as in ordinary course of justice it ought,) as nothing could be found in, by any one testimony, to be of criminal
nature, nor could the matter of the suit, with all damages,
have amounted to forty shillings. But two things appeared
to carry men on in this course as it were in captivity. One
was, the deputies stood only upon this, that their towns
were not satisfied in the cause (which by the way shows plainly
the democratical spirit which acts our deputies, etc.). The
other was, the desire of the name of victory; whereas on the
other side the magistrates, etc., were content for peace sake,
and upon the elders' advice, to decline that advantage, and to
let the cause fall for want of advice to sway it either way.

Now that which made the people so unsatisfied, and unwilling the cause should rest as it stood, was the 20 pounds
which the defendant had recovered against the plaintiff in an
action of slander for saying he had stolen the sow, etc., and
many of them could not distinguish this from the principal
cause, as if she had been adjudged to pay 20 pounds for de-
manding her sow, and yet the defendant never took of this

more than 3 pounds, for his charges of witnesses, etc., and offered to remit the whole, if she would have acknowledged the wrong she had done him. But he being accounted a rich man, and she a poor woman, this so wrought with the people, as being blinded with unreasonable compassion, they could not see, or not allow justice her reasonable course. This being found out by some of the court, a motion was made, that some who had interest in the defendant would undertake to persuade him to restore the plaintiff the 3 pounds (or whatever it were) he took upon that judgment, and likewise to refer other matters to reference which were between the said Story and him. This the court were satisfied with, and proceeded no further.

There was yet one offence which the elders desired might also be removed, and for that end some of them moved the governor in it, and he easily consented to them so far as they had convinced him of his failing therein. The matter was this. The governor had published a writing about the case of the sow, as is herein before declared, wherein some passages gave offence, which he being willing to remove, so soon as he came into the general court, he spake as followeth, (his speech is set down verbatim to prevent misrepresentation, as if he had retracted what he had wrote in the point of the case:)

I understand divers have taken offence at a writing I set forth about the sow business; I desire to remove it, and to begin my year in a reconciled estate with all. The writing is of two parts, the matter and the manner. In the former I had the concurrence of others of my brethren, both magistrates and deputies; but for the other, viz., the manner, that was wholly mine own, so as whatsoever was blame-worthy in it I must take it to myself. The matter is point of judgment, which is not at my own disposing. I have examined it over and again by such light as God hath afforded me from the rules of religion, reason, and common practice, and truly I can find no ground to retract any thing in that, therefore I desire I may enjoy my liberty herein, as every of yourselves do, and justly may. But for the manner, whatsoever I might allege for my justification before men, I now pass it over: I now set myself before another judgment seat. I will first speak to the manner in general and then to two particulars.  For the general.  Howsoever that which I wrote was upon great provocation by some of the adverse party, and upon invitation from others to vindicate ourselves from that aspersion which was cast upon us, yet that was no sufficient warrant for me to break out into any distemper.  I confess I was too prodigal of my brethren's reputation: I might have obtained the cause I had in hand without casting such blemish upon others as I did.  For the particulars.  1.  For the conclusion, viz., now let religion and sound reason give judgment in the case; whereby I might seem to conclude the other side to be void both of religion and reason.  It is true a man may (as the case may be) appeal to the judgment of religion and reason, but, as I there carried it, I did arrogate too much to myself and ascribe too little to others.  The other particular was the profession I made of maintaining what I wrote before all the world, which, though it may modestly be professed, (as the case may require,) yet I confess it was now not so beseeming me, but was indeed a fruit of the pride of mine own spirit.  These are all the Lord hath brought me to consider of, wherein I acknowledge my failings, and humbly intreat you will pardon and pass them by; if you please to accept my request, your silence shall be a sufficient testimony thereof unto me, and I hope I shall be more wise and watchful hereafter.

The sow business had started another question about the magistrates' negative vote in the general court.  The deputies generally were very earnest to have it taken away; whereupon one of the magistrates wrote a small treatise, wherein he laid down the original of it from the patent, and the establishing of it by order of the general court in 1634, showing thereby how it was fundamental to our government, which, if it were taken away, would be a mere democracy.  He showed also the necessity and usefulness of it by many arguments from scripture, reason, and common practice, etc.  Yet this would not satisfy, but the deputies and common people would have it taken away; and yet it was apparent (as some of the deputies themselves confessed) the most did not understand it.  An answer also was written (by one of the magistrates as was conceived) to the said treatise, undertaking to avoid all the arguments both from the patent and from the order, etc.  This the deputies made great use of in this court, supposing they had now enough to carry the cause clearly with them, so as they pressed earnestly to have it presently determined. But the magistrates told them the matter was of great concernment, even to the very frame of our government; it had been established upon serious consultation and consent of all the elders; it had been continued without any inconvenience or apparent mischief these fourteen years, therefore it would not be safe nor of good report to alter on such a sudden, and without the advice of the elders: offering withal, that if upon such advice and consideration it should appear to be inconvenient, or not warranted by the patent and the said order, etc., they should be ready to join with them in taking it away. Upon these propositions they were stilled, and so an order was drawn up to this effect, that it was desired that every member of the court would take advice, etc., and that it should be no offence for any, either publicly or privately, to declare their opinion in the case, so it were modestly, etc., and that the elders should be desired to give their advice before the next meeting of this court. It was the magistrates' only care to gain time, that so the people's heat might be abated, for then they knew they would hear reason, and that the advice of the elders might be interposed; and that there might be liberty to reply to the answer, which was very long and tedious, which accordingly was done soon after the court, and published to good satisfaction. One of the elders also wrote a small treatise, wherein scholastically and religiously he handled the question, laying down the several forms of government both simple and mixt, and the true form of our government, and the unavoidable change into a democracy, if the negative voice were taken away; and answered all objections, and so concluded for the continuance of it, so as the deputies and the people also, having their heat moderated by time, and their judgments better informed by what they had learned about it, let the cause fall, and he who had written the answer to the first defence, appeared no further in it.

Our supplies from England failing much, men began to look about them, and fell to a manufacture of cotton, whereof we had store from Barbados, and of hemp and flax, wherein Rowley, to their great commendation, exceeded all other towns.

The governor acquainted the court with a letter he received from Mr. Wheelwright, to intreat the favor of the court that he might have leave to come into the Bay upon especial occasions, which was readily granted him for 14 days, whereupon he came and spake with divers of the elders, and gave them such satisfaction as they intended to intercede with the court for the release of his banishment. See more (3) 44.[1]

Sacononoco and Pumham, two sachems near Providence, having under them between 2 and 300 men, finding themselves overborne by Miantunnomoh, the sachem of Naragansett and Gorton and his company, who had so prevailed with Miantunnomoh, as he forced one of them to join with him in setting his hand or mark to a writing, whereby a part of his land was sold to Gorton and his company, for which Miantunnomoh received a price, but the other would not receive that which was for his part, alleging that he did not intend to sell his land, though through fear of Miantunnomoh he had put his mark to the writing, they came to our governor, and by Benedict Arnold[2] their interpreter, did desire we would receive them under our government, and brought withal a small present of wampom, about ten fathom. The governor gave them encouragement, but referred them to the court, and received their present, intending to return it them again, if the court should not accord to them; but at the present he acquainted another of the magistrates with it. So it was agreed, and they wrote

[1] *I. e.*, under May, 1644.

[2] Benedict Arnold, long a trusted and useful man, especially helpful for his knowledge of Indian tongues and his faculty for dealing with the tribes, afterward eleven times governor of Rhode Island. The area described in the deed of January 12, 1642/3, was about equivalent to that of the present townships of Warwick and Coventry, R. I.

to Gorton and his company to let them know what the sachems had complained of, and how they had tendered themselves to come under our jurisdiction, and therefore if they had any thing to allege against it, they should come or send to our next court. We sent also to Miantunnomoh to signify the same to him. Whereupon, in the beginning of the court, Miantunnomoh came to Boston, and being demanded in open court, before divers of his own men and Cutshamekin and other Indians, whether he had any interest in the said two sachems as his subjects, he could prove none. Cutshamekin also in his presence affirmed, that he had no interest in them, but they were as free sachems as himself; only because he was a great sachem, they had sometime sent him presents, and aided him in his war against the Pequots: and Benedict Arnold affirmed, partly upon his own knowledge, and partly upon the relation of divers Indians of those parts, that the Indians belonging to these sachems did usually pay their deer skins (which are a tribute belonging to the chief sachem) always to them, and never to Miantunnomoh or any other sachem of Naragansett, which Miantunnomoh could not contradict. Whereupon it was referred to the governor and some other of the magistrates and deputies to send for the two sachems after the court, and to treat with them about their receiving in to us.

But before this, Gorton and his company (12 in number) sent a writing to our court of four sheets of paper, full of reproaches against our magistrates, elders and churches, of familistical and absurd opinions, and therein they justified their purchase of the sachems' land, and professed to maintain it to the death. They sent us word also after, (as Benedict Arnold reported to us,) that if we sent men against them, they were ready to meet us, being assured of victory from God, etc. Whereupon the court sent two of the deputies to speak with them, to see whether they would own that writing which was subscribed by them all. When they came, they with much difficulty came to find out Gorton and two or three more of them, and upon conference they did own and justify the said writing. They spake also with the two sachems, as they had commission, and giving them to understand upon what terms they must be received under us, they found them very pliable to all, and opening to them the ten commandments, they received this answer, which I have set down as the commissioners took it in writing from their mouths.

1. Quest. Whether they would worship the true God that made heaven and earth, and not blaspheme him? Ans. We desire to speak reverently of Englishman's God and not to speak evil of him, because we see the Englishman's God doth better for them than other Gods do for others.

2. That they should not swear falsely. Ans. We never knew what swearing or an oath was.

3. Not to do any unnecessary work on the Lord's day within the gates of proper towns. Ans. It is a small thing for us to rest on that day, for we have not much to do any day, and therefore we will forbear on that day.

4. To honor their parents and superiors. Ans. It is our custom so to do, for inferiors to be subject to superiors, for if we complain to the governor of the Massachusetts that we have wrong, if they tell us we lie, we shall willingly bear it.

5. Not to kill any man but upon just cause and just authority. Ans. It is good, and we desire so to do.

6. 7. Not to commit fornication, adultery, bestiality, etc. Ans. Though fornication and adultery be committed among us, yet we allow it not, but judge it evil, so the same we judge of stealing.

8. For lying, they say it is an evil, and shall not allow it.

9. Whether you will suffer your children to read God's word, that they may have knowledge of the true God and to worship him in his own way? Ans. As opportunity serveth by the English coming amongst us, we desire to learn their manners.

After the court, the governor, etc., sent for them, and they came to Boston at the day appointed, viz., the 22d of the 4th month (*June*), and a form of submission being drawn up, and they being by Benedict Arnold, their neighbor, and interpreter, (who spake their language readily,) made to understand every particular, in the presence of divers of the elders and many others, they freely subscribed the submission, as it here follow-eth verbatim. Being told that we did not receive them in as confederates but as subjects, they answered, that they were so little in respect of us, as they could expect no other. So they dined in the same room with the governor, but at a table by themselves; and having much countenance showed them by all present, and being told that they and their men should be al-ways welcome to the English, provided they brought a note from Benedict Arnold, that we might know them from other Indians, and having some small things bestowed upon them by the governor, they departed joyful and well satisfied. We looked at it as a fruit of our prayers, and the first fruit of our hopes, that the example would bring in others, and that the Lord was by this means making a way to bring them to civility, and so to conversion to the knowledge and embracing of the gospel in his due time.

Soon after their departure, we took order that Miantunno-moh and the English in those parts should have notice of their submission to us, that they might refrain from doing them injury.

*Their Submission was as followeth.*

This writing is to testify, That we Pumham, sachem of Shawomock, and Saconococo, sachem of Patuxet, etc., have, and by these presents do, voluntarily and without any constraint or persuasion, but of our own free motion, put ourselves, our subjects, lands and estates under the govern-ment and jurisdiction of the Massachusetts, to be governed and protected by them, according to their just laws and orders, so far as we shall be made capable of understanding them: and we do promise for ourselves and our subjects, and all our posterity, to be true and faithful to the said government, and aiding to the maintenance thereof to our best ability, and from time to time to give speedy notice of any conspiracy, attempt, or evil intention of any which we shall know or hear of, against the same: and we do promise to be willing, from time to time, to be instructed in the knowledge and worship of God.   In witness whereof, etc.[1]

The lady Moodye, a wise and anciently religious woman, being taken with the error of denying baptism to infants, was dealt withal by many of the elders and others, and admonished by the church of Salem, (whereof she was a member,) but persisting still, and to avoid further trouble, etc., she removed to the Dutch against the advice of all her friends.   Many others, infected with anabaptism, removed thither also.   She was after excommunicated.[2]

5. (*July*) 5.]   There arose a sudden gust at N. W. so violent for half an hour, as it blew down multitudes of trees.   It lifted up their meeting house at Newbury, the people being in it.   It darkened the air with dust, yet through God's great mercy it did no hurt, but only killed one Indian with the fall of a tree. It was straight between Linne and Hampton.

2.]   Here arrived one Mr. Carman, master of the ship called [*blank*] of 180 tons.   He went from New Haven in 10ber (*December*) last, laden with clapboards for the Canaries, being earnestly commended to the Lord's protection by the church there.   At the Island of Palma, he was set upon by a Turkish pirate of 300 tons and 26 pieces of ordnance and 200 men.   He fought with her three hours, having but 20 men and but 7 pieces of ordnance that he could use, and his muskets were unserviceable with rust.   The Turk lay across his hawse, so as he was forced to shoot through his own hoodings, and by these shot killed many Turks.   Then the Turk lay by his side and

---

[1] These Indian lands at Shawomet and Patuxit lay south of Providence and were much beyond the bounds of the Massachusetts charter.   We have here in unusual detail a specimen of the Massachusetts treatment of the Indians.

[2] The Lady Deborah Moody, a person highly connected, occupied for a time the estate at Saugus once owned by Humfrey.   She acquired influence in the parts to which she emigrated and rendered help to Peter Stuyvesant.

boarded him with near 100 men, and cut all his ropes, etc., but his shot having killed the captain of the Turkish ship and broken his tiller, the Turk took in his own ensign and fell off from him, but in such haste as he left about 50 of his men aboard him, then the master and some of his men came up and fought with those 50 hand to hand, and slew so many of them as the rest leaped overboard. The master had many wounds on his head and body, and divers of his men were wounded, yet but one slain; so with much difficulty he got to the island, (being in view thereof,) where he was very courteously entertained and supplied with whatsoever he wanted.

## *Continuation about La Tour.*

The governor, with the advice of some of the magistrates and elders, wrote a letter to D'Aulnay, taking occasion in answer to his letter in 9ber (*November*) last to this effect, viz. Whereas he found by the arrest he sent last autumn, that La Tour was under displeasure and censure in France, thereupon we intended to have no further to do with him than by way of commerce which is allowed, and if he had made prize of any of our vessels in that way, as he threatened, we should have righted ourselves so well as we could, without injury to himself or just offence to his majesty of France, whom we did honor as a great and mighty prince, and should endeavor always to behave ourselves towards his majesty and all his subjects as became us, etc. But La Tour coming now to us, and acquainting us how it was with him, etc., and here mentioning the vice admiral's commission and the letters, etc., though we thought not fit to give him aid, as being unwilling to intermeddle in the wars of any of our neighbors, yet considering his urgent distress, we could not in Christianity or humanity deny him liberty to hire for his money any ships in our harbor, either such as came to us out of England or others. And whereas some of our people were willing to go along with him, (though without any

commission from us,) we had charged them to labor by all
means to bring matters to a reconciliation, etc., and that they
should be assured, that if they should do or attempt any thing
against the rules of justice and good neighborhood, they must
be accountable therefor unto us at their return.[1]

Beside the former arguments, there came since to Boston
one Mr. Hooke, a godly gentleman, and a deputy of the court
for Salisbury, who related of the good usage and great courtesy
which La Tour had showed to himself and other passengers,
who were landed at his fort about nine years since as they
came from England, and how the ship leaving them there, and
only a small shallop to bring them to these parts, and a dangerous bay of 12 leagues to be passed over, he would not suffer
them to depart before he had provided his own pinnace to
transport them.

And whereas he was charged to have killed two Englishmen
at Machias not far from his fort, and to have taken away their
goods to the value of 500 pounds, Mr. Vines of Saco, who
was part owner of the goods and principal trader, etc., being
present with La Tour, the governor heard the cause between
them, which was thus: Mr. Vines being in a pinnace trading
in those parts, La Tour met him in another pinnace, and
bought so many of his commodities as Mr. Vines received
then of him 400 skins, and although some of Mr. Vines his
company had abused La Tour, whereupon he had made them
prisoners in his pinnace, yet at Mr. Vines' intreaty he discharged them with grave and good counsel, and acquainted Mr.
Vines with his commission to make prize of all such as should
come to trade in those parts, and thereupon desired him peaceably to forbear, etc., yet at his request he gave him leave to
trade the goods he had left, in his way home, so as he did not
fortify or build in any place within his commission, which he

---

[1] Savage thinks the inexpedient and calamitous policy of Winthrop as regards
La Tour referable to pressure brought to bear upon him by the Boston merchants,
who saw a chance to make money out of the Frenchman.

said he could not answer it if he should suffer it; whereupon they parted friendly. Mr. Vines landed his goods at Machias, and there set up a small wigwam, and left five men and two murderers[1] to defend it, and a shallop, and so returned home. Two days after La Tour comes, and casting anchor before the place, one of Mr. Vines' men came on board his pinnace, and while they were in parley, four of La Tour his men went on shore. One of the four which were in the house, seeing them, gave fire to a murderer, but it not taking fire, he called to his fellow to give fire to the other murderer, which he going to do, the four French retreated, and one of their muskets went off, (La Tour sayeth it was by accident, and that the shot went through one of his fellow's clothes, but Mr. Vines could say no thing to that). It killed two of the men on shore, which La Tour then professed himself innocent of, and very sorry for; and said further, that the five men were at that time all drunk, and not unlikely, having store of wine and strong water, for had they been sober, they would not have given fire upon such as they had conversed friendly with but two days before, without once bidding them stand, or asking them wherefore they came. After this La Tour coming to the house, and finding some of his own goods, (though of no great value,) which had a little before been taken out of his fort at St. Johns by the Scotch and some English of Virginia, (when they plundered all his goods to a great value and abused his men,) he seized the three men and the goods and sent them into France according to his commission, where the men were discharged, but the goods adjudged lawful prize. Mr. Vines did not contradict any of this, but only that he did not build or fortify at Machias, but only set up a shelter for his men and goods. For the value of the goods Mr. Vines showed an invoice which came to 3 or 400 pounds, but La Tour said he had another under the men's hands that were there, which came not to half so much. In conclusion he promised that he would refer the

---

[1] "Murderers" were small cannon.

cause to judgment, and if it should be found that he had done them wrong, he would make satisfaction.

5. (*July*) 14.]   In the evening La Tour took ship, the governor and divers of the chief of the town accompanying him to his boat.   There went with him four of our ships and a pinnace. He hired them for two months, the chiefest, which had 16 pieces of ordnance, at 200 pounds the month; yet she was of but 100 tons, but very well manned and fitted for fight, and the rest proportionable.  The owners took only his own security for their pay.   He entertained also about 70 land soldiers, volunteers, at 40s. per month a man, but he paid them somewhat in hand.

Of the two friars which came in this ship, the one was a very learned acute man.   Divers of our elders who had conference with him reported so of him.   They came not into the town, lest they should give offence, but once, being brought by some to see Mr. Cotton and confer with him, and when they came to depart, the chief came to take leave of the governor and the two elders of Boston, and showed himself very thankful for the courtesy they found among us.

In the afternoon they set sail from Long Island, the wind N. and by W. and went out at Broad Sound at half flood, where no ships of such burthen had gone out before, or not more than one.

Three errors the governor, etc., committed in managing this business.  1. In giving La Tour an answer so suddenly (the very next day after his arrival).   2. In not advising with any of the elders, as their manner was in matters of less consequence. 3. In not calling upon God, as they were wont to do in all public affairs, before they fell to consultation, etc.

The occasions of these errors were, first, their earnest desire to despatch him away, and conceiving at first they should have given him the same answer they gave his lieutenant the last year, for they had not then seen the Vice Admiral's commission. 2. Not then conceiving any need of counsel, the elders never

came into the governor's thoughts.  3. La Tour and many of
the French coming into them at first meeting, and some taking
occasion to fall in parley with them, there did not appear then
a fit opportunity for so solemn an action as calling upon God,
being in the midst of their business before they were aware of
it.   But this fault hath been many times found in the governor
to be over sudden in his resolutions, for although the course
were both warrantable and safe, yet it had beseemed men of
wisdom and gravity to have proceeded with more deliberation
and further advice.

Those about Ipswich, etc., took great offence at these proceedings, so as three of the magistrates and the elders of
Ipswich and Rowley, with Mr. Nathaniel Ward, wrote a letter
to the governor and assistants in the bay, and to the elders
here, protesting against the proceedings, and that they would
be innocent of all the evil which might ensue, etc., with divers
arguments against it, whereof some were weighty, but not to
the matter, for they supposed we had engaged the country
in a war, as if we had permitted our ships, etc., to fight with
D'Aulnay, whereas we only permitted them to be hired by
La Tour to conduct him home.   The governor made answer
to this protestation, so did Mr. Dudley and the pastor of
Boston.[1]

5. (*July*).]   Letters came to our governor from Mr. Haynes,
governor at Hartford, certifying of a war begun between Onkus,
sachem of Mohigen, and Sequasson, sachem upon Connecticut,
and that upon Onkus' complaint of the other's assaulting him,
etc., he sent for Sequasson and endeavored to make them
friends, but Sequasson chose rather to have war, so they were
forced to leave them to themselves, promising to be aiding
to neither, etc.   Soon after Onkus set upon Sequasson and
killed seven or eight of his men, wounded 13, burnt his wigwams and carried away the booty.   Upon this Miantunno-

[1] The papers in the controversy are preserved in Hutchinson, *Collection of Papers*, 115-134 (pp. 129-149 of Prince Society edition).

moh (being allied to Sequasson) sent to Mr. Haynes to complain of Onkus.  He answered that the English had no hand in it, nor would encourage them, etc.  Miantunnomoh gave notice hereof also to our governor by two of our neighbor Indians who had been with him, and was very desirous to know if we would not be offended, if he made war upon Onkus. Our governor answered, if Onkus had done him or his friends wrong and would not give satisfaction, we should leave him to take his own course.

5. (*July*) 22.]  A Dutch sloop arrived with letters in Latin, signed by the secretary there in the name and by the command of the governor and senate, directed to the governor and senate of U. P.[1] of New England, wherein 1st, he congratulates our late confederation, then he complains of unsufferable wrongs done to their people upon Connecticut, more of late than formerly, and of misinformation given by some of ours to the States' ambassador in London, and desires to know by a categorical answer, whether we will aid or desert them, (meaning of Hartford,) that so they may know their friends from their enemies, etc.  The governor appointed a meeting of some of the next magistrates on the second day next, but the rain hindering some of them, it was put off to the fifth day.

Here arrived a bark of the Earl of Warwick from Trinidado. She came for people and provisions, but our people, being well informed of the state of those places, were now become wiser, and could stay here where they were in better condition than they could be in those parts, so he altered his design and went toward Canada, and by the way guarded home a pinnace of La Tour's which came hither for provisions.

The wife of one [*blank*] Hett, of whom mention was made before, being cast out of the church of Boston, the Lord was pleased so to honor his own ordinance, that whereas before no means could prevail with her either to reclaim her from her

[1] United Provinces.

wicked and blasphemous courses and speeches, etc., or to bring
her to frequent the means, within a few weeks after her casting
out, she came to see her sin and lay it to heart, and to frequent
the means, and so was brought to such manifestation of repentance and a sound mind, as the church received her in again.

The day appointed for considering of the letter from the
Dutch proved again so wet as but few met, and of those some
would have another day appointed, and all the magistrates to
be called to it, but others thought it not fit both in regard the
messenger hasted away, and also, for that no direct answer
could be returned without a general court. At length advising with some of the elders who were at hand, and some
of the deputies, we returned answer to this effect, (in the name
of the governor only,) viz. After gratulation, etc., of their
friendly respect and our earnest desire of the continuance of
that good correspondency which hath been between themselves
and us, ever since our arrival in these parts, That our chief
council, to whom their letters were directed, being far dispersed,
etc., he was necessitated, with the advice of some other of the
magistrates, to return this answer to them for the present, being
rather a declaration of their own conceptions than the determination of our chiefest authority, from which they should
receive further answer in time convenient. We declared our
grief for the difference between them and our brethren of Hartford, which we conceived might be composed by arbiters, either
in England or Holland, or here; that by our confederation we
were bound to seek the good and safety of each other as our
own, which we hoped would not hinder the continuance of that
amity and correspondency between themselves and us; and
that the ground of their difference, being only for a small parcel of land, was a matter of so little value in this vast continent,
as was not worthy to cause a breach between two people so
nearly related, both in profession of the same Protestant
religion and otherwise; therefore we would seriously request
them, as we would do also the others, that until the justice

of the cause were decided by one of the ways before named, there might be abstinence on both sides from injury and provocation, and if any should happen on their part, that it might be duly examined, and we were assured (they being a people fearing God, they durst not allow themselves in any unrighteous course) they should receive equal satisfaction. See more page [*blank*.]

We received news of a great defeat given the Narragansetts by Onkus, and of 15 Dutch slain by the Indians, and much beaver taken, and of Mr. Lamberton, etc.

6. (*August*).] Onkus, being provoked by Sequasson, a sachem of Connecticut, who would not be persuaded by the magistrates there to a reconciliation, made war upon him, and slew divers of his men and burnt his wigwams; whereupon Miantunnomoh, being his kinsman, took offence against Onkus, and went with near 1,000 men and set upon Onkus before he could be provided for defence, for he had not then with him above 3 or 400 men. But it pleased God to give Onkus the victory, after he had killed about 30 of the Narragansetts, and wounded many more, and among these two of Canonicus' sons and a brother of Miantunnomoh, who fled, but having on a coat of mail, he was easily overtaken, which two of his captains perceiving, they laid hold on him and carried him to Onkus, hoping thereby to procure their own pardon. But so soon as they came to Onkus, he slew them presently; and Miantunnomoh standing mute, he demanded of him why he would not speak. If you had taken me, sayeth he, I would have besought you for my life. The news of Miantunnomoh's captivity coming to Providence, Gorton and his company, who had bought of him the lands belonging to the sachems who were come under our jurisdiction, wrote a letter to Onkus, willing him to deliver their friend Miantunnomoh, and threatened him with the power of the English if he refused, and they sent their letter in the name of the governor of Massachusetts. Upon this Onkus carries Miantunnomoh to Hartford to take advice of the mag-

istrates there, and at Miantunnomoh's earnest entreaty he left
him with them, yet as a prisoner.   They kept him under guard,
but used him very courteously, and so he continued till the
commissioners of the United Colonies met at Boston, who
taking into serious consideration what was safest and best
to be done, were all of opinion that it would not be safe to set
him at liberty, neither had we sufficient ground for us to put
him to death.   In this difficulty we called in five of the most
judicious elders, (it being in the time of the general assembly
of the elders,) and propounding the case to them, they all agreed
that he ought to be put to death.   Upon this concurrence we
enjoined secrecy to ourselves and them, lest if it should come to
the notice of the Narragansetts, they might set upon the commissioners, etc., in their return, to take some of them to redeem
him, (as Miantunnomoh himself had told Mr. Haynes had been
in consultation amongst them;) and agreed that, upon the
return of the commissioners to Hartford, they should send for
Onkus and tell him our determination, that Miantunnomoh
should be delivered to him again, and he should put him to
death so soon as he came within his own jurisdiction, and that
two English should go along with him to see the execution,
and that if any Indians should invade him for it, we would
send men to defend him:   If Onkus should refuse to do it, then
Miantunnomoh should be sent in a pinnace to Boston, there
to be kept until further consideration.

The reasons of this proceeding with him were these.   1.
It was now clearly discovered to us, that there was a general
conspiracy among the Indians to cut off all the English, and
that Miantunnomoh was the head and contriver of it.   2.
He was of a turbulent and proud spirit, and would never be at
rest.   3. Although he had promised us in the open court to
send the Pequod to Onkus, who had shot him in the arm with
intent to have killed him, (which was by the procurement of
Miantunnomoh as it did probably appear,) yet in his way
homeward he killed him.   4. He beat one of Pumham's men

and took away his wampom, and then bid him go and complain to the Massachusetts.

According to this agreement the commissioners, at their return to Connecticut, sent for Onkus, and acquainted him therewith, who readily undertook the execution, and taking Miantunnomoh along with him, in the way between Hartford and Windsor, (where Onkus hath some men dwell,) Onkus' brother, following after Miantunnomoh, clave his head with an hatchet, some English being present. And that the Indians might know that the English did approve of it, they sent 12 or 14 musketeers home with Onkus to abide a time with him for his defence, if need should be.[1]

Mo. 6 (*August*).] About the 20th of this month the ships which went with La Tour came back safe, not one person missing or sick. But the report of their actions was offensive and grievous to us; for when they drew near to La Tour's place, D'Aulnay, having discovered them, set sail with his vessels (being two ships and a pinnace) and stood right home to Port Royal. Ours pursued them, but could not fetch them up, but they ran their ships on ground in the harbor and began to fortify themselves: whereupon ours sent a boat to D'Aulnay with the governor's letter and a letter from Captain Hawkins, who by agreement among themselves was commander in chief. The messenger who carried the letters, being one who could speak French well, was carried blindfold into the house, and there kept six or seven hours, and all D'Aulnay's company plied for their fortifying with palisadoes, and the friars as busy as

----

[1] The conduct of Massachusetts toward Miantonomo seems to students in general ungrateful and cruel. No Indian character of that time is more dignified and engaging. The most powerful of New England chieftains, he was friendly to the new-comers. He resisted the Pequot blandishments in 1636, which saved the colonies from destruction. His treatment of Providence and Rhode Island in particular had been kind. Possibly Massachusetts was influenced by his kindness to the outcast Gorton; but no sufficient reason appears why he should have been given over to death. Still, there may have been undercurrents of treachery, and we must not forget that the English hold was then very precarious, and remained so until after Philip's war.

any, and encouraging the women, who cried pitifully, telling them we were infidels and heretics.   D'Aulnay would not open La Tour's letter, because he did not style him Lieutenant General, etc., but he returned answer to the governor and to Captain Hawkins, and sent him a copy of the arrest against La Tour, and showed the original to the messenger, but refused to come to any terms of peace.   Upon this La Tour urged much to have our men to assault him, but they refused.   Then he desired that some of ours might be landed with his to do some mischief to D'Aulnay.   Captain Hawkins would send none, but gave leave to any that would go; whereupon some 30 of ours went with La Tour's men, and were encountered by D'Aulnay's men, who had fortified themselves by his mill, but were beaten out with loss of three of their men, and none slain on our side nor wounded, only three of La Tour's men were wounded.   They set the mill on fire and burnt some standing corn, and retired to their ships with one prisoner whom they took in the mill.   D'Aulnay shot with his ordnance at their boats as they went aboard, but missed them, nor did our ships make one shot at him again, but set sail and went to La Tour's fort.   While they lay there, D'Aulnay's pinnace came, supposing he and his ships had been still there, and brought in her 400 moose skins and 400 beaver skins.   These they took without any resistance and divided them; one third La Tour had and the pinnace, one third to the ships, and the other to the men.   So they continued there till their time was near expired, and were paid their hire and returned, one ship coming a good time before the other; and the pinnace went up John's river some 20 leagues and loaded with coal.   They brought a piece of white marble, whereof there is great store near his fort, which makes very good lime.[1]

Mo. 7 (*September*).]   The Indians near the Dutch, having killed 15 men, as is before related, proceeded on and began to

---

[1] The English thus became much farther involved in the quarrel between the Frenchmen than was intended.

set upon the English who dwelt under the Dutch.  They came
to Mrs. Hutchinson's in way of friendly neighborhood, as they
had been accustomed, and taking their opportunity, killed her
and Mr. Collins, her son-in-law, (who had been kept prisoner
in Boston, as is before related,) and all her family, and such of
Mr. Throckmorton's and Mr. Cornhill's families as were at
home; in all sixteen, and put their cattle into their houses
and there burnt them.  By a good providence of God, there
was a boat came in there at the same instant, to which some
women and children fled, and so were saved, but two of the
boatmen going up to the houses were shot and killed.[1]

These people had cast off ordinances and churches, and now
at last their own people, and for larger accommodation had
subjected themselves to the Dutch and dwelt scatteringly near
a mile asunder: and some that escaped, who had removed
only for want (as they said) of hay for their cattle which
increased much, now coming back again to Aquiday, they
wanted cattle for their grass.  These Indians having killed
and driven away all the English upon the main as far as Stamford, (for so far the Dutch had gained possession by the English,) they passed on to Long Island and there assaulted the
Lady Moodey in her house divers times, for there were 40 men
gathered thither to defend it.

These Indians at the same time set upon the Dutch with
an implacable fury, and killed all they could come by, and
burnt their houses and killed their cattle without any resistance, so as the governor and such as escaped betook themselves to their fort at Monhaton, and there lived and eat up their
cattle.

4.]   There was an assembly at Cambridge of all the elders
in the country, (about 50 in all,) such of the ruling elders as

---

[1] Here ends the painful tragedy of Anne Hutchinson's life.  The location
was the point now known as Pelham Neck, near New Rochelle, New York.  It
is still marked by the local nomenclature, for though the name of Anne's Hoeck
has disappeared, Hutchinson Creek still perpetuates her memory.

would were present also, but none else. They sat in the college, and had their diet there after the manners of scholars' commons, but somewhat better, yet so ordered as it came not to above sixpence the meal for a person. Mr. Cotton and Mr. Hooker were chosen moderators. The principal occasion was because some of the elders went about to set up some things according to the presbytery, as of Newbury, etc. The assembly concluded against some parts of the presbyterial way, and the Newbury ministers took time to consider the arguments, etc.[1]

7.] Upon the complaint of the English of Patuxet near Providence, who had submitted to our jurisdiction, and the two Indian sachems there, of the continual injuries offered them by Gorton and his company, the general court sent for them, by letter only, not in way of command, to come answer the complaints, and sent them letters of safe conduct. But they answered our messengers disdainfully, refused to come, but sent two letters full of blasphemy against the churches and magistracy, and other provoking terms, slighting all we could do against them. So that having sent three times, and receiving no other answer, we took testimonies against them both of English and Indians, and determined to proceed with them by force. And because they had told our messengers the last time, that if we had anything to say to them, if we would come to them, they would do us justice therein, therefore we wrote to them to this effect, viz.; To the end that our justice and moderation might appear to all men, we would condescend so far to them as to send commissioners to hear their answers and allegations, and if thereupon they would give us such satisfaction as should be just, we would leave them in peace, if otherwise, we would proceed by force of arms; and signified withal that we would send a sufficient guard with our commissioners. For seeing they would not trust themselves with us upon our

[1] An echo of the dispute between Presbyterianism and the rising Independency, which in England had now become acute.

safe conduct, we had no reason to trust ourselves with them upon their bare courtesy.  And accordingly we sent the next week Captain George Cook, Lieutenant Atherton, and Edward Johnson,[1] with commission and instructions, (the instructions would here be inserted at large,) and with them 40 soldiers.

They came to Providence, and by the way received another letter from Gorton, of the like contents with the former, and told them plainly they were prepared for them, etc.  Being come near, they found they had put themselves all into one house, which they had made musket-proof with two flankers. But by the mediation of others of Providence, they came to parley, and then offered to refer their cause to arbitrators, (alleging that we were parties, and so not equal judges,) so as some of them might be of Providence or of Aquiday, and offered their cattle for security to abide the order, etc.  Our commissioners, through importunity of themselves and others of Providence, were content to send to us to know our minds about it.  Their letter came to us, when a committee, appointed by the general court, were met about the tidings of Miantunnomoh's death; so calling into us five or six of the elders who were near at hand, we considered of the motion, and agreed that it was neither seasonable nor reasonable, neither safe nor honorable, for us to accept of such a proposition.  1. Because they would never offer us any terms of peace before we had sent our soldiers.  2. Because the ground of it was false, for we were not parties in the case between the Indians and them, but the proper judges, they being all within our jurisdiction by the Indians and English their own grant. 3. They were no state, but a few fugitives living without law or government, and so not honorable for us to join with them in

---

[1] Cook returning to England became a colonel in Cromwell's army.  Atherton at a later time became major-general of the colonial forces, and while holding that position was killed by a fall from his horse in 1665.  Johnson was the author of the *Wonder-Working Providence*.

such a course. 4. The parties whom they would refer it unto were such as were rejected by us, and all the governments in the country, and besides, not men likely to be equal to us, or able to judge of the cause. 5. Their blasphemous and reviling writings, etc., were not matters fit to be compounded by arbitrament, but to be purged away only by repentance and public satisfaction, or else by public punishment.

And lastly, the commission and instructions being given them by the general court, it was not in our power to alter them; so accordingly we wrote to our commissioners to proceed, which accordingly they did, and approached the house, where they had fortified themselves, with trenches so near as they might fire the house, which they attempted two or three times, but they within quenched it. At last three of them escaped out and ran away, and the rest yielded and were brought to Boston, and were committed to the prison. It was a special providence of God that neither any of them nor of ours were slain or hurt, though many shot passed between them, but every man returned safe and hale. See more, page [*blank*].

Here wants the beginning which may be supplied out of the records, 64.

Other affairs were transacted by the commissioners of the United Colonies, as writing letters to the Swedish governor in Delaware river, concerning the foul injuries offered by him to Mr. Lamberton and those people whom New Haven had planted there, and also to the Dutch governor about the injuries his agent there had also offered and done to them, as burning down their trading house, joining with the Swedes against them, etc. But this was inserted in the letter which the general court sent to him in further answer of that which he sent to them, as is expressed herebefore; in which letter we declared the complaints which had been made by our confederates both of Hartford and New Haven, of their injurious dealings, as well at Hartford and New Haven as at Delaware:

also our opinion of the justice of the cause of Hartford in respect of title of the land in question between them, which we could not change, except we might see more light than had yet appeared to us by the title the Dutch insisted upon, nor might we desert either of our confederates in a righteous cause. And we gave also commission to Mr. Lamberton to go treat with the Swedish governor about satisfaction for those injuries and damages, and to agree with him about settling their trade and plantation. This Swedish governor demeaned himself as if he had neither Christian nor moral conscience, getting Mr. Lamberton into his power by feigned and false pretences, and keeping him prisoner and some of his men, laboring by promises and threats to draw them to accuse him to have conspired with the Indians to cut off the Swedes and Dutch, and not prevailing these ways, then by attempting to make them drunk, that so he might draw something from them: and in the end, (though he could gain no testimony,) yet he forced him to pay [*blank*] weight of beaver before he would set him at liberty. He is also a man very furious and passionate, cursing and swearing, and also reviling the English of New Haven as runagates, etc., and himself with his own hands put irons upon one of Mr. Lamberton's men, and went also to the houses of those few families planted there, and forced some of them to swear allegiance to the crown of Sweden, though he had no color of title to that place, and such as would not, he drave away, etc. All these things were clearly proved by Mr. Lamberton's relation, and by other testimony upon oath, but this was before he was sent with commission.[1]

About this time our governor received letters from Philip Bell, Esq., governor of Barbados, complaining of the distracted condition of that island in regard of divers sects of familists

---

[1] The settlement of the New Haven men was near the present site of Salem, New Jersey. The story is told by Professor Keen in Winsor's *Narrative and Critical History*, IV. 451-457, from the reports of Governor Johan Printz and other Swedish sources.

sprung up there, and their turbulent practices, which had
forced him to proceed against some of them by banishment,
and others of mean quality by whipping; and earnestly desiring us to send them some godly ministers and other good people.
The governor imparted the letter to the court and elders, but
none of our ministers would go thither, and the governor
returned answer accordingly.

8. (*October*) 12.] The new sachem of Narraganset, Miantunnomoh's brother called Pesecus, a young man about 20, sent
a present to our governor, viz., an otter coat and girdle of
wampom, and some other wampom, in all worth about 15
pounds, and desired peace and friendship with us, and withal
that we would not aid Onkus against him, whom he intended
to make war upon in revenge of his brother's death. Our
governor answered the messengers, that we were willing to have
peace and friendship with him, and to that end had sent messengers to Canonicus, (whom it seemed they met with by the
way,) but we desired withal that there might be peace with all
Indians also, both Onkus and others, and that we had also sent
to Ousamekin to that end; therefore except their sachem would
agree to it, we could not receive his present. They replied that
they had no instructions about the matter, but would return
back and acquaint their sachem with it, and return to us again,
and desired to leave their present with our governor in the
mean time, which he agreed unto.

13.] Captain Cook and his company, which were sent
out against Gorton, returned to Boston, and the captives,
being nine, were brought to the governor his house in a military order, viz., the soldiers being in two files, and after every
five or six soldiers a prisoner. So being before his door, the
commissioners came in, and after the governor had saluted
them, he went forth with them, and passing through the files,
welcomed them home, blessing God for preserving and pros-
pering them, and gave them all thanks for their pains and good
carriage, and desired of the captain a list of their names, that

the court, etc., might know them if hereafter there should be occasion to make use of such men. This good acceptance and commendation of their service gave many of them more content than their wages, (which yet was very liberal, ten shillings per week, and they to victual themselves, and it is needful in all such commonwealths where the state desires to be served by volunteers). Then having conferred privately with the commissioners, he caused the prisoners to be brought before him in his hall, where was a great assembly, and there laid before them their contemptuous carriage towards us, and their obstinacy against all the fair means and moderation we had used to reform them and bring them to do right to those of ours whom they had wronged, and how the Lord had now justly delivered them into our hands. They pleaded in their excuse that they were not of our jurisdiction, and that though they had now yielded themselves to come and answer before us, yet they yielded not as prisoners. The governor replied, they were brought to him as taken in war, and so our commissioners had informed, but if they could plead any other quarter or agreement our commissioners had made with them, we must and would perform it; to which they made no answer. So the governor committed them to the marshal to convey to the common prison, and gave order they should be well provided for both for lodging and diet. Then he went forth again with the captain, and the soldiers gave him three vollies of shot and so departed to the inn, where the governor had appointed some refreshing to be provided for them above their wages.

The next Lord's day in the forenoon, the prisoners would not come to the meeting, so as the magistrates determined they should be compelled. They agreed to come, so as they might have liberty after sermon to speak, if they had occasion. The magistrates' answer was, that they did leave the ordering of things in the church to the elders, but there was no doubt but they might have leave to speak, so as they spake the words of truth and sobriety. So in the afternoon they came, and

were placed in the fourth seat right before the elders. Mr.
Cotton (in his ordinary text) taught then out of Acts 19. of
Demetrius pleading for Diana's silver shrines or temples, etc.
After sermon Gorton desired leave to speak, which being granted, he repeated the points of Mr. Cotton's sermon, and coming
to that of the silver shrines, he said that in the church there
was nothing now but Christ, so that all our ordinances, ministers, sacraments, etc., were but men's inventions for show and
pomp, and no other than those silver shrines of Diana. He
said also that if Christ lived eternally, then he died eternally;
and it appeared both by his letters and examinations that he
held that Christ was incarnate in Adam, and that he was that
image of God wherein Adam was created, and that the chief
work and merit was in that his incarnation, in that he became
such a thing, so mean, etc., and that his being born after of the
Virgin Mary and suffering, etc., was but a manifestation of his
sufferings, etc., in Adam. Likewise in his letter he condemned
and reviled magistracy, calling it an idol, alleging that a man
might as well be a slave to his belly as to his own species: yet
being examined he would acknowledge magistracy to be an
ordinance of God in the world as marriage was, viz., no other
magistracy but what was natural, as the father over his wife
and children, and an hereditary prince over his subjects.

When the general court was assembled, Gorton and his company were brought forth upon the lecture day at Boston, and
there, before a great assembly, the governor declared the cause
and manner of our proceeding against them, and their letters
were openly read, and all objections answered. As 1. That
they were not within our jurisdiction. To this was answered.
1. That they were either within Plymouth or Mr. Fenwick,[1] and
they had yielded their power to us in this cause. 2. If they
were under no jurisdiction, then had we none to complain unto
for redress of our injuries, and then we must either right ourselves and our subjects by force of arms, or else we must sit

[1] *I. e.*, Saybrook.

still under all their reproaches and injuries, among which
they had this insolent passage.—"We do more disdain that
you should send for us to come to you, than you could do, if
we should send for the chiefest among you to come up to us,
and be employed according to our pleasure in such works as
we should appoint you."

As for their opinions, we did not meddle with them for those,
otherwise than they had given us occasion by their letters to us,
and by their free and open publishing them amongst us, for we
wrote to them only about civil controversies between them and
our people, and gave them no occasion to vent their blasphem-
ings and revilings, etc.   And for their title to the Indians' land,
we had divers times desired them to make it appear, but they
always refused, even to our commissioners whom we sent last
to them; and since they were in prison, we offered to send for
any witnesses they would desire, but still they refused, so that
our title appearing good and we having now regained our possession, we need not question them any more about that.
Their letters being read, they were demanded severally if they
would maintain those things which were contained therein.
They answered they would in that sense wherein they wrote
them.

After this they were brought before the court severally to be
examined, (divers of the elders being desired to be present,)
and because they had said they could give a good interpretation of all they had written, they were examined upon the particular passages.   But the interpretation they gave being con-
tradictory to their expressions, they were demanded then if
they would retract those expressions, but that they refused, and
said still that they should then deny the truth.   For instance
in one or two; their letters were directed, one to their neighbors of the Massachusetts, and the other of them to the great
honored idol general of the Massachusetts, and by a messenger
of their own delivered to our governor, and many passages
in both letters particularly applied to our courts, our magis-

trates, our elders, etc., yet in their examinations about their reproachful passages, they answered, that they meant them of the corrupt estate of mankind in general and not of us, etc. So whereas in their letters they impute it to us as an error, that we teach that Christ died actually only when he suffered under Pontius Pilate, and before only in types, upon their examination they say that their meaning was, that his death was actual to the faith of the fathers under the law, which is in effect no other than we hold, yet they account it an error in us, and would not retract that charge. One of the elders had been in the prison with them, and had conferred with them about their opinions, and they expressed their agreement with him in every point, so as he intended to move for favor for them, but when he heard their answer upon their examination, he found how he had been deluded by them; for they excel the jesuits in the art of equivocation, and regard not how false they speak to all other men's apprehensions, so they keep to the rules of their own meaning. Gorton maintained, that the image of God wherein Adam was created was Christ, and so the loss of that image was the death of Christ, and the restoring of it in regeneration was Christ's resurrection, and so the death of him that was born of the Virgin Mary was but a manifestation of the former. In their letters, etc., they condemned all ordinances in the church, calling baptism an abomination, and the Lord's supper the juice of a poor silly grape turned into the blood of Christ by the skill of our magicians, etc. Yet upon examination they would say they did allow them to be the ordinances of Christ; but their meaning was that they were to continue no longer than the infancy of the church lasted, (and but to novices then,) for after the revelation was written they were to cease, for there is no mention of them, say they, in that book.

They were all illiterate men, the ablest of them could not write true English, no not common words, yet they would take upon them the interpretation of the most difficult places of scripture, and wrest them any way to serve their own turns: as to give one instance for many. Mr. Cotton pressing them with that in Acts 10. "Who can forbid water why these should not be baptized? so he commanded them to be baptized" they interpret thus. Who can deny but these have been baptized, seeing they have received the Holy Ghost, etc., so he allowed them to have been baptized. This shift they were put to, that they might maintain their former opinion, That such as have been baptized with the Holy Ghost need not the outward baptism.

The court and the elders spent near a whole day in discovery of Gorton's deep mysteries which he had boasted of in his letters, and to bring him to conviction, but all was in vain. Much pains was also taken with the rest, but to as little effect. They would acknowledge no error or fault in their writings, and yet would seem sometimes to consent with us in the truth.

After all these examinations the court began to consult about their sentence. The judgment of the elders also had been demanded about their blasphemous speeches and opinions, what punishment was due by the word of God. Their answer was first in writing, that if they should maintain them as expressed in their writings, their offence deserved death by the law of God. The same some of them declared after in open court. But before the court would proceed to determine of their sentence, they agreed first upon their charge, and then calling them all publicly they declared to them what they had to charge them with, out of their letter and speeches. Their charge was this, viz. They were charged to be blasphemous enemies of the true religion of our Lord Jesus Christ, and of all his holy ordinances, and likewise of all civil government among his people, and particularly within this jurisdiction. Then they were demanded whether they did acknowledge this charge to be just, and did submit to it, or what exceptions they had against it. They answered they did not acknowledge it to be just, but they took no particular exceptions to it, but fell into some cavilling speeches, so they were returned to prison again. Being in prison they behaved insolently towards their keeper, and spake evil of the magistrates. Whereupon some of the magistrates were very earnest to have irons presently put upon them. Others thought it better to forbear all such severity till their sentence were passed. This latter opinion prevailed.

After divers means had been used both in public and private to reclaim them, and all proving fruitless, the court proceeded to consider of their sentence, in which the court was much divided. All the magistrates, save three, were of opinion that Gorton ought to die, but the greatest number of the deputies dissenting, that vote did not pass. In the end all agreed upon this sentence, for seven of them, viz., that they should be dispersed into seven several towns, and there kept to work for their living, and wear irons upon one leg, and not to depart the limits of the town, nor by word or writing maintain any of their blasphemous or wicked errors upon pain of death, only with exception for speech with any of the elders, or any other licensed by any magistrate to confer with them; this censure to continue during the pleasure of the court.

There were three more taken in the house with them, but because they had not their hands to the letters, they were dismissed, two of them upon a small ransom, as captives taken in war, and the third freely, for that he was but in his master's house, etc. A fourth, being found to be an ignorant young man, was only enjoined to abide in Watertown upon pain of the court's displeasure only.

At the next court they were all sent away, because we found that they did corrupt some of our people, especially the women, by their heresies.

About a week after, we sent men to fetch so many of their cattle as might defray our charges, both of the soldiers and of the court, which spent many days about them, and for their expenses in prison. It came to in all about 160 pounds. There were three who escaped out of the house; these being sent for to come in, two of them did so, and one of them, because his hand was not to the letters, was freely discharged, the other was sent home upon his own bond to appear at the next court, (only some of his cattle were taken towards the charges). There was a fourth who had his hand to the first letter, but he died before our soldiers went, and we left his whole estate to his wife and children. Their arms were all taken from them, and of their guns the court gave one fowling piece to Pumham and another to Saconoco, and liberty granted them to have powder as being now within our jurisdiction.[1]

The Lord Bartemore being owner of much land near Virginia, being himself a papist, and his brother Mr. Calvert the governor there a papist also, but the colony consisted both of Protestants and papists, he wrote a letter to Captain Gibbons of Boston, and sent him a commission, wherein he made tender of land in Maryland to any of ours that would transport themselves thither, with free liberty of religion, and all other privileges which the place afforded, paying such annual rent as should be agreed upon; but our captain had no mind to further his desire herein, nor had any of our people temptation that way.[2]

5. (July) 13.] One Captain John Chaddock, son of him that was governor of Bermuda, a godly gentleman, but late removing from them with his family and about 100 more to Trinidado, where himself and wife and most of his company

---

[1] The treatment of Gorton and his associates, given in such detail by Winthrop, is also the subject of numerous scattered entries in the *Records of Massachusetts*, Vol. II., p. 51, etc. Though the story is repulsive, the procedure is consistent with Massachusetts custom. The come-outers were severely punished, but their offence was great: the New England magistrates were "just asses," they declared, and denunciation and contempt were poured out upon what the colonists revered. There was danger that Gorton might secure a numerous following. In England, at last, he found a tolerance such as New England was not yet ready to grant.

[2] The liberality of Maryland contrasts remarkably with the narrowness of Massachusetts. For a consideration of Maryland toleration see John Fiske, *Old Virginia and her Neighbors*, I. 319.

died, arrived here in a man of war of about 100 tons, set forth
by the Earl of Warwick. He came hither for planters for
Trinidado, (Mr. Humfrey having told the Earl that he might be
supplied from hence,) but here was not any that would enter
upon that voyage, etc. So La Tour having a pinnace here at
the same time, they hired Captain Chaddock for two months at
200 pounds the month, partly to convoy the pinnace home
from the danger of D'Aulnay his vessels, and partly for other
service against D'Aulnay there. But when they came, they
found D'Aulnay gone into France, and a new fort raised at
Port Royal, and a pinnace ready to go forth to trade, so they
kept her in so long till the season was over and his two months
out, and then he returned to Boston. When he was come in
near the town, his men going up upon the main yard to hand
in the sail, the main tie brake, and the yard falling down shook
off five men into the sea, and though it were calm and smooth
water, yet not having their boat out, three of them were
drowned. One of these had taken some things out of the deserted castle, as they went out. Notwithstanding this sad
accident, yet so soon as they came on shore, they fell to drinking, etc., and that evening, the captain and his master being at
supper and having drank too much, the captain began to speak
evil of the country, swearing fearfully, that we were a base
heathen people. His master answered that he had no reason
to say so, for it was the best place that ever he came in. Upon
these and other speeches the captain arose and drew his sword,
and the master drew forth his pistol, but the company staying
them from doing any mischief, the captain sware blood and
wounds he would kill him. For this they were brought before
the court, and the captain fined 20 pounds and committed to
the marshal till he gave security for it. The master for that
he was in drink, as he ingenuously acknowledged, etc., was
fined only 10 shillings, but was set at liberty from the captain,
who had formerly misused other of his men, and was a very
proud and intemperate man. But because the ship was the

Earl of Warwick's, who had always been forward to do good to our colony, we wrote to him, that the fine should be reserved to be at his lordship's disposing, when he should please to command or call for it.   See the next page.

10. (*December*) 27.]   By order of the general court all the magistrates and the teaching elders of the six nearest churches were appointed to be forever governors of the college, and this day they met at Cambridge and considered of the officers of the college, and chose a treasurer, H. Pelham, Esq., being the first in that office.

This day five ships set sail from Boston; three of them were built here, two of 300 tons and the other of 160.   One of them was bound for London with many passengers, men of chief rank in the country, and great store of beaver.   Their adventure was very great, considering the doubtful estate of the affairs of England, but many prayers of the churches went with them and followed after them.

# 1644

**11.** (*January*) 2.] Captain Chaddock having bought from the French a pinnace of about 30 tons, (which La Tour sold him for a demiculverin and was the same which was taken before from D'Aulnay,) he had manned and fitted her to go in her to Trinidado, and riding before Boston ready to depart, and eight men aboard her, one striking fire with a pistol, two barrels of powder took fire and blew her up: five of the men being in the cabin were destroyed, and the other three being in the other part were much scorched and hurt, but got into their boat and were saved. The captain himself was then on shore at Boston. It is observable that these men making no use of the sudden loss of three of their company, but falling to drinking, etc., that very evening this judgment came thus upon them. It is also to be observed that two vessels have thus been blown up in our harbor, and both belonging to such as despised us and the ordinance of God amongst us. See more, page [*blank*].

About this time Captain Daniel Patrick was killed at Stamford by a Dutchman, who shot him dead with a pistol. This captain was entertained by us out of Holland (where he was a common soldier of the Prince's guard) to exercise our men. We made him a captain, and maintained him. After, he was admitted a member of the church of Watertown and a freeman. But he grew very proud and vicious, for though he had a wife of his own, a good Dutch woman and comely, yet he despised her and followed after other women; and perceiving that he was discovered, and that such evil courses would not be endured here, and being withal of a vain and unsettled disposition, he went from us, and sat down within twenty miles of the Dutch, and put himself under their protection, and joined

153

to their church, without being dismissed from Watertown: but when the Indians arose in those parts, he fled to Stamford and there was slain.  The Dutchman who killed him was apprehended, but made an escape; and this was the fruit of his wicked course and breach of covenant with his wife, with the church, and with that state who had called him and maintained him, and he found his death from that hand where he sought protection.  It is observable that he was killed upon the Lord's day in the time of afternoon exercise (for he seldom went to the public assemblies).  It was in Captain Underhill's house. The Dutchman had charged him with treachery, for causing 120 men to come to him upon his promise to direct them to the Indians, etc., but deluded them.  Whereupon the captain gave him ill language and spit in his face, and turning to go out, the Dutchman shot him behind in the head, so he fell down dead and never spake.  The murderer escaped out of custody.

10. (*December*) 3.][1]  The *Hopewell*, a ship of Boston, about 60 tons, arrived; the freight was wines, pitch, sugar, ginger, etc. She had her lading at Palma an island near Teneriffe.  The Spaniards used our people courteously, but put them to give security by some English merchants residing there to discharge their cargoes at Boston, for they would not have the Portugals of the Madeiras to have any goods from them.[2]  She performed her voyage in four months.  She went a second voyage thither soon after, but was never heard of.  Her lading was corn in bulk.

At this time came over Thomas Morton, our professed old adversary, who had set forth a book against us, and written reproachful and menacing letters to some of us.[3]

Some of Watertown began a plantation at Martin's Vineyard beyond Cape Cod, and divers families going thither, they

[1] *I. e.*, December 3, 1643.
[2] Portugal had revolted from Spain, and war existed between the two.
[3] Thomas Morton of Merry Mount, author of the *New English Canaan*.

procured a young man, one Mr. Green, a scholar, to be their minister, in hopes soon to gather a church there.   He went not.

Others of the same town began also a plantation at Nasha-way[1] some 15 miles N. W. from Sudbury.

11. (*January*) 18.] About midnight, three men, coming in a boat to Boston, saw two lights arise out of the water near the north point of the town cove, in form like a man, and went at a small distance to the town, and so to the south point, and there vanished away. They saw them about a quarter of an hour, being between the town and the governor's garden. The like was seen by many, a week after, arising about Castle Island and in one fifth of an hour came to John Gallop's point.

The country being weary of the charge of maintaining Castle Island, the last general court made an order to have it deserted and the ordnance fetched away; but Boston and other towns in the bay finding that thereupon the masters of some ships which came from England took occasion to slight us and to offer injury to our people, having liberty to ride and go out under no command, and considering also how easily any of our towns in the bay might be surprised, we having no strength without to stop them or to give notice of an enemy, they chose certain men out of the several towns who met at Boston to consider of some course of repairing and maintaining it at their proper charge: but the difficulty was, how to do it without offence to the general court who had ordered the deserting of it, etc.

The 18th of this month two lights were seen near Boston, (as is before mentioned,) and a week after the like was seen again. A light like the moon arose about the N. E. point in Boston, and met the former at Nottles Island, and there they closed in one, and then parted, and closed and parted divers times, and so went over the hill in the island and vanished. Sometimes they shot out flames and sometimes sparkles.   This

---

[1] Now Lancaster, Mass.

was about eight of the clock in the evening, and was seen by many. About the same time a voice was heard upon the water between Boston and Dorchester, calling out in a most dreadful manner, boy, boy, come away, come away: and it suddenly shifted from one place to another a great distance, about twenty times. It was heard by divers godly persons. About 14 days after, the same voice in the same dreadful manner was heard by others on the other side of the town towards Nottles Island.

These prodigies having some reference to the place where Captain Chaddock's pinnace was blown up a little before, gave occasion of speech of that man who was the cause of it, who professed himself to have skill in necromancy, and to have done some strange things in his way from Virginia hither, and was suspected to have murdered his master there; but the magistrates here had not notice of him till after he was blown up. This is to be observed that his fellows were all found, and others who were blown up in the former ship were also found, and others also who have miscarried by drowning, etc., have usually been found, but this man was never found.

12. (*February*) 5.] Cutshamekin, and Agawam, and Josias, Chickatabot his heir, came to the governor, and in their own name and the names of all the sachems of Watchusett,[1] and all the Indians from Merrimack to Tecticutt,[2] tendered themselves to our government, and gave the governor a present of 30 fathom of wampom, and offered to come to the next court to make their acknowledgment, etc. The governor received their present to keep it till the court, etc., and if the court and they did agree, then to accept it. We now began to conceive hope that the Lord's time was at hand for opening a door of light and grace to those Indians, and some fruit appeared of our kind dealing with Pumham and Saconococo, protecting them against the Narragansett, and righting them against Gorton, etc., who had taken away their land: for this example gave encourage-

[1] Princeton.                                   [2] Taunton.

ment to all these Indians to come in and submit to our government, in expectation of the like protection and benefit.

16.] Pesacus, the Narragansett sachem, sent again a message to the governor with another present by Washose, a
sachem who came before, and his errand was, that seeing they,
at our request, had sitten still this year, that now this next year
we would grant their request, and suffer them to fight with
Onkus, with many arguments. The governor refused his
present, and told him that if they sent us 1000 fathom of
wampom and 1000 skins, yet we would not do that which we
judged to be unjust, viz. to desert Onkus, but our resolution
was, and that they must rest upon, that if they made war upon
Onkus, the English would all fall upon them.

1. (*March*) 23.] The *Trial* (the first ship built in Boston)
being about 160 tons, Mr. Thomas Graves, an able and a godly
man, master of her, was sent to Bilboa in the 4th month last,
with fish, which she sold there at a good rate, and from thence
she freighted to Malaga, and arrived here this day laden with
wine, fruit, oil, iron, and wool, which was a great advantage to
the country, and gave encouragement to trade.  So soon as she
was fitted (3.) (*May*) she was set forth again to trade with La
Tour, and so along the eastern coast towards Canada.

One Mr. Rigby, a lawyer and a parliament man, wealthy
and religious, had purchased the Plough Patent lying at Sagad-
ahock, and had given commission to one Mr. Cleaves, as his
deputy, to govern the people there, etc.   He, landing at Boston,
and knowing how distasteful this would be to the governor of
Sir Ferdinand Gorges' province of New Somersetshire, who
challenged jurisdiction in a great part of Ligonia or the Plough
patent, petitioned the general court to write to them on his
behalf, but the court thought not fit so to do, but rather that
the governor should write in his own name only, which he did
accordingly.   But when Mr. Cleaves came to set this commission on foot, and called a court at Casco, Mr. Richard Vines
and other of Sir Ferdinand Gorges' commissioners opposed,

and called another court at Saco the same time: whereupon
the inhabitants were divided; those of Casco, etc., wrote to
Mr. Vines that they would stand to the judgment of the
magistrates of the bay till it were decided in England, to
which government they should belong, and sent this letter by
one Tucker. Mr. Vines imprisoned him, and the next day took
his bond for his appearance at Saco and his good behavior.
Upon this Mr. Cleaves and the rest, about thirty persons, wrote
to our governor for assistance against Mr. Vines, and tendered
themselves to the consociation of the United Colonies. The
governor returned answer, that he must first advise with
the commissioners of the United Colonies. And beside, they
had an order not to receive any but such as were in a church
way, etc.[1]

Not long after, viz. (2.) (*April*) 24, Mr. Vines came to Boston
with a letter from himself and the other of Sir F. Gorges' commissioners, and other inhabitants of the province, between 20
and 30.

Three fishermen of a boat belonging to Isle of Shoals were
very profane men, and scorners of religion, and were drinking
all the Lord's day, and the next week their boat was cast upon
the rocks at the Isle of Shoals, and they drowned.

There was little rain this winter, and no snow till the 3d of
the 1st month, the wind continuing W. and N. W. near six
weeks, which was an occasion that very many houses were
burned down, and much chattels (in some of them) to a greater
value than in 14 years before.

1. (*March*) 7.]     Boston, Charlestown, Roxbury, Dorchester,
Cambridge, and Watertown, conceiving that the want of fortification at Castle Island would leave them open to an enemy,
appointed a committee to consider how it might be fortified,
and coming to some conclusion about it, they advised with the

---

[1] The arrival of the *Plough* with the "Husbandmen", who were to occupy a
tract at Casco Bay, afterward called Ligonia, and the Plough Patent, are described in Vol. I., p. 65, note 2.

governor and some other of the magistrates, who encouraged
them in it, as the elders also did in their sermons; but because
the general court had given order for fetching off the ordnance,
etc., it was thought fit not to attempt any thing without the
advice of the same.   It fell out also that five of the neighboring
Indian sachems came at the same time to the governor with a
present of wampom about 30 fathom, worth some 8 pounds, and
desired to come under our government as Pumham and Sacononoco had done.   For these two occasions the governor summoned a general court to be held at Boston this day, (the court
of assistants being to begin the 5th day before,) where the
committees of the said six towns exhibited a petition for fortifying of the said Island, craving help also from the country,
though they had agreed to do it at their own charge rather than
fail.   The court refusing to undertake it, they gave in certain
propositions whereby they craved some aid, at least for maintaining of the garrison, and some privileges and immunities.
These coming to be debated in the court, some opposition there
was, which had almost discouraged the committee.   The arguments brought against it were chiefly these.   1. The great
charge.   2. The little help it could afford against a strong
enemy.   3. The opportunity left of another passage by Bird
Island.   But these objections were so far removed, as after
much debate, the court voted for the fortification, and granted
100 pounds pay for the maintenance of it, when it should be in
defence and a garrison of 20 men residing there; and 50 pounds
towards the securing the other passage.   And a committee was
appointed to draw up a commission for him who should have
command in chief, etc.   But this allowance was yielded rather
out of a willingness to gratify these six towns (being near one
half of the commonwealth for number of people and substance)
and to keep loving correspondency among all the towns, rather
than out of any confidence of safety by it.   Many also of good
judgment did conceive that the fortifications would not be
accomplished according to the dimensions propounded, nor

so great a garrison maintained, for the people were known generally to be more willing and forward in such public engagements, than able, upon trial, to perform them: for in such cases, the major part, which carries the vote, is of such as can afford least help to the work.

The court finding that Gorton and his company did harm in the towns where they were confined, and not knowing what to do with them, at length agreed to set them at liberty, and gave them 14 days to depart out of our jurisdiction in all parts, and no more to come into it upon pain of death. This censure was thought too light and favorable, but we knew not how in justice we could inflict any punishment upon them, the sentence of the court being already passed, etc.

At this court Cutshamekin and squaw sachem, Masconono-co, Nashacowam, and Wassamagoin, two sachems near the great hill to the west called Wachusett, came into the court, and according to their former tender to the governor, desired to be received under our protection and government upon the same terms that Pumham and Sacononoco were; so we causing them to understand the articles, and all the ten commandments of God, and they freely assenting to all, they were solemnly received, and then presented the court with 26 fathom more of wampom, and the court gave each of them a coat of two yards of cloth, and their dinner; and to them and their men every of them a cup of sack at their departure, so they took leave and went away very joyful.

At this court came letters from New Haven, and withal an answer from the Swedes and Dutch to the letters of the commissioners of the union, sent in the 7th month last. The Dutch still maintained their right to the land at Hartford, and their complaint of injuries. The Swedes denied what they had been charged with, and sent copies of divers examinations upon oath taken in the cause, with a copy of all the proceeding between them and our friends of New Haven from the first; and in their letters used large expressions of their respect to

the English, and particularly to our colony. And Mr. Eaton
desired a copy of our patent to show the Swedish governor
(at his request) and a new commission from the commissioners
of the union, allowing them to go on with their plantation and
trade in Delaware river and bay (for the governor had told
their agent that upon such a commission they should have liberty, etc.). This coming at the sitting of the general court, the
commissioners advised with the court about it, who granted
both, but the commission with a salvo jure: we were then informed also of a Dutch ship lately arrived at Hudson's river
sent to the free boors at Fort Orange,[1] which brought them
4,000 weight of powder, and 700 pieces to trade with the
natives, which the Dutch governor having notice of, did seize
and confiscate to the use of the company.

We had the news also that the Dutch had entertained Captain Underhill, who with 120 men, Dutch and English, had
killed 120 Indians upon Long Island, and 300 more upon the
main, which was found to be a plot of the Dutch governor to
engage the English in that quarrel with the Indians, which we
had wholly declined, as doubting of the justice of the cause.

At this court of assistants one James Britton, a man ill
affected both to our church discipline and civil government, and
one Mary Latham, a proper young woman about 18 years of
age, whose father was a godly man and had brought her up
well, were condemned to die for adultery, upon a law formerly
made and published in print. It was thus occasioned and
discovered. This woman, being rejected by a young man
whom she had an affection unto, vowed she would marry the
next that came to her, and accordingly, against her friends'
minds, she matched with an ancient man who had neither
honesty nor ability, and one whom she had no affection unto.

[1] Fort Orange was later Albany. For a late and clear account of the relations of the Dutch and English colony, see John Fiske, *Dutch and English Colonies
in America*, I., chap. IX.; for the fortunes of the Swedish colony on the Delaware,
see same volume, p. 277. "Freeboors," *vrije boeren*, means the free settlers, as
distinguished from the feudal tenants of the adjoining colony of Rensselaerswyck.

Whereupon, soon after she was married, divers young men solicited her chastity, and drawing her into bad company, and giving her wine and other gifts, easily prevailed with her, and among others this Britton. But God smiting him with a deadly palsy and fearful horror of conscience withal, he could not keep secret, but discovered this, and other the like with other women, and was forced to acknowledge the justice of God in that having often called others fools, etc., for confessing against themselves, he was now forced to do the like. The woman dwelt now in Plymouth patent, and one of the magistrates there, hearing she was detected, etc., sent her to us. Upon her examination, she confessed he did attempt the fact, but did not commit it, and witness was produced that testified (which they both confessed) that in the evening of a day of humiliation through the country for England, etc., a company met at Britton's and there continued drinking sack, etc., till late in the night, and then Britton and the woman were seen upon the ground together, a little from the house. It was reported also that she did frequently abuse her husband, setting a knife to his breast and threatening to kill him, calling him old rogue and cuckold, and said she would make him wear horns as big as a bull. And yet some of the magistrates thought the evidence not sufficient against her, because there were not two direct witnesses; but the jury cast her, and then she confessed the fact, and accused twelve others, whereof two were married men. Five of these were apprehended and committed, (the rest were gone,) but denying it, and there being no other witness against them than the testimony of a condemned person, there could be no proceeding against them. The woman proved very penitent, and had deep apprehension of the foulness of her sin, and at length attained to hope of pardon by the blood of Christ, and was willing to die in satisfaction to justice. The man also was very much cast down for his sins, but was loth to die, and petitioned the general court for his life, but they would not grant it, though some of the magistrates spake much for it, and questioned the letter, whether adultery was death by God's law now.[1] This Britton had been a professor in England, but coming hither he opposed our church government, etc., and grew dissolute, losing both power and profession of godliness.

1. (*March*) 21.] They were both executed, they both died very penitently, especially the woman, who had some comfortable hope of pardon of her sin, and gave good exhortation to all young maids to be obedient to their parents, and to take heed of evil company, etc.

The Earl of Warwick and other lords, etc., being appointed by the parliament commissioners for regulating the West Indies and all other English plantations in America, sent commission to Virginia to free them from all former taxations and all other charges but such as should be needful for their own occasions, and gave them liberty to choose their own governor; and sent command to all English ships there (which were then to the number of sixteen, most of them great ships) to assist them if need were. But the king sending a countermand to Sir Robert Berkley, the governor, he withstood the parliament's commissioners, and drew most of the other magistrates to take oath upon the sacrament to maintain the king's authority, etc., so that the whole country was like to rise in parties, some for the king, and others for the parliament.[2]

A proposition was made this court for all the English within the united colonies to enter into a civil agreement for the maintenance of religion and our civil liberties, and for yielding some more of the freeman's privileges to such as were no

[1] The death penalty was provided in the "Body of Liberties."

[2] Sir William Berkeley (not Robert) the ultra cavalier, who thus in Virginia upholds the King in opposition to the Houses, is the official who writes, "I thank God there are no free schools nor printing, and I hope we shall not have these hundred years." The Civil War was now at its height, just before the battle of Marston Moor, and naturally there were echoes of it in the colonies. For a description of Virginia conditions see L. G. Tyler, *England in America* ("American Nation" series), chaps. V., VI.

church members that should join in this government. But nothing was concluded, but referred to next court, and in the mean time, that letters should be written to the other colonies to advise with them about it. Nothing was effected for want of opportunity of meeting, etc.

At the same court in the first month, upon the motion of the deputies, it was ordered that the court should be divided in their consultations, the magistrates by themselves, and the deputies by themselves, what the one agreed upon they should send to the other, and if both agreed, then to pass, etc. This order determined the great contention about the negative voice.[1]

Divers of the merchants of Boston being desirous to discover the great lake, supposing it to lie in the north-west part of our patent, and finding that the great trade of beaver, which came to all the eastern and southern parts, came from thence, petitioned the court to be a company for that design, and to have the trade which they should discover, to themselves for twenty-one years. The court was very unwilling to grant any monopoly, but perceiving that without it they would not proceed, granted their desire; whereupon, having also commission granted them under the public seal, (3) and letters from the governor to the Dutch and Swedish governors, they sent out a pinnace well manned and furnished with provisions and trading stuff, which was to sail up Delaware river so high as they could go, and then some of the company, under the conduct of Mr. William Aspenwall, a good artist, and one who had been in those parts, to pass by small skiffs or canoes up the river so far as they could.

Many of Watertown and other towns joined in the plantation at Nashaway, and having called a young man, an university scholar, one Mr. Norcross, to be their minister, seven

---

[1] The momentous issue of "the sow business" is here noted. Another important business of the present court Winthrop fails to notice,—the gathering of the Massachusetts townships into the four counties of Suffolk, Norfolk, Essex, and Middlesex. *Records of Massachusetts*, II. 38.

of them, who were no members of any churches, were desirous
to gather into a church estate; but the magistrates and elders
advised them first to go and build them habitations, etc., (for
there was yet no house there,) and then to take some that were
members of other churches, with the consent of such churches,
as formerly had been done, and so proceed orderly.  But the
persons interested in this plantation, being most of them poor
men, and some of them corrupt in judgment, and others profane, it went on very slowly, so as that in two years they had
not three houses built there, and he whom they had called to
be their minister left them for their delays.

One Dalkin and his wife dwelling near Meadford coming
from Cambridge, where they had spent their Sabbath, and
being to pass over the river at a ford, the tide not being fallen
enough, the husband adventured over, and finding it too deep,
persuaded his wife to stay a while, but it raining very sore,
she would needs adventure over, and was carried away with the
stream past her depth.   Her husband not daring to go help her,
cried out, and thereupon his dog, being at his house near by,
came forth, and seeing something in the water, swam to her,
and she caught hold on the dog's tail, so he drew her to the
shore and saved her life.

At the general court (8.) (*October*) 4. there came a letter to
the governor from Mr. Wheelwright, (who was now moved
from Exeter to Wells, near Cape Porpoise, where he was pastor
of a church,) the contents whereof were as followeth:—

RIGHT WORSHIPFUL.

Upon the long and mature consideration of things, I perceive that
the main difference between yourselves and some of the reverend elders
and me, in point of justification and the evidencing thereof, is not of that
nature and consequence as was then presented to me in the false glass of
Satan's temptations and mine own distempered passions, which makes me
unfeignedly sorry that I had such an hand in those sharp and vehement
contentions raised thereabouts to the great disturbance of the churches
of Christ.   It is the grief of my soul that I used such vehement censorious

speeches in the application of my sermon, or in any other writing, whereby I reflected any dishonor upon your worships, the reverend elders, or any of contrary judgment to myself. It repents me that I did so much adhere to persons of corrupt judgment, to the countenancing of them in any of their errors or evil practices, though I intended no such thing; and that in the synod I used such unsafe and obscure expressions falling from me as a man dazzled with the buffetings of Satan, and that I did appeal from misapprehension of things. I confess that herein I have done very sinfully, and do humbly crave pardon of this honored state. If it shall appear to me, by scripture light, that in any carriage, word, writing, or action, I have walked contrary to rule, I shall be ready, by the grace of God, to give satisfaction: thus hoping that you will pardon my boldness, I humbly take leave of your worship, committing you to the good providence of the Almighty; and ever remain, your worship's in all service to be commanded in the Lord.

J. WHEELWRIGHT.

Wells, (7) 10–43.[1]

Upon this letter the court was very well inclined to release his banishment; and thereupon ordered that he might have a safe conduct to come to the court, etc. Hereof the governor certified him by letter, and received this answer from him.

RIGHT WORSHIPFUL.

I have received the letter wherein you signify to me that you have imparted my letter to the honorable court, and that it finds good applause, for which I rejoice with much thankfulness. I am very thankful to your worship for the letter of safe conduct which I formerly received, as likewise for the late act of court, granting me the same liberty in case I desire letters to that end. I should very willingly, upon letters received, express by word of mouth openly in court, that which I did by writing, might I, without offence, explain my true intent and meaning more fully to this effect: that notwithstanding my failings, for which I humbly crave pardon, yet I cannot with a good conscience condemn myself for such capital crimes, dangerous revelations and gross errors, as have been charged upon me, the concurrence of which (as I take it) make up the very substance of the cause of all my sufferings. I do not see, but in so mixt a cause I am bound to use, may it be permitted, my just defence so far as I apprehend

[1] *I. e.*, September 10, 1643.

myself to be innocent, as to make my confession where I am convinced of
any delinquency; otherwise I shall seemingly and in appearance fall under
guilt of many heinous offences, for which my conscience doth acquit me.
If I seem to make suit to the honorable court for relaxation to be granted,
by an act of mercy, upon my sole confession, I must offend my conscience;
if by an act of justice, upon mine apology and lawful defence, I fear lest
I shall offend your worships.    I leave all things to your wise and godly
consideration, hoping that you will pardon my simplicity and plainness
which I am forced unto by the power of an over-ruling conscience.    I
rest your worship's in the Lord.

J. WHEELWRIGHT.

Wells, (1) 1–43.[1]


To this the governor replied to this effect, viz., that though
his liberty might be obtained without his personal appearance,
yet that was doubtful, nor did he conceive that a wise and
modest apology would prejudice the acceptance of his free and
ingenuous confession, seeing the latter would justify the sentence of the court, which looked only at his action, and yet by
the former, he might maintain the liberty of his conscience in
clearing his intention from those ill deserving crimes which the
court apprehended by his action:  and withal (because there
might want opportunity of conveyance before the court) he
sent him inclosed a safe conduct, etc.    The next court released
his banishment without his appearance.[2]

3. (*May*) 20.]    A ship coming from Virginia certified us of
a great massacre lately committed by the natives upon the
English there, to the number of 300 at least, and that an Indian
whom they had since taken confessed, that they did it because
they saw the English took up all their lands from them, and
would drive them out of the country, and they took this season
for that they understood that they were at war in England, and

[1] *I. e.*, March 1, 1643/4.
[2] The restoration of this able man to the colonies was a great benefit.  In
later life he went to England, where he is said to have been in high favor with
Cromwell.  Returning, he survived till 1680, being at his death the oldest minister
in the country.

began to go to war among themselves, for they had seen a fight
in the river between a London ship which was for the parliament and a Bristol ship which was for the king. He confessed
further that all the Indians within 600 miles were confederate
together to root all strangers out of the country.

It was very observable that this massacre came upon them
soon after they had driven out the godly ministers we had sent
to them, and had made an order that all such as would not conform to the discipline of the church of England should depart
the country by a certain day,[1] which the massacre now prevented: and the governor (one Sir Robert Berkeley, a courtier,
and very malignant towards the way of our churches here) and
council had appointed a fast to be kept through the country
upon good Friday (as they call it) for the good success of the
king, etc., and, the day before, this massacre began in the out-
parts of the country round about, and continued two days, for
they killed all, by sudden surprisal, living amongst them, and
as familiar in their houses as those of the family. This massacre was accompanied with a great mortality. Upon these
troubles divers godly disposed persons came from thence to
New England, and many of the rest were forced to give glory
to God in acknowledging, that this evil was sent upon them
from God for their reviling the gospel and those faithful ministers he had sent among them.[2]

A letter came to the governor, under the marks of Pesecus
and Canonicus, the sachem of Narragansett, but written by
Gorton's company, to this effect: That they were purposed to
make war upon Onkus in revenge of the death of Onkus[3] and
others of their people whom he had slain, and that they marvelled why we should be against it; that they had put them-

---

[1] The act may be seen in Hening, *Statutes of Virginia*, I. 277.

[2] Among these refugees from Virginia was probably Daniel Gookin, afterward major-general, honorably distinguished in various ways, and especially for
his humane spirit toward the Indians at a time when humanity could not be
shown without risk.

[3] For Uncas must be read Miantonomo.

selves under the government and protection of the king of England, and so were now become our fellow-subjects, and therefore if any difference should fall between us and them, it ought to be referred to him; professing withal their willingness to continue all friendly correspondency with us.

The general court being assembled, when Mr. Endecott was chosen governor[1] and Mr. Winthrop deputy governor, they took this letter into consideration, together with another from Gorton's company to the same effect, and sent two messengers to the Narragansetts with instructions to this purpose, viz. to know whether they did own that letter, etc., and by whose advice they had done as they wrote, and why they would countenance and take counsel from such evil men, and such as we had banished from us and to persuade them to sit still, and to have more regard to us than such as Gorton, etc. When our messengers came to them, Canonicus would not admit them into his wigwam for two hours, but suffered them to stay in the rain. When he did admit them, he lay along upon his couch, and would not speak to them more than a few froward speeches, but referred them to Pesacus, who, coming after some four hours, carried them into an ordinary wigwam, and there had conference with them most part of the night. Their answers were witty and full to the questions; and their conclusion was, that they would presently go to war upon Onkus, but not in such manner as Miantunnomoh had done, by a great army, but by sending out parties of 20 or more or less, to catch his men, and keep them from getting their living, etc.

At this court Passaconaway, the Merrimack sachem, came in and submitted to our government, as Pumham, etc. had done before.

4. (*June*) 5.] Two of our ministers' sons, being students in the college, robbed two dwelling houses in the night of some 15 pounds. Being found out, they were ordered by the

---

[1] Endicott now becomes governor for the first time, though before the formal organization he was chief agent in the inchoate colony.

governors of the college to be there whipped, which was performed by the president himself—yet they were about 20 years of age; and after they were brought into the court and ordered to two fold satisfaction, or to serve so long for it.  We had yet no particular punishment for burglary.[1]

At this court there arose some troubles by this occasion. Those of Essex had procured at the court before, that the deputies of the several shires should meet before this court to prepare business, etc., which accordingly they did, and propounded divers things which they agitated and concluded among themselves, without communicating them to the other shires, who conceived they had been only such things as had concerned the commonwealth, but when they came now to be put to this court, it appeared that their chief intent was to advantage their own shire.  As, 1. By drawing the government thither.  2. By drawing the courts thither.  3. By drawing a good part of the country stock thither.  4. By procuring four of those parts to be joined in commission with the magistrates. And for this end they had made so strong a party among the deputies of the smaller towns (being most of them mean men, and such as had small understanding in affairs of state) as they easily carried all these among the deputies.  But when the two bills came to the magistrates, they discerning the plot, and finding them hurtful to the commonwealth, refused to pass them, and a committee of both being appointed to consider the reasons of both sides, those of the magistrates prevailed.

But the great difference was about a commission, which the deputies sent up, whereby power was given to seven of the magistrates and three of the deputies and Mr. Ward (some time pastor of Ipswich, and still a preacher) to order all affairs of the commonwealth in the vacancy of the general court, which

---

[1] The young men were the sons of Nathaniel Ward and Thomas Welde. The latter was already in England, whither the former also returned in 1646. Ward left the college six hundred acres of land in Andover, which he had received from the governor, thus showing he bore no grudge for the treatment of his son.

the magistrates returned with this answer: That they conceived such commission did tend to the overthrow of the foundation of our government, and of the freemen's liberty, and therefore desired the deputies to consider of a way how this danger might be avoided, and the liberty of the freemen preserved inviolable, otherwise they could not comfortably proceed in other affairs.

Upon this return all the deputies came to confer with the magistrates. The exceptions the magistrates took were these. 1. That this court should create general officers which the freemen had reserved to the court of elections. 2. That they should put out four of the magistrates from that power and trust which the freemen had committed to them. 3. At the commission itself, seeing they ought not to accept that power by commission which did belong to them by the patent and by their election. They had little to answer to this, yet they alleged a precedent or two where this court had ordered some of the magistrates and some others to be a council of war, and that we had varied from our patent in some other things, and therefore were not bound to it in this.

But they chiefly stood upon this, that the governor and assistants had no power out of court but what was given them by the general court. To this the magistrates replied: 1. That such examples as were against rules or common right were errors and no precedents. 2. That council was for one particular case only, and not of general extent. 3. In those things wherein we had varied from our patent we did not touch the foundation of our government. To the last it was said, that the governor and assistants had power of government before we had any written laws or had kept any courts; and to make a man a governor over a people, gives him, by necessary consequence, power to govern that people, otherwise there were no power in any commonwealth to order, dispose, or punish in any case where it might fall out, that there were no positive law declared in.

It was consented to that this court had authority to order and direct the power of these magistrates for time, place, persons, etc., for the common good, but not wholly to deprive them of it, their office continuing: so as these being chosen by the people, by virtue of the patent to govern the people, a chief part whereof consists in counsel, they are the standing council of the commonwealth, and therefore in the vacancy of this court, may act in all the affairs thereof without any commission.

Upon this they withdrew, and after a few hours came again, and then they tendered a commission for war only, and none of the magistrates to be left out. But the magistrates refused to accept of any commission, but they would consent the same should pass by order so as the true power of the magistrates might be declared in it: or to a commission of association, to add three or four others to the magistrates in that council: or to continue the court a week longer, and send for the elders to take their advice in it; but none of these would be accepted. But they then moved, that we would consent that nothing might be done till the court met again, which was before agreed to be adjourned to the 28th of (8) (*October*). To this was answered, that, if occasion required, they must act according to the power and trust committed to them; to which their speaker replied—You will not be obeyed.[1]

4. (*June*) 23.] Two days after the court was broken up, Pumham sent two men to Boston to tell us that the Narragansetts had taken and killed six of Onkus' men and five women, and had sent him two hands and a foot to engage him in the war, but he refused to receive them and sent to us for counsel, etc. This occasioned such of the magistrates and deputies as were at hand (advising also with some of the near elders) to meet to consult about calling the court, and agreed, both in regard of this news from the Indians, and especially for speedy reconciling the magistrates and deputies, to write to

[1] The Democracy was pressing with Anglo-Saxon sturdiness toward power.

the governor that the court might be called the 28th following, which the governor assented unto.

The court being assembled, they took order for ten men to be sent to Pumham according to his desire, to help him make a fort of palisadoes, etc., but the men, being volunteers, asked 10s. per week for each man, and such spoil as they should get, if they were put to fight, and arms fixed and powder and shot. Whereupon the court, fearing it would be an ill precedent, staid, and sent word to Pumham that the men were ready, but he must pay them, etc.

The commission also for the serjeant major general was agreed and sealed, and in it he was referred to receive his instructions, etc., from the council of the commonwealth, but who were this council was not agreed. Whereupon the magistrates (all save two) signed a declaration in maintenance of their authority, and to clear the aspersions cast upon them, as if they intended to bring in an arbitrary government, etc. This they sent first to the deputies, with intimation that they intended to publish it, whereupon the deputies sent to desire that it might not be published, and desired a committee might meet to state the difference between us, which was done, and the difference was brought under this question: whether the magistrates are by patent and election of the people the standing council of the commonwealth in the vacancy of the general court, and have power accordingly to act in all cases subject to government, according to the said patent and the laws of this jurisdiction; and when any necessary occasions call for action from authority, in cases where there is no particular express law provided, there to be guided by the word of God, till the general court give particular rules in such cases? This difference being thus stated, they drew up this following order and sent it to us, viz.

Whereas there is a difference between the governor, assistants, and deputies in this court, concerning the power of the magistrates in the vacancy of the general court,—we therefore (salvo jure) for the peace and safety of this colony do consent, that the governor and assistants shall take order for the welfare of this commonwealth in all sudden cases that may happen within our jurisdiction, until the next session of this court, when we desire this question may be determined.

This we accepted (with the salvo jure) but we had refused to accept of another they sent us before in these words,—we do authorize those three which are of the standing council to proceed, etc.

Upon this agreement the magistrates consented, that the declaration should remain with the secretary, and not be published without the consent of the major part of the magistrates, which we intended not to do, except we were necessitated thereto by the deputies' misreport of our proceedings. And indeed some of the magistrates did decline the publishing thereof, upon this apprehension, that it would cause a public breach throughout the country: and if it should come to that, the people would fall into factions, and the non-members would certainly take part with the magistrates, (we should not be able to avoid it,) and this would make us and our cause, though never so just, obnoxious to the common sort of freemen, the issue whereof must needs have been very doubtful.[1]

5. (*July*) 2.]   Mr. George Phillips was buried.   He was the first pastor of the church of Watertown, a godly man, specially gifted, and very peaceful in his place, much lamented of his own people and others.

Another great error the deputies committed, which also arose out of the same false bottom, viz., the choosing one of the younger magistrates, (though a very able man,) Mr. Bradstreet,[2]

---

[1] The theocracy, in which a privileged body exercised a power that was oppressive, the people, except the church members, being without franchise, was not a polity agreeable to Englishmen.   In 1665 came what Brooks Adams calls the "Emancipation of Massachusetts," with a form of government much freer and better, though introduced under the auspices of the restored Stuarts.

[2] Simon Bradstreet, already useful and distinguished, and destined to become more so, was born in 1603, and received part of his education at Emmanuel

and one of the deputies, Mr. Hathorne, (the principal man in all these agitations,) a young man also, to be commissioners for the united colonies; both eastern men, quite out of the way of opportunity of correspondency with the other confederates; whereas all the rest had chosen either their governors or other chief magistrates; and ourselves had formerly chosen the governor and Mr. Dudley. Thus usual it is for one error in state to beget others.

This also was a failing in them, that, when the governor of Plymouth (our brethren and confederates) wrote earnestly to us, in their great want of powder, to supply them out of our store, and the magistrates had granted them two barrels, the deputies stopped it, and would not consent they might have liberty to buy for their money.

Those also of Aquiday Island, being in great fear of the Indians, wrote to us for some powder and other ammunition, but the court was then adjourned; and because the deputies had denied our confederates, the magistrates thought not fit to supply them: but certainly it was an error (in state policy at least) not to support them, for though they were desperately erroneous and in such distraction among themselves as portended their ruin, yet if the Indians should prevail against them, it would be a great advantage to the Indians, and danger to the whole country by the arms, etc., that would there be had, and by the loss of so many persons and so much cattle and other substance belonging to above 120 families. Or, if they should be forced to seek protection from the Dutch, who would be ready to accept them, it would be a great inconvenience to all the English to have

College, Cambridge, before his immigration. He performed a noble service ten years later in opposing a war by New England against the New Netherlands, the English Commonwealth at the time being engaged in their unfortunate struggle with Holland. He was elected, as one of the best men of the colony, to accompany John Norton to England, to establish good relations after the Restoration. He died, full of years and honors, in 1697. At this time Bradstreet and Hathorne lived respectively at Ipswich and Salem.

so considerable a place in the power of strangers so potent as they are.

Another error also was this, that, when by the articles of confederation we were bound, if any of our confederates upon any pressing occasion should send to us for aid, we should forthwith send them such a number of men as is agreed upon in the articles, yet the deputies would not consent, that upon any such occasion the magistrates should raise any man, without calling a general court, which would put the country to great charge, and might occasion the loss of the opportunity; and when they should be assembled, there would be no use of council, the thing being already determined by the articles of confederation.

5. (*July*) 15.] Upon the earnest importunity of Pumham who feared the Narragansetts because of their threatenings, that it might really appear that we did own them and would protect them, we sent 10 men and an officer, a discreet man, to command them, and gave them commission to stay there one, two, or three days, as etc., with charge not to enter into the limits of the Narragansett, nor to provoke them, etc., and if they were forced, to defend themselves, yet they should not pursue the enemy, if he retired, etc.

Two new ships, one of 250 [*tons*], built at Cambridge, the other of 200, built at Boston, set sail towards the Canaries laden with pipe staves, fish, etc.

The court, breaking up in haste, (it being on the evening of the fast appointed,) gave order to the magistrates in the bay to return answer to the Dutch governor's letter of (12) (*February*) 11. which accordingly was done, to this effect, viz., Gratulation of his respect and correspondency with us, manifestation of our good will to him, and desire of continuance of all friendly intercourse, etc.,—acknowledging that he had largely and prudently discoursed of the matters in difference: but we are also to attend the allegations on the other part. But seeing proofs were not yet had on either side, he could expect no further answer than before: but if he would please to send commissioners to Hartford to treat with the commissioners for the colonies, it would be very acceptable, and a hopeful means to prepare for a good issue.

Anabaptistry increased and spread in the country, which occasioned the magistrates, at the last court, to draw an order for banishing such as continued obstinate after due conviction. This was sent to the elders, who approved of it with some mitigations, and being voted, and sent to the deputies, it was after published.[1]

A poor man of Hingham, one Painter, who had lived at New Haven and at Rowley and Charlestown, and been scandalous and burdensome by his idle and troublesome behavior to them all, was now on the sudden turned anabaptist, and having a child born, he would not suffer his wife to bring it to the ordinance of baptism, for she was a member of the church, though himself were not. Being presented for this, and enjoined to suffer the child to be baptized, he still refusing, and disturbing the church, he was again brought to the court not only for his former contempt, but also for saying that our baptism was antichristian; and in the open court he affirmed the same. Whereupon after much patience and clear conviction of his error, etc., because he was very poor, so as no other but corporal punishment could be fastened upon him, he was ordered to be whipped, not for his opinion, but for reproaching the Lord's ordinance, and for his bold and evil behavior both at home and in the court. He endured his punishment with much obstinacy, and when he was loosed, he said boastingly, that God had marvellously assisted him. Whereupon two or three honest men, his neighbors, affirmed before all the company, that he was of very loose behavior at home,

---

[1] Though Winthrop now connived at such intolerance, later he is said to have grown wiser. When pressed on his death-bed by Dudley to sign an order banishing a heterodox offender, he is said to have replied: "I have done too much of that work already." Hutchinson, *History of Massachusetts Bay*, I. 142.

and given much to lying and idleness, etc. Nor had he any great occasion to gather God's assistance from his stillness under the punishment, which was but moderate, for divers notorious malefactors had showed the like, and one the same court.

5. (*July*) 15.] Here arrived Monsieur La Tour, who understood by letters from his lady, that Monsieur D'Aulnay had prevailed against him in France, and was coming with great strength to subdue him: whereupon he came to desire some aid, if need should be.

Natascott being formerly made a town, and having now twenty houses and a minister, was by the last general court named Hull.

At this court Captain Jenyson, captain of the military company in Watertown, an able man who had been there from the first settling of that town, having a year before, (being then a deputy,) in private conference, questioned the lawfulness of the parliament's proceeding in England, was sent for by the deputies, and examined about it, and after before the magistrates. He ingenuously confessed his scruple, but took offence, that being a church member, and in public office, he should be openly produced merely for matter of judgment, not having been first dealt with in private, either in a church way or by some of the magistrates, which seemed to some of the court to have been a failing. The court was unwilling to turn him out of place, having been a very useful man, etc., yet not seeing how he might be trusted, being of that judgment, yet professing that he was assured that those of the parliament side were the more godly and honest part of the kingdom, and that though, if he were in England, he should be doubtful whether he might take their part against their prince, yet, if the king or any party from him should attempt any thing against this commonwealth, he should make no scruple to spend estate and life and all in our defence against them, he was dismissed to further consideration; and the court being broken up, he came soon after to some of the magistrates and told them, that this questioning in the court had occasioned him to search further into the point, and he was now satisfied that the parliament's cause was good, and if he were in England he would assist in defence of it.[1]

The contentions in Hampton were grown to a great height, the whole town was divided into two factions, one with Mr. Batchellor their late pastor, and the other with Mr. Dalton their teacher, both men very passionate, and wanting discretion and moderation. Their differences were not in matters of opinion, but of practice. Mr. Dalton's party being the most of the church, and so freemen, had great advantage of the other, though a considerable party, and some of them of the church also, whereby they carried all affairs both in church and town according to their own minds, and not with that respect to their brethren and neighbors which had been fit. Divers meetings had been both of magistrates and elders, and parties had been reconciled, but brake out presently again, each side being apt to take fire upon any provocation. Whereupon Mr. Batchellor was advised to remove, and was called to Exeter, whither he intended to go, but they being divided, and at great difference also, when one party had appointed a day of humiliation to gather a new church, and call Mr. Batchellor, the court sent order to stop it, for they considered they were not in a fit condition for such a work, and beside, Mr. Batchellor had been in three places before, and through his means, as was supposed, the churches fell to such divisions, as no peace could be till he was removed. And at this court there came petition against petition both from Hampton and Exeter; whereupon the court ordered two or three magistrates to be sent to Hampton with full power to hear and determine all differences there.

At Wenham also there was a public assembly for gathering a church, but the magistrates and elders present, finding upon trial, that the persons appointed were not fit for

---

[1] The better prospects of the Parliament, now helped by Scotland, made concealment of sympathy with it no longer necessary.

foundation stones, they advised them not to proceed, which they obeyed.

4. and 5 (*June* and *July*).] About this time, Mr. Vines of Saco, Mr. Short of Pemaquid, and Mr. Wannerton of Pascataquack, went to La Tour to call for some debts, etc. In their way they put in at Penobscott, and were there detained prisoners a few days; but after, for Mr. Short's sake, to whom D'Aulnay was in debt, they were dismissed: and going to La Tour, Mr. Wannerton and some other Englishmen of the eastern parts were entertained by him, and sent with some twenty of his men to try if they could not take Penobscott, for he understood the fort was weakly manned and in want of victual. They went first to a farm house of D'Aulnay's, about six miles off, and there Wannerton and two more went and knocked at the door, with their swords and pistols ready. One opens the door, and another presently shoots Wannerton dead, and a third shoots his second in the shoulder, but he withal discharged his pistol upon him that shot him, and killed him. Then other of Wannerton's company came in and took the house and the two men (for there were no more) prisoners, and they burnt the house and killed the cattle they found there, and so embarked themselves and came to Boston to La Tour. This Thomas Wannerton was a stout man, and had been a soldier many years: he had lived very wickedly in whoredom, drunkenness and quarrelling, so as he had kept the Pascataquack men under awe of him divers years, till they came under this government, and since that he was much restrained, and the people freed from his terror. He had of late come under some terrors, and motions of the spirit, by means of the preaching of the word, but he had shaken them off, and returned to his former dissolute course, and so continued till God cut him off by this sudden execution. But this hostile action being led on by an Englishman of our jurisdiction, it was like to provoke D'Aulnay the more against us.

3. (*May*) 3.] There was mention made before of a pinnace

sent by the company of discoverers to Delaware river, with
letters from the governor to the Dutch and Swedish governors
for liberty to pass. The Dutch promised to let them pass, but
for maintaining their own interest he must protest against them.
When they came to the Swedes, the fort shot at them, ere they
came up: whereupon they cast forth anchor, and the next
morning, being the Lord's day, the lieutenant came aboard
them, and forced them to fall down lower; when Mr. Aspenwall
came to the governor and complained of the lieutenant's ill
dealing, both in shooting at them before he had hailed them,
and in forcing them to weigh anchor on the Lord's day. The
governor acknowledged he did ill in both, and promised all
favor, but the Dutch agent, being come down to the Swedes'
fort, showed express order from the Dutch governor not to let
him pass, whereupon they returned. But before they came out
of the river, the Swedish lieutenant made them pay 40 shillings
for that shot which he had unduly made. The pinnace arrived
at Boston (5) 20.—44.[1] See page.

A Dutch ship came from the West Indies and brought to
Monhatoes 200 soldiers from Curassou,[2] which was taken by
the Portugal and the Indians and 300 slain of the Dutch part,
as was reported.

23.] La Tour having been with the governor at Salem,
and made known his condition to him, he was moved with
compassion towards him, and appointed a meeting of the
magistrates and elders at Boston this day. In opening La
Tour's case, it appeared that the place, where his fort was, had
been purchased by his father of Sir William Alexander, and he
had a free grant of it, and of all that part of New Scotland,
under the great seal of Scotland, and another grant of a Scotch
Baronetcy under the same seal; and that himself and his father
had continued in possession, etc., about thirty years,[3] and that
Port Royal was theirs also, until D'Aulnay had dispossessed

[1] *I. e.*, July 20, 1644.   [2] Manhattan; Curaçao.
[3] Alexander's own grant was only of date 1621.

him of it by force within these five years. Most of the magistrates and some of the elders were clear in the case that he was to be relieved, both in point of charity, as a distressed neighbor, and also in point of prudence, as thereby to root out, or at least weaken, an enemy or a dangerous neighbor. But because many of the elders were absent, and three or four of the magistrates dissented, it was agreed the rest of the elders should be called in, and that another meeting should be at Salem the next week.

When they were met, the governor propounded the case to them, and it was brought to the two former questions. 1. Whether it were lawful for true Christians to aid an antichristian. 2. Whether it were safe for us in point of prudence. After much disputation, some of the magistrates and elders remaining unsatisfied, and the rest not willing to conclude any thing in this case without a full consent, a third way was propounded, which all assented to, which was this, that a letter should be sent to D'Aulnay to this effect, viz.: That by occasion of some commissions of his (which had come to our hands) to his captains to take our people, etc., and not knowing any just occasion we had given him, to know the reason thereof, and withal to demand satisfaction for the wrongs he had done us and our confederates in taking Penobscott, and our men and goods at Isle Sable, and threatening to make prize of our vessels if they came to Penobscott, etc., declaring withal that although our men, which went last year to aid La Tour, did it without any commission from us, or any counsel or act of permission of our state, yet if he made it appear to us that they had done him any wrong, (which yet we knew not of,) we should be ready to do him justice; and requiring his express answer by the bearer, and expecting that he should call in all such commissions, etc. We subscribed the letter with the hands of eight of the magistrates, and directed it to Monsieur D'Aulnay, Knight, General for the King of France in L'Acady at Port Royal. We sent it in English, because he had written to our

governor in French, but understanding that he had been formerly scrupulous to answer letters in English, we therefore
gave the messenger a copy of it in French.  We sent also in
the letter a copy of an order published by the governor and
council, whereby we forbade all our people to use any act of
hostility, otherwise than in their own defence, towards French
or Dutch, etc., till the next general court, etc.  In our letter
we also mentioned a course of trade our merchants had entered
into with La Tour, and our resolution to maintain them in it.

Before this letter was sent, we had intelligence from the
West Indies, that D'Aulnay was met at sea by some Biscayers
and his ship sunk, yet being not certain hereof, when La Tour
went home, we sent the letter by a vessel of our own which accompanied him, to be delivered if occasion were.  This news
proved false, and no such thing was; and indeed it was so
usual to have false news brought from all parts, that we were
very doubtful of the most probable reports.

At the same meeting there were three other questions on
foot.  The first was upon this occasion.

Captain Stagg arriving at Boston in a ship of London, of
24 pieces of ordnance, and finding here a ship of Bristol
of 100 tons, laden with fish for Bilboa, he made no speech of
any commission he had, but having put on shore a good part
of his lading, which was wine from Teneriffe, he suddenly
weighed anchor, and with the sea turn sailed from before
Boston to Charlestown, and placed his ship between Charlestown and the Bristol ship, and moored himself abreast her.
Then he called the master of the Bristol ship, and showed him
his commission, and told him, if he would yield, himself and all
his should have what belonged to them and their wages to that
day, and turning up the half hour glass, set him in his own
ship again, requiring to have his answer by that time of half
an hour.  The master coming aboard acquainted his men
with it, and demanded their resolution.  Two or three would
have fought, and rather have blown up their ship than have

yielded; but the greater part prevailed, so she was quietly taken, and all the men save three sent to Boston, and there order was taken by the captain for their diet.[1]

In this half hour's time much people gathered together upon Windmill hill to see the issue, and some who had interest in the ship, especially one Bristol merchant, (a very bold malignant person,) began to gather company and raise a tumult. But some of the people present laid hold of them and brought them to the deputy governor, who committed the merchant and some others who were strangers to a chamber in an ordinary, with a guard upon them, and others who were town dwellers he committed to prison, and sent the constable to require the people to depart to their houses; and then hearing that the ship was taken, he wrote to the captain to know by what authority he had done it in our harbor, who forthwith repaired to him with his commission, which was to this effect:

Robertus Comes Warwici, etc., magnus Admirallus Angliae, etc., omnibus cujuscunque status honoris, etc., salutem. Sciatis quod in registro curiæ Admiralitatis, etc.,—and so recites the ordinance of parliament, in English, to this effect: That it should be lawful for all men, etc., to set forth ships and to take all vessels in or outward bound to or from Bristol, Barnstable, Dartmouth, etc., in hostility against the king and parliament, and to visit all ships in any port or creek, etc., by force, if they should refuse, etc., and they were to have the whole prize to themselves, paying the tenth to the admiral, provided, before they went forth, they should give security to the admiral to observe their commission, and that they should make a true invoice of all goods, and not break bulk, but bring the ship to the admiral and two or three of the officers, and that they should not rob or spoil any of the parliament's

---

[1] The Civil War, as appears here, came near to actual battle on this side of the Atlantic. London was strong for the Houses; the west of England, of which Bristol was the metropolis, long held for the King, and ships were Roundhead or Cavalier according to the ports whence they sailed.

friends, and so concludes thus: Stagg Capitaneus obligavit
se, etc., in bis mille libris, etc.   In cujus rei testimonium sigil-
lum Admiralitatis presentibus apponi feci.

Dat. March, 1644.

Upon sight of this commission, the deputy appointed Captain Stagg to bring or send it to the meeting at Salem; and
the tumult being pacified, he took bond, with sureties, of the
principal stirrers, to appear at the meeting and to keep the
peace in the mean time.   The captain brought his commission
to Salem, and there it was read and considered.   Some of the
elders, the last Lord's day, had in their sermons reproved
this proceeding, and exhorted the magistrates, etc., to maintain the people's liberties, which were, they said, violated by
this act, and that a commission could not supersede a patent.
And at this meeting some of the magistrates and some of the
elders were of the same opinion, and that the captain should
be forced to restore the ship.   But the greater part of both were
of a different judgment.—Their reasons were these.

1. Because this could be no precedent to bar us from opposing any commission or other foreign power that might indeed
tend to our hurt and violate our liberty; for the parliament
had taught us, that salus populi is suprema lex.

2. The king of England was enraged against us, and all that
party, and all the popish states in Europe: and if we should
now, by opposing the parliament, cause them to forsake us, we
could have no protection or countenance from any, but should
lie open as a prey to all men.

3. We might not deny the parliament's power in this case,
unless we should deny the foundation of our government by
our patent; for the parliament's authority will take place in all
peculiar and privileged places, where the king's writs or commissions will not be of force, as in the Dutchy of Lancaster,
the Cinque ports, and in London itself, the parliament may
fetch out any man, even the Lord Mayor himself, and the
reason is, because what the parliament doth is done by them·

selves, for they have their burgesses, etc., there; nor need they fear that the parliament will do any man wrong: and we have consented to hold our land of the manor of E. Greenwich, and so such as are burgesses or knights for that manor, are our burgesses also. This only might help us, that the king giving us land which was none of his, but we were forced to purchase it of the natives, or subdue it as vacuum domicilium, we are not bound to hold that of him which was not his. But if we stand upon this plea, we must then renounce our patent and England's protection, which were a great weakness in us, seeing their care hath been to strengthen our liberties and not over-throw them: and if the parliament should hereafter be of a malignant spirit, etc., then if we have strength sufficient, we may make use of salus populi to withstand any authority from thence to our hurt.

4. Again, if we who have so openly declared our affection to the cause of the parliament by our prayers, fastings, etc., should now oppose their authority, or do any thing that might make such an appearance, it would be laid hold on by those in Virginia and the West Indies to confirm them in their rebellious course; and it would grieve all our godly friends in England, or any other of the parliament's friends.

5. Lastly, if any of our people have any goods in the ship, it is not to be questioned, but upon testimony the parliament will take order for their satisfaction.

It was objected by some, that our's is perfecta respublica and so not subject to appeals, and consequently to no other power but among ourselves. It was answered, that though our patent frees us from appeals in cases of judicature, yet not in point of state; for the king of England cannot erigere per-fectam rempublicam in such a sense: for nemo potest plus juris in alios transferre quam in se habet; he hath not an absolute power without the parliament.[1]

Upon these and other considerations, it was not thought fit

[1] The spirit of independence is notable here.

to oppose the parliament's commission, but to suffer the captain to enjoy his prize. But because some of our merchants had put goods aboard her, wherein they claimed property, they desired to try their right by action, to which the captain consented to appear. So a court was called of purpose, the issue whereof follows after.[1]

The third matter which fell into consideration, at the said meeting at Salem, was about one Franklin, who at the last court of assistants was found guilty of murder, but, some of the magistrates doubting of the justice of the case, he was reprieved till the next court of assistants. The case was this. He had taken to apprentice one Nathaniel Sewell, one of those children sent over the last year for the country; the boy had the scurvy, and was withal very noisome, and otherwise ill disposed. His master used him with continual rigor and unmerciful correction, and exposed him many times to much cold and wet in the winter season, and used divers acts of rigor towards him, as hanging him in the chimney, etc., and the boy being very poor and weak, he tied him upon an horse and so brought him (sometimes sitting and sometimes hanging down) to Boston, being five miles off, to the magistrates, and by the way the boy calling much for water, would give him none, though he came close by it, so as the boy was near dead when he came to Boston, and died within a few hours after. Those who doubted whether this were murder or not, did stick upon two reasons chiefly. 1. That it did not appear that the master's intention was to hurt him, but to reform him. 2. In that which was most likely to be the occasion or cause of his death, he was busied about an action which in itself was lawful, viz., the bringing of him before the magistrates; and murder cannot be committed but where the action and intention both are evil. To this it was answered, that this continual act of cruelty did bring him to death by degrees, and the last act was the consummation of it; and that this act, in regard to

[1] See *post*, p. 190.

the subject, who, to the apprehension of all that saw him, was more fit to be kept in his bed than to be haled to correction, was apparently unlawful.  As in case a man had a servant sick in bed of the small pox, newly come forth, and that his master knowing and seeing these upon his body should, against the physician's advice, hale him forth of his bed into the open air in frosty weather, upon pretence that he might ease nature, etc., this act, in regard of the state of the subject, were utterly unlawful, and if the servant should die under his hand, etc., it were murder in him.  As for the intention, though prima intentio might be to reform him, yet sure proxima intentio was evil because it arose from distemper of passion; and if a man in a sudden passion kill his dear friend or child, it is murder, though his prima intentio were to instruct or admonish him: and in some cases where there appears no intention to hurt, as where a man knowing his ox to have used to push, shall not keep him in, so as he kills a man, he was to die for it, though to keep an ox were a lawful act, and he did not intend hurt, but because he did not what he reasonably ought to prevent, etc., therefore he was a murderer.  And that in Exodus      if a master strike his servant with a rod, which is a lawful action, and he die under his hand, (as this servant did,) he was to die for it:— And that in Deut.      if a man strike with a weapon or with his hand, or any thing wherewith he may die, and he die, he is a murderer,—shows plainly, that let the means be what it may, if it be voluntarily applied to an evil intent, it is murder; according to that judgment given      against her that gave a potion to one to procure his love, and it killed him, it was adjudged murder.

All the magistrates seeming to be satisfied upon this confer-ence, warrant was signed by the governor for his execution a week after, which was not approved by some, in regard of his reprieval to the next court of assistants.  But it was without any good reason, for a condemned man is in the power of the magistrate to be executed when he please, and the reprieval was no stipulation or covenant with him, but a determination among the magistrates for the satisfaction of some who were doubtful, which satisfaction being attained, currat lex etc. Pro. 22. He shall go to the pit, let no man hinder him.

This man had been admitted into the church of Roxbury about a month before, and upon this he was cast out; but the church, in compassion to his soul, after his condemnation, procured license for him to come to Roxbury, intending to receive him in again before he died, if they might find him truly penitent. But though presently after his condemnation he judged himself, and justified God and the court, yet then he quarrelled with the witnesses, and justified himself, and so continued even to his execution, professing assurance of salvation, and that God would never lay the boy his death to his charge, but the guilt of his blood would lie upon the country. Only a little before he was turned off the ladder, he seemed to apprehend some hardness of heart, that he could not see himself guilty of that which others did.

A fourth matter then in consideration was upon a speech, which the governor made to this effect, viz. 1. That he could not but bewail the great differences and jarrings which were upon all occasions, among the magistrates, and between them and the deputies; that the ground of this was jealousies and misreports; and thereupon some elders siding, etc., but not dealing with any of them in a way of God; but hearing them reproached and passing it in silence: also their authority questioned, as if they had none out of court but what must be granted them by commission from the general court, etc.,—and the way to redress hereof was, that the place and power of magistrates and deputies might be known; and so the elders were desired (which they willingly assented to) to be mediators of a thorough reconciliation, and to go about it presently, and to meet at Boston two or three days before the next court to perfect the same. But indeed the magistrates did all agree very well together, except two only, viz., Mr. Bellingham and **Mr. Saltonstall**, who took part with the deputies against the other ten magistrates about their power, and in other cases where any difference was. And some of the elders had done no good offices in this matter, through their misapprehensions both of the intentions of the magistrates, and also of the matters themselves, being affairs of state, which did not belong to their calling.[1]

The merchants which had to do with the goods in the ship which was seized by Captain Stagg, being desirous to do their utmost to save their principals in England from damage, knowing them to be honest men and faithful to the parliament, intended to have a trial at law about it, and procured an attachment against the captain; but they were dissuaded from that course, and the deputy sent for Captain Stagg and acquainted him with it, and took his word for his appearance at the next court which was called of purpose. When the governor and six other of the magistrates were met, (for the governor did not send for such as dwelt far off,) and the jury, the merchants were persuaded not to put it to a jury, for the jury could find no more but the matter of fact, viz., whose the goods were, whether the merchants' in England, or theirs who shipped them, in regard they had not yet made any consignment of them, nor taken any bills of lading: and this the magistrates could as well determine upon proof, and certify accordingly: for it was resolved not to use any force against the parliament's authority; and accordingly they certified the Lord Admiral of the true state of the case, as they found it upon examination and oath of the factors.

The pinnace, which went to Delaware upon discovery, returned with loss of their voyage. The occasion was, the Dutch governor made a protest against them, yet promised them leave to pass, etc., provided they should not trade with the Indians: also the Swedish governor gave them leave to pass, but would not permit them to trade; and for that end

[1] And yet the elders were constantly dealing with affairs of state.

each of them had appointed a pinnace to wait upon our pinnace, but withal the master of their vessel proved such a drunk-
en sot, and so complied with the Dutch and Swedes, as they
feared, when they should have left the vessel to have gone up
to the lake in a small boat, he would in his drunkenness have
betrayed their goods, etc., to the Dutch, whereupon they gave
over and returned home; and bringing their action against the
master both for his drunkenness and denial to proceed as they
required, and as by charter party he was bound, they recovered
200 pounds of him, which was too much, though he did deal
badly with them, for it was very probable they could not have
proceeded.

There fell out a troublesome business at Boston, upon this
occasion. There arrived here a Portugal ship with salt, having
in it two Englishmen only. One of these happened to be
drunk, and was carried to his lodging, and the constable, (a
godly man, and zealous against such disorders,) hearing of it,
found him out, being upon his bed asleep, so he awaked him,
and led him to the stocks, there being no magistrate at home.
He being in the stocks, one of La Tour's gentlemen lifted up
the stocks and let him out. The constable, hearing of it, went
to the Frenchman, (being then gone and quiet,) and would
needs carry him to the stocks; the Frenchman offered to yield
himself to go to prison, but the constable, not understanding
his language, pressed him to go to the stocks: the Frenchman
resisted and drew his sword; with that company came in and
disarmed him, and carried him by force to the stocks, but soon
after the constable took him out and carried him to prison, and
presently after took him forth again and delivered him to La
Tour. Much tumult there was about this: many Frenchmen
were in town, and other strangers, which were not satisfied
with this dealing of the constable, yet were quiet. In the
morning the magistrates examined the cause and sent for La
Tour, who was much grieved for his servant's miscarriage, and
also for the disgrace put upon him, (for in France it is a most

ignominious thing to be laid in the stocks,) but yet he complained not of any injury, but left him wholly to the magistrates to do with him what they pleased. The magistrates
told him, they were sorry to have any such occasion against
any of his servants, but they must do justice, and therefore
they must commit him to prison, except he could find sureties
to be forth coming, to answer, etc., and to keep the peace.
La Tour's gentlemen offered to engage themselves for him.
They answered, they might not take security of strangers in
this case, otherwise they would have desired no more than
La Tour's own word. Upon this two Englishmen, members of
the church of Boston, standing by, offered to be his sureties,
whereupon he was bailed till he should be called for, because
La Tour was not like to stay till the court. This was thought
too much favor for such an offence by many of the common
people, but by our law bail could not be denied him; and beside the constable was the occasion of all this in transgressing
the bounds of his office, and that in six things. 1. In fetching
a man out of his lodging that was asleep upon his bed, and
without any warrant from authority. 2. In not putting a
hook upon the stocks, nor setting some to guard them. 3.
In laying hands upon the Frenchman that had opened the
stocks, when he was gone and quiet, and no disturbance of the
peace then appearing. 4. In carrying him to prison without
warrant. 5. In delivering him out of prison without warrant.
6. In putting such a reproach upon a stranger and a gentleman,
when there was no need, for he knew he would be forthcoming,
and the magistrate would be at home that evening; but such
are the fruits of ignorant and misguided zeal. It might have
caused much blood and no good done by it, and justice might
have had a more fair and safe way, if the constable had kept
within his own bounds, and had not interfered upon the authority of the magistrate. But the magistrates thought not
convenient to lay these things to the constable's charge before
the assembly, but rather to admonish him for it in private, lest

they should have discouraged and discountenanced an honest officer, and given occasion to the offenders and their abettors to insult over him.  The constable may restrain, and, if need be, imprison in the stocks, such as he sees disturbing the peace, but, when the affray is ended and the parties departed and in quiet, it is the office of the magistrate to make inquiry and to punish it, and the persons so wrongfully imprisoned by the constable might have had their action of false imprisonment against him.

6. (*August*) 26.] About nine in the evening there fell a great flame of fire down into the water towards Pullen Point; it lighted the air far about: it was no lightning, for the sky was very clear.

At Stamford an Indian came into a poor man's house, none being at home but the wife, and a child in the cradle, and taking up a lathing hammer as if he would have bought it, the woman stooping down to take her child out of the cradle, he struck her with the sharp edge upon the side of her head, wherewith she fell down, and then he gave her two cuts more which pierced into her brains, and so left her for dead, carrying away some clothes which lay at hand.  This woman after a short time came to herself and got out to a neighbor's house, and told what had been done to her, and described the Indian by his person and clothes, etc.  Whereupon many Indians of those parts were brought before her, and she charged one of them confidently to be the man, whereupon he was put in prison with intent to have put him to death, but he escaped, and the woman recovered, but lost her senses.  A good time after the Indians brought another Indian whom they charged to have committed that fact, and he, upon examination, confessed it, and gave the reason thereof, and brought forth some of the clothes which he had stolen.  Upon this the magistrates of New Haven, taking advice of the elders in those parts, and some here, did put him to death.  The executioner would strike off his head with a falchion, but he had eight blows at it before he could effect it, and the Indian sat upright and stirred not all the time.

7. (*September*) 7.]   Here came a pinnace from Virginia with
letters from the governor and council there, for procuring
powder and shot to prosecute their war against the Indians,
but we were weakly provided ourselves, and so could not afford
them any help in that kind.

9.]   Mr. La Tour departed from Boston; all our train bands
(it being then the ordinary training day) made a guard for him
to his boat; and the deputy governor and many others accompanied him to the wharf.   When he was aboard his bark, he
weighed, and set sail and shot off all his guns, which were six,
and our small shot gave him a volley and one piece of ordnance,
and all the ships, viz., four, saluted him, each of them with three
pieces.

At the court of assistants, Thomas Morton[1] was called forth
presently after the lecture, that the country might be satisfied
of the justice of our proceeding against him.   There was laid
to his charge his complaint against us at the council board,
which he denied.   Then we produced the copy of the bill exhibited by Sir Christopher Gardiner, etc., wherein we were
charged with treason, rebellion, etc., wherein he was named as
a party or witness.   He denied that he had any hand in
the information, only was called as a witness.   To convince
him to be the principal party, it was showed:  1. That Gardiner had no occasion to complain against us, for he was kindly
used, and dismissed in peace, professing much engagement for
the great courtesy he found here.  2. Morton had set forth
a book against us, and had threatened us, and had prosecuted a quo warranto against us, which he did not deny.  3.
His letter was produced, written soon after to Mr. Jeffery, his
old acquaintance and intimate friend, in these words.

MY VERY GOOD GOSSIP,

If I should commend myself to you, you reply with this proverb,
propria laus sordet in ore: but to leave impertinent salute, and really to
proceed.—You shall hereby understand, that, although, when I was first

[1] Morton of Merry Mount, whose return to America has been mentioned.

sent to England to make complaint against Ananias and the brethren, I
effected the business but superficially, (through the brevity of time,) I
have at this time taken more deliberation and brought the matter to a
better pass.    And it is thus brought about, that the king hath taken the
business into his own hands.    The Massachusetts Patent, by order of
the council, was brought in view; the privileges there granted well scanned
upon, and at the council board in public, and in the presence of Sir
Richard Saltonstall and the rest, it was declared, for manifest abuses there
discovered, to be void.    The king hath reassumed the whole business into
his own hands, appointed a committee of the board, and given order for
a general governor of the whole territory to be sent over.    The commission
is passed the privy seal, I did see it, and the same was 1 mo. Maii[1] sent to
the Lord Keeper to have it pass the great seal for confirmation; and I
now stay to return with the governor, by whom all complainants shall
have relief: So that now Jonas being set ashore may safely cry, repent
you cruel separatists, repent, there are as yet but forty days.    If Jove
vouchsafe to thunder, the charter and kingdom of the separatists will
fall asunder.    Repent you cruel schismatics, repent.    These things have
happened, and I shall see (notwithstanding their boasting and false
alarms in the Massachusetts, with feigned cause of thanksgiving) their
merciless cruelty rewarded, according to the merit of the fact, with con-
dign punishment for coming into those parts, like Sampson's foxes with
fire-brands at their tails.    The king and council are really possessed of
their preposterous loyalty and irregular proceedings, and are incensed
against them: and although they be so opposite to the catholic axioms,
yet they will be compelled to perform them, or at leastwise suffer them to
be put in practice to their sorrow.    In matter of restitution and satisfaction, more than mystically, it must be performed visibly, and in such sort
as may be subject to the senses in a very lively image.    My Lord Canter-
bury having, with my Lord Privy Seal, caused all Mr. Cradock's letters
to be viewed, and his apology in particular for the brethren here, protested
against him and Mr. Humfrey, that they were a couple of imposterous
knaves; so that, for all their great friends, they departed the council
chamber in our view with a pair of cold shoulders.    I have staid long,
yet have not lost my labor, although the brethren have found their hopes
frustrated; so that it follows by consequence, I shall see my desire upon
mine enemies: and if John Grant had not betaken him to flight, I had

---

[1] *I. e.*, primo Maii, on the first of May.    The "committee of the board"
is doubtless the well-known colonial committee of April 28, 1634, whose commission is given in Bradford, appendix.

taught him to sing clamavi in the Fleet before this time, and if he return before I depart, he will pay dear for his presumption.   For here he finds me a second Perseus:  I have uncased Medusa's head, and struck the brethren into astonishment.   They find, and will yet more to their shame, that they abuse the word and are to blame to presume so much,—that they are but a word and a blow to them that are without.   Of these particulars I thought good, by so convenient a messenger, to give you notice, lest you should think I had died in obscurity, as the brethren vainly intended I should, and basely practised, abusing justice by their sinister practices, as by the whole body of the committee, una voce, it was concluded to be done, to the dishonor of his majesty.   And as for Ratcliffe, he was comforted by their lordships with the cropping of Mr. Winthrop's ears:[1] which shows what opinion is held amongst them of King Winthrop with all his inventions and his Amsterdam fantastical ordinances, his preachings, marriages, and other abusive ceremonies, which do exemplify his detestation to the church of England, and the contempt of his majesty's authority and wholesome laws, which are and will be established in those parts, invita Minerva.   With these I thought fit to salute you, as a friend, by an epistle, because I am bound to love you, as a brother, by the gospel, resting your loving friend.

                                                          THOMAS MORTON.
Dated 1 mo. Maii, 1634.


Having been kept in prison about a year, in expectation of further evidence out of England, he was again called before the court, and after some debate what to do with him, he was fined 100 pounds, and set at liberty.   He was a charge to the country, for he had nothing, and we thought not fit to inflict corporal punishment upon him, being old and crazy, but thought better to fine him and give him his liberty, as if it had been to procure his fine, but indeed to leave him opportunity to go out of the jurisdiction, as he did soon after, and he went to Acomenticus, and living there poor and despised, he died within two years after.

7. (*September*) 16.]   Here arrived a ship from Dartmouth. She was impressed into the king's service, and sent to sea in the

----

[1] Ratcliffe's ears had been cropped by order of the Massachusetts authorities for speaking abusively of the magistracy and church government.

Earl of Marlborough's fleet, but she left the fleet, and took in wine and salt at the Spanish Islands, and went to Virginia, where he left his merchants and divers of his men; and not putting off his goods there, he came to Boston, where the London ship, Captain Bayley commander, having commission from the parliament, would have taken him, but he stood upon his defence, and was able to keep his ship against the other. But another question arose about her, upon this occasion; our merchants of Boston had set out a small ship worth 1500 pounds, which, being trading in Wales, was taken by the king's ships, whereupon the merchants desired leave to seize this ship for their satisfaction. On the other side, the master, being come under our command, desired our protection. Our answer was, that, if he would deliver his sailors on shore, we would protect him till the court, etc. See more next leaf.

17.] The Lady La Tour arrived here from London in a ship commanded by Captain Bayley. They had been six months from London, having spent their time in trading about Canada, etc. They met with D'Aulnay near Cape Sable, and told him they were bound for the Bay, and had stowed the lady and her people under hatches, so he not knowing it was Captain Bayley, whom he earnestly sought for, to have taken or sunk him, he wrote by the master to the deputy governor to this effect: That his master the king of France, understanding that the aid La Tour had here the last year was upon the commission he showed from the Vice Admiral of France, gave him in charge not to molest us for it, but to hold all good correspondency with us and all the English, which he professed he was desirous of, so far as might stand with his duty to his master, and withal that he intended to send to us so soon as he had settled his affairs, to let us know what further commission he had, and his sincerity in the business of La Tour, etc.

Here arrived also Mr. Roger Williams of Providence, and

with him two or three families.   He brought with him a letter from divers lords and others of the parliament, the copy whereof ensueth.

OUR MUCH HONORED FRIENDS:

Taking notice, some of us of long time, of Mr. Roger Williams his good affections and conscience, and of his sufferings by our common enemies and oppressors of God's people, the prelates, as also of his great industry and travail in his printed Indian labors in your parts, the like whereof we have not seen extant from any part of America, and in which respect it hath pleased both houses of Parliament freely to grant unto him and friends with him a free and absolute charter of civil government for those parts of his abode:[1] and withal sorrowfully resenting, that amongst good men (our friends) driven to the ends of the world, exercised with the trials of a wilderness, and who mutually give good testimony each of other, as we observe you do of him  and he abundantly of you, there should be such a distance; we thought it fit, upon divers considerations, to profess our great desires of both your utmost endeavors of nearer closing, and of ready expressing of those good affections, which we perceive you bear each to other, in the actual performance of all friendly offices; the rather because of those bad neighbors you are like to find too near unto you in Virginia, and the unfriendly visits from the West of England and from Ireland: that howsoever it may please the Most High to shake our foundations, yet the report of your peaceable and prosperous plantations may be some refreshing to

Your true and faithful friends,

| | |
|---|---|
| NORTHUMBERLAND, | P. WHARTON, |
| ROB. HARLEY, | THOS. BARRINGTON, |
| WM. MASHAM, | OL. ST. JOHN, |
| JOHN GURDON, | ISAAC PENNINGTON, |
| COR. HOLLAND, | GIL. PYKERING, |
| J. BLAKISTON, | MILES CORBET. |

To the Right Worshipful the Governor and Assistants and the rest of our worthy friends in the plantation of Massachusetts Bay, in New England.[2]

[1] The Rhode Island charter of 1644.

[2] This letter is strong evidence of the respect in which Roger Williams was held.   He had just before put humanity in his debt by writing *The Bloudy Tenent*, his famous defence of toleration, which appeared in 1644.

19.] Two churches were appointed to be gathered, one at Haverhill and the other at Andover, both upon Merrimack river. They had given notice thereof to the magistrates and elders, who desired, in regard of their far remoteness and scarcity of housing there, the meeting might be at Rowley, which they assented unto, but being assembled, most of those who were to join, refused to declare how God had carried on the work of his grace in them, upon this reason, because they had declared it formerly in their admission into other churches; whereupon the assembly brake up without proceeding, etc.

The governor and others of the magistrates met at Boston upon two special occasions; the one was for trial of an action between the Lady La Tour and Captain Bayley for not carrying her, etc., to her own place, and for some injuries done her aboard his ship. See more after.

The other was upon the request of some merchants of Boston, who, having a ship taken in Wales by the king's party, desired recompence by a ship of Dartmouth riding in our harbor. Whereupon we sent for the master of the Dartmouth ship, who delivered his ship into our hands, till the cause should be tried, which he did the more willingly, for that some London ships of greater force, riding also in our harbor, had threatened to take him; and the next morning Captain Richardson (having commission from the Lord Admiral) fitted his ship to take her, notwithstanding that he had been forbidden over night by the deputy governor to meddle with her, being under our protection, and lying so before Boston as their shot must needs do harm. Whereupon the governor and the other magistrates (sitting then in court) arose and went to take order about it, and having over night given commission to some to make seizure of the Dartmouth ship, they went aboard her with their commission, and an officer was sent with warrant to stay Captain Richardson, but he being then come to anchor close by the other ship, he could not (or would not) stay, but suffered his men to enter the other ship, and the master coming aboard him at his request, he detained him prisoner. Whereupon the governor, etc., sent two other masters of ships to him to command him ashore, but he seeing his men so unruly, and fearing they would fall to fight or pillage in his absence, (as he after told us,) excused himself for not coming upon that command. Upon which fire was given to a warning piece from the battery, which cut a rope in the head of his ship: and upon that one of his men, without any command, ran down hastily to fire upon our battery; but it pleased God that he hurt himself in the way, and so was not able to go on. A stranger also (unbidden) gave fire to another piece on the battery, which levelled at the bow of his ship, but it struck against the head of a bolt in the cutwater of the Dartmouth ship, and went no further. Then we sent forty men armed aboard the Dartmouth ship, and upon that Captain Richardson came ashore and acknowledged his error, and his sorrow for what he had done, yet withal alleging some reasons for his excuse. So we only ordered him to pay a barrel of powder, and to satisfy the officers and soldiers we had employed, etc., and dismissed him. The reason was, because (through the Lord's special providence) there was no hurt done, nor had he made one shot; for if he had, we were resolved to have taken or sunk him, which we might easily have done, lying close under our battery, so as we could have played upon him with whole culverin or demi culverin six hours together, nor had he yet showed to us or to the master of the Dartmouth ship any commission. But after, he showed only an ordinary commission from the Lord Admiral, not under the great seal, nor grounded upon any ordinance of parliament, as Captain Stagg's was: therefore we forbade him to meddle with any ship in our harbor, for he could not by that commission take a ship in any place exempt from the Admiral's jurisdiction.

Having thus seized this ship, we were to consult what to do with her. Upon examination, we found that the master and company were Dartmouth men, and that the ship had formerly been employed in the parliament's service, but, Dartmouth being taken by the king, she had been employed for taking a vessel or two of the parliament's under the same master, but a captain put over him and many soldiers, and was since sold to a merchant of Christopher Island, and by his agent sent forth upon merchant affairs to divers places, and to repair at last to St. Maloes in France, where the agent dwelt, who was an Englishman and had used to trade at Dartmouth, whose letter of advice and the bill of sale of the ship were produced by the master. It appeared further to us, that Dartmouth had been cordial to the parliament, and stood out seven days against 12,000 men; and after it was surrendered did generally refuse to take the oath to the king, and the master among others, and that they had many better ships there which lay still at home, and such as they sent forth they were not to come home but by advice. Yet it appeared after by divers testimonies, that she belonged to Dartmouth, and the charter party also, and that the master was part owner. Divers of the elders, being called in for advice, agreed (near all) that she might be seized to satisfy for our two ships which the king's party had taken from us, and accordingly commission was given by the governor and council to the merchant to seize and use her, giving security to be responsible and 8 pounds per 100 if she should be lawfully recovered within thirteen months, but the company to have their wages and goods.

While the governor and other of the magistrates were at Boston, a boat sent from Mr. D'Aulnay with ten men arrived at Salem, hearing that the governor dwelt there. There was in her one Marie, supposed to be a friar, but habited like a gentleman. He wrote a letter to our governor by a gentleman of his company to know where he should attend him: and upon our governor's answer to him, he came the next day to Boston, and with letters of credence and commission from Mr. D'Aulnay; he showed us the king of France his commission under the great seal of France, with the privy seal annexed,

wherein the proceedings against La Tour were verified, and he
condemned as a rebel and traitor, etc., with command for the
apprehension of himself and lady, who had fled out of France
against special order, under, etc.   He complained also of the
wrong done by our men the last year in assisting of La Tour
etc., and proffered terms of peace and amity.   We answered to
the 1.  That divers of the ships and most of the men were
strangers to us, and had no commission from us, nor any permission to use any hostility, and we were very sorry when we
heard what had been done.  This gave him satisfaction.  To
the other proposition we answered, that we could not conclude
any league with him, without the advice of the commissioners
of the united colonies; but if he would set down his propositions in writing, we would consider further of them: and withal
we acquainted him with what we had lately written to Mr.
D'Aulnay, and the injuries we had complained of to him.   So
he withdrew himself to his lodging at Mr. Fowle's, and drew
out both his propositions and answers to our complaints in
French, and returned to us.  He added two propositions
more, one that we would aid him against La Tour, and the
other that we would not assist him, and gave reasonable answer
to our demands.  Upon these things [he] discoursed half the
day, sometimes with our governor in French, and otherwhile
with the rest of the magistrates in Latin.  We urged much for
a reconciliation with La Tour, and that he would permit his
lady to go to her husband.  His answer was, that if La Tour
would voluntarily submit and come in, he would assure him his
life and liberty, but if he were taken, he were sure to lose his
head in France; and for his lady, she was known to be the
cause of his contempt and rebellion, and therefore they could
not let her go to him, but if we should send her in any of our
vessels he must take her, and if we carried any goods to La
Tour he would take them also, but he would give us satisfaction
for them.  In the end we came to this agreement, which
was drawn up in Latin in these words, and signed by the

governor and six other magistrates, and Mr. Marie, whereof one copy we kept and the other he carried with him. He came to Boston the sixth day very late, and made great haste away, so he departed on the third day following. We furnished him with horses and sent him to Salem well accompanied, and offered him a bark to carry him home, but he refused it. We entertained him with all courteous respect, and he seemed to be surprised with his unexpected entertainment, and gave a very liberal testimony of his kind acceptance thereof, and assurance of Mr. D'Aulnay's engagement to us for it. The agreement between us was this.

The agreement between John Endecott, Esq., Governor of the Massachusetts in New England, and the rest of the magistrates there, and Mr. Marie, commissioner of Mr. D'Aulnay, Knight, Governor and Lieutenant General of his Majesty the king of France, in Acadie, a province of New France, made and ratified at Boston in the Massachusetts aforesaid, 8 die mensis 8, (*October* 8) An. Dom. 1644.

The governor and the rest of the magistrates do promise to Mr. Marie, that they and all the English within the jurisdiction of the Massachusetts aforesaid shall observe and keep firm peace with Mr. D'Aulnay, etc., and all the French under his command in Acadie: and likewise the said Mr. Marie doth promise for Mr. D'Aulnay, that he and all his people shall also keep firm peace with the governor and magistrates aforesaid, and with all the inhabitants of the jurisdiction of the Massachusetts aforesaid; and that it shall be lawful for all men, both French and English, to trade each with other: so that if any occasion of offence shall happen, neither party shall attempt any thing against the other in any hostile manner before the wrong be first complained of, and due satisfaction not given. Provided always, the governor and magistrates aforesaid be not bound to restrain their merchants to trade with their ships with any persons, either French or other, wheresoever they dwell: provided also, that the full ratification and conclusion of this agreement be referred to the next meeting of the commissioners of the united colonies of New England, for the continuation or abrogation of the same; and in the mean time to remain firm and inviolate.[1]

---

[1] The treaty is given in full in Hazard, *State Papers*, I. 536; also in Hutchinson, *Collections*, 146.

By this agreement we were freed from the fear our people were in, that Mr. D'Aulnay would take revenge of our small vessels or out plantations, for the harm he sustained by our means the last year; and also from any further question about that business.

We were now also freed from as great a fear of war with the Narragansetts. For the commissioners, meeting at Hartford, sent for Onkus and some from Narragansett, (a sachem and a chief captain were sent,) and whereas the Narragansett's plea against Onkus was, that he had put their sachem to death after he had received a ransom for his life, it was clearly proved otherwise, and that the things he received were part of them given him for his courteous usage of the said Miantunnomoh and those sachems which were slain in the battle, and another part, that Miantunnomoh might be given to the English. In the end it was agreed by all parties, that there should be peace on all sides till planting time were over the next year; and then neither of them should attempt any hostile act against the other, without first acquainting the English, etc. therewith.

The Lady La Tour, being arrived here, commenced her action against Captain Bayley and the merchant, (brother and factor to Alderman Berkley, who freighted the ship,) for not performing the charter party, having spent so much time upon the coast in trading, as they were near six months in coming, and had not carried her to her fort as they ought and might have done: and upon a full hearing in a special court four days, the jury gave her 2,000 pounds. For had they come in any reasonable time, it might have been much more to her advantage in her trade and safety against D'Aulnay: whereas now it was like to occasion her utter ruin: for she knew not how to get home without hiring two or three ships of force.

La Tour, and a vessel of ours in his company laden with provision, went hence with a fair wind, which if he had made use of, he had met with D'Aulnay, and after he had touched at divers places by the way, and staid there some time, he passed by Penobscott soon after D'Aulnay was gone into the harbor, and so escaped, whereas if he had passed any time many days before, he must needs have been taken. This vessel of ours in her return was met by D'Aulnay, who stayed her, and taking the master aboard his ship, manned the other with Frenchmen, and telling the master his intention, and assuring him of all good usage and recompense for the stay of his vessel, (all which he really performed,) he brought her with him to the mouth of St. John's river; and then sent her boat with one gentleman of his own to La Tour to show his commission, and withal desired the master to write to La Tour to desire him to dismiss the messenger safely, for otherwise D'Aulnay would keep him for hostage (yet he assured him he would not do it). So La Tour dismissed the messenger in peace, which he professed he would not have done but for our master's sake. D'Aulnay carried our ketch with him to Port Royal, where he used the master very courteously and gave him credit for fish, etc., he bought of him, and recompense for keeping his vessel, and so dismissed him. Presently after their return, we sent another vessel to trade with D'Aulnay, and by it the deputy governor wrote to D'Aulnay to show the cause of sending her, with profession of our desire of holding good correspondency with him, etc., and withal persuading him by divers arguments to entertain peace with La Tour. That vessel found courteous entertainment with him, and he took off all her commodities, but not at so good rates as they expected.

The Lady La Tour having arrested the captain and merchant of the ship, they were forced to deliver their cargo on shore to free their persons, by which means she laid her execution upon them to the value of 1100 pounds; more could not be had without unfurnishing the ship, which must have been by force, for otherwise the master and seamen would deliver ncne. The master petitioned the general court for his freight and wages, for which the goods stood bound by charter party. The general court was much divided about it, but the magistrates voted that none was due here, nor the goods bound for them; but the major part of the deputies being of another judgment, they made use of their negative vote, and so nothing was ordered. Whereupon the master brought his action at the next court of assistants. When it came to be tried, two of the assistants were of opinion that it ought not to be put to trial, because the general court had the hearing and voting of it: but it was answered by the rest, (the governor being absent,) that, seeing the general court had made no order in it, this court might hear and determine it, as if the general court had never taken cognizance of it. Accordingly it was put to the jury upon this issue: Whether the goods were security for the freight, etc. And the jury found for the defendant, and yet in the charter party the merchants bound themselves, their executors, etc., and goods, as the owners had bound their ship, etc., to the merchants.

This business caused much trouble and charge to the country, and made some difference between the merchants of Charlestown, (who took part with the merchants and master of the ship,) and the merchants of Boston, who assisted the lady, (some of them being deeply engaged for La Tour,) so as offers were made on both sides for an end between them. Those of Charlestown offered security for the goods, if upon a review within thirteen months the judgment were not reversed, or the parliament in England did not call the cause before themselves. This last clause was very ill taken by the court, as making way for appeals, etc., into England, which was not reserved in our charter. The other offered them all the goods save 150 pounds to defray the lady's expenses in town, and security for that, if the judgment was reversed, so as the other would give security to answer the whole 2,000 pounds if the judgment were not reversed, etc.

10. (*December*) 8.] The parties not agreeing, the lady took the goods and hired three ships which lay in the harbor, be-longing to strangers, which cost her near 800 pounds, and set

sail for her fort.   And the merchants, against whom she had execution for their bodies for satisfaction of the rest of the judgment, got into their ship and fell down beyond the castle, (where they were out of command,) and took aboard some thirty passengers, and so, (26,) in company of one of our own ships which carried about seventy passengers, they set sail for London.

When our ship, etc., arrived at London, Alderman Berkley arrested the goods of two of the passengers.

# A CONTINUATION OF THE HISTORY OF NEW ENGLAND[1]

## PART III

## 1644

17. 7. (*September*) 17.] THE Lady La Tour arrived here in ship set forth from London by Alderman Berkley and Captain Bayley. They were bound for La Tour's fort, and set forth in the spring, but spent so much time in trading by the way, etc., as when they came at Cape Sable, Monsieur D'Aulnay came up to them in a ship from France, so as they durst not discover what they were, but stood along for Boston. The lady, being arrived, brought her action against them for delaying her so long at sea, whereby she lost the opportunity of relieving her fort, and must be at excessive charges to get thither. The cause was openly heard at a special court at Boston before all the magistrates, and a jury of principal men impannelled, (most merchants and seamen,) and the charter party being read, and witnesses produced, it appeared to the court, that they had broken charter party, so as the jury gave her 2000 pounds damages. Whereupon the cargo of the ship was seized in execution, (so much of it as could be found,) and being meal, and peas, and trading stuff, etc., and being appraised by four men, sworn, etc., it was found to the value of

---

[1] This is the part of *Winthrop's Journal* discovered in the year 1816, in the tower of the Old South Meeting House in Boston, the part unknown to the Hartford transcribers, and first published by Savage in 1825. While part II. of the *Journal* was destroyed by fire in 1825, part III. as well as part I. are preserved in the archives of the Massachusetts Historical Society, so that the accuracy of Savage's transcription may be verified.

about 1100 pounds.  The defendants desired liberty till the
next year to bring a review, pretending they had evidence in
England, etc.   It was granted them, and they were offered to
have all their goods again, (except 100 pounds for defraying the
lady's present charges in Boston, for which they should have
good security, etc.) so as they would put in security to answer
the whole 2000 pounds, if they did not reverse the judgment
within the year.   This they refused, and would give security
for no more than what they should receive back; whereupon
the execution proceeded.   But the master of the ship brought
his action upon the goods in execution for security for his
freight and men's wages (which did amount to near the whole
extended).  The jury found against him, whereupon at the next
general court he petitioned for redress.   A great part of the
court was of opinion, that the goods, being his security by
charter party, ought not to be taken from him upon the execution, and most of the deputies, and the deputy governor, and
some others of the magistrates voted that way; but the greater
part of the magistrates being of the other side, he would not be
relieved.   The lady was forced to give 700 pounds to three
ships to carry her home.[1]

It may be of use to mention a private matter or two, which
fell out about this time, because the power and mercy of the
Lord did appear in them in extraordinary manner.   One of the
deacons of Boston church, Jacob Eliot, (a man of a very sincere heart and an humble frame of spirit,) had a daughter[2]
of eight years of age, who being playing with other children
about a cart, the hinder end thereof fell upon the child's
head, and an iron sticking out of it struck into the child's head,
and drove a piece of the skull before it into the brain, so as the
brains came out, and seven surgeons (some of the country, very

[1] This opening passage of part III. Winthrop has crossed out in the manuscript, with the marginal comment, "this is before in the other book."   It is however worth while to retain the passage since it tells the story in somewhat different
shape.
[2] The little girl was a niece of the Apostle Eliot.

experienced men, and others of the ships, which rode in the harbor) being called together for advice, etc., did all conclude, that it was the brains, (being about half a spoonful at one time, and more at other times,) and that there was no hope of the child's life, except the piece of skull could be drawn out.  But one of the ruling elders of the church, an experienced and very skilful surgeon, liked not to take that course, but applied only plasters to it; and withal earnest prayers were made by the church to the Lord for it, and in six weeks it pleased God that the piece of skull consumed, and so came forth, and the child recovered perfectly; nor did it lose the senses at any time.

Another was a child of one Bumstead, a member of the church, had a child of about the same age, that fell from a gallery in the meeting house about eighteen feet high, and brake the arm and shoulder, (and was also committed to the Lord in the prayers of the church, with earnest desires, that the place where his people assembled to his worship might not be defiled with blood,) and it pleased the Lord also that this child was soon perfectly recovered.

The differences which fell out in the court, and still continued [blank].

A bark was set out from Boston with seven men to trade at Delaware.  They staid in the river near the English plantation all the winter, and in the spring they fell down, and traded three weeks, and had gotten five hundred skins, and some otter, etc., and being ready to come away, fifteen Indians came aboard, as if they would trade again, and suddenly they drew forth hatchets from under their coats, and killed the master and three others, and rifled the bark, and carried away a boy, and another man, who was the interpreter; and when they came on shore, they gave him forty skins, and twenty fathom of wampom, and other things, and kept them till about six weeks after.  The Swedish governor procured another sachem to fetch them to him, who sent them to New Haven by a bark of that place, and so they were brought to Boston (5) 14, 45,[1] the man as a prisoner.

(8) (*October*) 30.] The general court assembled again, and all the elders were sent for, to reconcile the differences between the magistrates and deputies. When they were come, the first question put to them was that which was stated by consent the last session, viz.

Whether the magistrates are, by patent and election of the people, the standing council of this commonwealth in the vacancy of the general court, and have power accordingly to act in all cases subject to government, according to the said patent and the laws of this jurisdiction; and when any necessary occasions call for action from authority, in cases where there is no particular express law provided, there to be guided by the word of God, till the general court give particular rules in such cases.

The elders, having received the question, withdrew themselves for consultation about it, and the next day sent to know, when we would appoint a time that they might attend the court with their answer. The magistrates and deputies agreed upon an hour, but the deputies came not all, but sent a committee of four (which was not well, nor respectively, that when all the elders had taken so much pains at their request, some having come thirty miles, they would not vouchsafe their presence to receive their answer). Their answer was affirmative on the magistrates' behalf, in the very words of the question, with some reasons thereof. It was delivered in writing by Mr. Cotton in the name of them all, they being all present, and not one dissentient.

Upon the return of this answer, the deputies prepared other questions to be propounded to the elders, and sent them to the magistrates to take view of. Likewise the magistrates prepared four questions, and sent them also to the deputies.

[1] July 14, 1645.

The magistrates' questions, with the elders' answers, were:

1. Whether the deputies in the general court have judicial and magistratical authority?

2. Whether by patent the general court, consisting of magistrates and deputies, (as a general court) have judicial and magistratical authority?

3. Whether we may warrantably prescribe certain penalties to offences, which may probably admit variable degrees of guilt?

4. Whether a judge be bound to pronounce such sentence as a positive law prescribes, in case it be apparently above or beneath the merit of the offence?

The elders answer to the two first.

1. The patent, in express words, giveth full power and authority, as to the governor and assistants, so to the freemen also assembled in general court.

2. Whereas there is a threefold power of magistratical authority, viz., legislative, judicial, and consultative or directive of the public affairs of the country for provision and protection. The first of these, viz., legislative is expressly given to the freemen, jointly with the governor and assistants. Consultative or directive power, etc., is also granted by the patent as the other. But now for power of judicature, (if we speak of the constant and usual administration thereof,) we do not find that it is granted to the freemen, or deputies, in the general court, either by the patent, or the elections of the people, or by any law of the country. But if we speak of the occasional administration thereof, we find power of judicature administrable by the freemen, jointly with the governor and assistants upon a double occasion. 1. In case of defect or delinquency of a magistrate, the whole court, consisting, etc., may remove him. 2. If by the law of the country there lie any appeal to the general court, or any special causes be reserved to their judgment, it will necessarily infer, that, in such cases, by such laws, the freemen, jointly with the governor and assistants,

have power of judicature, touching the appellant's cause of appeal and those reserved cases. What we speak of the power of freemen by patent, the same may be said of the deputies, so far forth as the power of the freemen is delegated to them by order of law.

To the third and fourth questions the elders answer.

1. Certain penalties may and ought to be prescribed to capital crimes, although they may admit variable degrees of guilt; as in case of murder upon prepensed malice, and upon sudden provocation, there is prescribed the same death in both, though murder upon prepensed malice be of a far greater guilt than upon sudden provocation, Numb. 35. 16. 18 with 20. 21. Also in crimes of less guilt, as in theft, though some theft may be of greater guilt than other, (as for some man to steal a sheep, who hath less need, is of greater guilt, than for another, who hath more need,) the Lord prescribed the same measure of restitution to both.

2. In case that variable circumstances of an offence do so much vary the degrees of guilt, as that the offence is raised to an higher nature, there the penalty must be varied to an higher answerable proportion. The striking of a neighbor may be punished with some pecuniary mulct, when the striking of a father may be punished with death. So any sin committed with an high hand, as the gathering of sticks on the Sabbath day, may be punished with death, when a lesser punishment may serve for gathering sticks privily, and in some need.

3. In case circumstances do so vary a sin, as that many sins are complicated or wrapped up in it, the penalty is to be varied, according to the penalties of those several sins. A single lie may be punished with a less mulct, than if it be told before the judgment seat, or elsewhere, to the damage of any person, whether in his good name, by slander, or in his estate, by detriment in his commerce; in which case, a lie aggravated by circumstances is to be punished with respect both to a lie and to a slander and to the detriment which another sustaineth thereby.

4. In case that the circumstances, which vary the degrees of guilt, concern only the person of the offender, (as whether it were the first offence, or customary, whether he were enticed thereto, or the enticer, whether he were principal or accessory, whether unadvised, or witting or willing, etc.) there it were meet the penalty should be expressed with a latitude, whereof the lowest degree to be expressed (suppose five shillings, or, as the case may be, five stripes) and the highest degree, twenty shillings or, etc., or stripes more or less; within which compass or latitude it may be free to a magistrate to aggravate or mitigate the penalty, etc.   Yet even here also care would be taken, that a magistrate attend, in his sentence, as much as may be, to a certain rule in these circumstances, lest some persons, whose sins be alike circumstanced with others, if their punishment be not equal, etc., may think themselves more unequally dealt withal than others.

5. In those cases wherein the judge is persuaded in conscience, that a crime deserveth a greater punishment than the law inflicteth, he may lawfully pronounce sentence according to the prescript penalty, etc., because he hath no power committed to him by law to go higher.   But where the law may seem to the conscience of the judge to inflict a greater penalty than the offence deserveth, it is his part to suspend his sentence, till by conference with the lawgivers, he find liberty, either to inflict the sentence, or to mitigate it.

6. The penalties of great crimes may sometimes be mitigated by such as are in chief power, out of respect to the public good service which the delinquent hath done to the state in former times, as Solomon did by Abiathar, 1 Kings 2. 26. 27.

Questions propounded to the elders by the deputies.

1. Whether the governor and assistants have any power by patent to dispense justice in the vacancy of the general court, without some law or order of the same to declare the rule?

The elders' answer was negative; and further, they conceived it meet, the rule should be express for the regulating of all particulars, as far as may be, and where such cannot be had, to be supplied by general rules.

2. Quest. Whether any general court hath not power by patent, in particular cases, to choose any commissioners, (either assistants or freemen,) exempting all others, to give them commission, to set forth their power and places? By "any particular case" we mean in all things, and in the choice of all officers, that the commonwealth stands in need of between election and election; not taking away the people's liberty in elections, nor turning out any officer so elected by them, without showing cause.

The elders answer.

1. If the terms, "all things," imply or intend all cases of constant judicature and counsel, we answer negatively, etc., because then it would follow, that the magistrates might be excluded from all cases of constant judicature and counsel, which are their principal work, whereby also the end of the people's election would be made frustrate.

2. But if these terms, "all things," imply or intend cases (whether occasional or others) belonging neither to constant judicature nor counsel, we answer affirmatively, etc., which yet we understand with this distinction, viz., that if the affairs committed to such officers and commissioners be of general concernment, we conceive the freemen, according to patent, are to choose them, the general court to set forth their power and places; but if they be of merely particular concernment, then we conceive the general court may choose them, and set forth their power and places. Whereas we give cases of constant judicature and council to the magistrates, we thus interpret the word "counsel." Counsel consists of care and action. In respect of care, the magistrates are not limited; in respect of action, they are to be limited by the general court, or by the supreme council. Finally, it is our humble request, that in case any difference grow in the general court, between magistrates and deputies, either in these, or any like weighty cases,

which cannot be presently issued with mutual peace, that both parties will be pleased to defer the same to further deliberation for the honor of God and of the court.

Upon other propositions made by the deputies, the elders gave this further answer, viz.

That the general court, consisting of magistrates and deputies, is the chief civil power of this commonwealth, and may act in all things belonging to such a power, both concerning counsel, in consulting about the weighty affairs of the commonwealth, and concerning making of laws, also concerning judicatures, in orderly impeaching, removing, and sentencing any officers, even the highest, according to law, likewise in receiving appeals, whether touching civil or criminal causes, wherein appeals are or shall be allowed by the general court; provided that all such appeals proceed orderly from an inferior court to the court of assistants, and from thence to the general court; or if the case were first depending in the court of assistants, then to proceed from thence to the general court, in all such cases as are appealable, "as in cases judged evidently against "law, or in cases wherein the subject is sentenced to banish-"ment, loss of limb, or life, without an express law, or in cases "weighty and difficult, (not admitting small matters, the pur-"suit whereof would be more burdensome to the court and "country, than behoveful to the appellant, nor needlessly in-"terrupting the ordinary course of justice in the court of as-"sistants, or other inferior courts;) provided also, that if it do "appear, that the appeal proceed not out of regard of right, but "from delay of justice, or out of contention, that a due and just "punishment be by law ordained, and inflicted upon such "appellant."

That no magistrate hath power to vary from the penalty of any law, etc., without consulting with the general court.

3. Quest.  Whether the titles of governor, deputy, and assistants do necessarily imply magistratical authority, in the patent?

The elders' answer was affirmative.

4. Quest.　Whether the magistratical power be not given by the patent to the people or general court, and by them to the governor, etc.

The elders answer, the magistratical power is given to the governor, etc., by the patent.　To the people is given, by the same patent, to design the persons to those places of government; and to the general court power is given to make laws, as the rules of their administration.

These resolutions of the elders were after put to vote, and were all allowed to be received, except those in the last page marked in the margin thus, " ".　Most of the deputies were now well satisfied concerning the authority of the magistrates, etc., but some few leading men (who had drawn on the rest) were still fixed upon their own opinions.　So hard a matter it is, to draw men (even wise and godly) from the love of the fruit of their own inventions.[1]

There fell out at this court another occasion of further trouble.　The deputy governor having formerly, and from time to time, opposed the deputies' claim of judicial authority, and the prescribing of set penalties in cases which may admit variable degrees of guilt, which occasioned them to suspect, that he, and some others of the magistrates, did affect an arbitrary government, he now wrote a small treatise about these points, showing what arbitrary government was, and that our government (in the state it now stood) was not arbitrary, neither in the ground and foundation of it, nor in the exercise and administration thereof.　And because it is of public, and (for the most part) of general concernment, and being a subject not formerly handled by any that I have met with, so as it may be of use to stir up some of more experience and more able parts to bestow their pains herein, I have therefore made bold to set down the

---

[1] This detailed and labored expounding of the patent by the elders for the benefit of the uneasy deputies is an incident in the long struggle in which the people conquered.

whole discourse, with the proceedings which happened about
it, in a treatise by itself, with some small alterations and additions (not in the substance of the matter) for clearer evidence
of the question.    And I must apologize this to the reader, that
I do not condemn all prescript penalties, although the argument
seem to hold forth so much, but only so far as they cross with
the rules of justice, and prudence, and mercy; also, in such
cases of smaller concernment, as wherein there may be lawful
liberty allowed to judges to use admonition, or to respite an
offender to further trial of reformation, etc.[1]

At this court Mr. Saltonstall moved very earnestly that he
might be left out at the next election, and pursued his motion
after to the towns.    It could not appear what should move him
to it; only Mr. Bellingham and he held together, and joined
with the deputies against the rest of the magistrates, but not
prevailing, and being oft opposed in public, might put some
discouragement upon his spirit, to see all differ from him save
one.    And indeed it occasioned much grief to all the elders,
and gave great offence through the country; and such as were
acquainted with other states in the world, and had not well
known the persons, would have concluded such a faction here
as hath been usual in the council of England and other states,
who walk by politic principles only.    But these gentlemen
were such as feared God, and endeavored to walk by the rules
of his word in all their proceedings, so as it might be conceived
in charity, that they walked according to their judgments and
conscience, and where they went aside, it was merely for want
of light, or their eyes were held through some temptation for a
time, that they could not make use of the light they had; for
in all these differences and agitations about them, they continued in brotherly love, and in the exercise of all friendly
offices each to other, as occasion required.

One Cornish, dwelling some time in Weymouth, removed to
Acomenticus, for more outward accommodation, and in the

[1] The tract is printed in Winthrop's *Winthrop*, II. 445.

[*blank*] month last was taken up in the river, his head bruised, and a pole sticking in his side, and his canoe laden with clay found sunk. His wife (being a lewd woman, and suspected to have fellowship with one Footman) coming to her husband, he bled abundantly, and so he did also, when Footman was brought to him;[1] but no evidence could be found against him. Then something was discovered against the son of Mr. Hull, their minister, and the woman was arraigned before the mayor, Mr. Roger Garde, and others of the province of Maine, and strong presumptions came in against her, whereupon she was condemned and executed. She persisted in the denial of the murder to the death, but confessed to have lived in adultery with divers. She charged two specially, the said Garde, the mayor, and one Edward Johnson, who confessed it openly at the time of her execution; but the mayor denied it, and it gave some likelihood that he was not guilty, because he had carried himself very zealously and impartially in discovery of the murder. But there might be skill in that; and he was but a carnal man, and had no wife in the country, and some witnesses came in against him of his acknowledgment to the woman, etc.

---

[1] That the body of a murdered man bleeds afresh in presence of the murderer is an inveterate superstition of the Teutonic race. In the *Nibelungen Lied*, the body of Siegfried bleeds afresh in the presence of Hagen; the belief still persists in the ruder communities of the United States.

# 1645

12. (*February*) 17.]   Mr. Allerton coming from New Haven in a ketch, with his wife and divers other persons, were taken in a great storm at northeast with much snow, and cast away at Scituate, but the persons all saved.

12. (*February*) 16.]   The winter was very mild hitherto, and no snow lay, so as ploughs might go most part of the winter, but now there fell so great a snow in several days, as the ways were unpassable for three weeks, so as the court of assistants held not (the magistrates and juries not coming to Boston (1) 4 (*March*) being the usual day for that court).   And withal the weather was cold, and the frost as fierce as is at any time of the winter; and the snow was not off the ground till the end of the first month.

1645.]   2. (*April*) 6.]   Two great fires happened this week, one at Salem; Mr. Downing having built a new house at his farm, he being gone to England, and his wife and family gone to the church meeting upon the Lord's day, the chimney took fire, and burnt down the house, and bedding, apparel, and household to the value of 200 pounds.   The other was at Roxbury this day.   John Johnson, the surveyor general of the ammunition, a very industrious and faithful man in his place, having built a fair house in the midst of the town, with divers barns and other out houses, it fell on fire in the day time, (no man knowing by what occasion,) and there being in it seventeen barrels of the country's powder and many arms, all was suddenly burnt and blown up, to the value of 4 or 500 pounds, wherein a special providence of God appeared, for he being from home, the people came together to help, and many were in the house, no man thinking of the powder, till one of the company put them in mind of it, whereupon they all withdrew, and soon after the powder took fire, and blew up all about it, and shook the houses in Boston and Cambridge, so as men thought it had been an earthquake, and carried great pieces of timber a great way off and some rags and such light things beyond Boston meeting house. There being then a stiff gale at south, it drove the fire from the other houses in the town, (for this was the most northerly,) otherwise it had endangered the greatest part of the town. This loss of our powder was the more observable in two respects, 1. Because the court had not taken that care they ought to pay for it, having been owing for divers years; 2. In that, at the court before, they had refused to help our countrymen in Virginia, who had written to us for some for their defence against the Indians, and also to help our brethren of Plymouth in their want.

Mr. Wheelwright being removed from Exeter to Wells, the people remaining fell at variance among themselves. Some would gather a new church, and call old Mr. Batchellor from Hampton to be their pastor, and for that purpose appointed a day, and gave notice thereof to the magistrates and churches, but the court, understanding of their divisions and present unfitness for so solemn and sacred a business, sent and wrote to them (by way of direction only) to desist for that time, and not to proceed until upon satisfaction given to this court, or the court at Ipswich, of their reconciliation, they might proceed with allowance of authority, according to order. To this they submitted, and did not proceed.

The question about Seacunk, now Rehoboth, being revived this court, whether it should belong to this jurisdiction (upon the submission of the purchasers, etc.) or to Plymouth by right of their patent, the court (by order) referred it to the judgment of the commissioners of the union, who decreed it for Plymouth, with reservation, if better evidence should appear by the next meeting.

Some malignant spirits began to stir, and declare themselves for the king, etc., whereupon an order was made to restrain such courses, and to prevent all such turbulent practices, either by action, word, or writing.

The court ordered letters of thanks to be sent to Mr. Richard Andrews of London, haberdasher, for his gift of 500 pounds, and to the Lady Armine for her gift of 20 pounds per annum, and to the Lady Moulson for her gift, which was done accordingly by the committee appointed.[1]

Upon advice from Mr. Weld, remaining still at London, a commission was sent under the public seal to Mr. Pocock and divers other our friends in London to this effect, 1. To answer for us upon all such occasions as may be presented to the parliament or any other court or officer, concerning us or our affairs, but not to engage us, without our consent, 2. To receive all letters and other despatches of public nature or concernment from us, 3. To advise us of all occurrents as may happen touching our colony, 4. To receive all moneys or other things due to us from any person in England, by gift or otherwise, and to dispose of them by direction under our public seal.

Mr. John Winthrop, the younger, coming from England two years since, brought with him 1000 pounds stock and divers workmen to begin an iron work, and had moved the court for some encouragement to be given the undertakers, and for the court to join in carrying on the work, etc. The business was well approved by the court, as a thing much conducing to the good of the country, but we had no stock in the treasury to give furtherance to it, only some two or three private persons joined in it, and the court granted the adventurers near all their demands, as a monopoly of it for twenty-one years, liberty to

[1] The last two gifts were to the college. Andrews had before shown himself generous. Lady Armine, granddaughter of the Earl of Shrewsbury, was wife of Sir William Armine, associated with Vane in the negotiation of the Solemn League and Covenant with the Scots, and a statesman of eminence. Lady Mowlson had, in 1643, by a gift of £100, founded the first scholarship in Harvard College. She was the daughter of a London alderman, and widow of a lord mayor. Her maiden name was Ann Radcliffe. Radcliffe College has been named for her.

make use of any six places not already granted, and to have three miles square in every place to them and their heirs, and freedom from public charges, trainings, etc., and this was now sent them over under the public seal this year.[1]

The court, finding that the over number of deputies drew out the courts into great length, and put the country to excessive charges, so as some one court hath expended more [than] 200 pounds, etc., did think fit to have fewer deputies, and so to have only five or six out of each shire; and because the deputies were still unsatisfied with the magistrates' negative vote, the magistrates consented to lay it down, so as the deputies might not exceed them in number, and those to be the prime men of the country, to be chosen by the whole shires; but they agreed first to know the mind of the country. But upon trial, the greater number of towns refused it, so it was left for this time.

At this court in the third month Passaconaway, the chief sachem of Merimack, and his sons came and submitted themselves and their people and lands under our jurisdiction, as Pumham and others had done before.

Mr. Shepherd, the pastor of the church in Cambridge, being at Connecticut when the commissioners met there for the United Colonies, moved them for some contribution of help towards the maintenance of poor scholars in the college, whereupon the commissioners ordered that it should be commended to the deputies of the general courts and the elders within the several colonies to raise (by way of voluntary contribution) one peck of corn or twelve pence money, or other commodity, of every family, which those of Connecticut presently performed.

5. (*July*) 3.] By order of the general court, upon advice with the elders, a general fast was kept. The occasions were,

---

[1] These mining operations proved successful, ore in considerable amounts being obtained. The enterprise receives much notice in the public records. Boston Town Records, *Second Report of the Record Commissioners* (1877), I. 77. 91, 92, 127; *Records of Massachusetts*, II. 61 (March 7, 1643/4).

the miseries of England, and our own differences in the general court, and also for the great drought. In this latter the Lord prevented our prayers in sending us rain soon after, and before the day of humiliation came.

Divers free schools were erected, as at Roxbury (for maintenance whereof every inhabitant bound some house or land for a yearly allowance forever) and at Boston (where they made an order to allow forever 50 pounds to the master and an house, and 30 pounds to an usher, who should also teach to read and write and cipher, and Indians' children were to be taught freely, and the charge to be by yearly contribution, either by voluntary allowance, or by rate of such as refused, etc., and this order was confirmed by the general court [*blank*]). Other towns did the like, providing maintenance by several means.[1]

By agreement of the commissioners, and the motions of the elders in their several churches, every family in each colony gave one peck of corn or twelve pence to the college at Cambridge.

1. (*March*) 25.] Another strange accident happened by fire about this time. One Mr. Peck and three others of Hingham, being about with others to remove to Seaconk, (which was concluded by the commissioners of the United Colonies to belong to Plymouth,) riding thither, they sheltered themselves and their horses in an Indian wigwam, which by some occasion took fire, and (although they were all four in it, and labored to their utmost, etc.) burnt three of their horses to death, and all their goods to the value of 50 pounds.

Also some children were killed, and others sore scorched with wearing cloaths of cotton, which was very apt to take fire, and hard to be quenched; so as one man of Watertown

---

[1] This passage is of interest as referring to the origin in New England of the common school, which may be traced farther back than the present date. In the *Boston Town Records*, p. 5 (April 13, 1635), Philemon Pormont is mentioned as "intreated" to undertake a school, and next year comes a list of subscribers, headed by Henry Vane, the governor. For reference to the sources of the common school system, see Winsor, *Memorial History of Boston*. I. 123.

being so cloathed, and taking fire by endeavoring to save his house being on fire, was forced to run into a well to save his life.

2. (*April*) 13.]   Mr. Hopkins, the governor of Hartford upon Connecticut, came to Boston, and brought his wife with him, (a godly young woman, and of special parts,) who was fallen into a sad infirmity, the loss of her understanding and reason, which had been growing upon her divers years, by occasion of her giving herself wholly to reading and writing, and had written many books.   Her husband, being very loving and tender of her, was loath to grieve her; but he saw his error, when it was too late.   For if she had attended her household affairs, and such things as belong to women, and not gone out of her way and calling to meddle in such things as are proper for men, whose minds are stronger, etc., she had kept her wits, and might have improved them usefully and honorably in the place God had set her.   He brought her to Boston, and left her with her brother, one Mr. Yale, a merchant, to try what means might be had here for her.   But no help could be had.[1]

The governor and assistants met at Boston, to consider what might lawfully be done for saving La Tour and his fort out of the hands of D'Aulnay, who was now before it with all his strength both of men and vessels.   So soon as we were met, word was brought us, that a vessel sent by some merchants to carry provisions to La Tour was fallen into the hands of D'Aulnay, who had made prize of her, and turned the men upon an island, and kept them there ten days, and then gave them an old shallop (not above two tons) and some provisions to bring them home, but denied them their clothes, etc. (which at first he had promised them) and any gun or compass, whereby it was justly conceived that he intended they should perish, either at sea, or by the Indians (who were at hand, and chased them next day, etc.).   Upon this news we presently despatched away a vessel to D'Aulnay with letters, wherein we expostulated with him about this act of his, complaining of it as a

---

[1] Mrs. Hopkins was aunt of Elihu Yale, founder of Yale University.

breach of the articles of our peace, and required the vessel and goods to be restored, or satisfaction for them. We gave answer also to some charges he laid upon us in a letter lately written to our governor, carried on in very high language, as if we had hired the ships, which carried home the lady La Tour, and had broken our articles by a bare sufferance of it, etc., which caused us to answer him accordingly, that he might see we took notice of his proud terms, and were not afraid of him. And whereas he oft threatened us with the king of France his power, etc., we answered that we did acknowledge him to be a mighty prince, but we conceived withal he would continue to be just, and would not break out against us, without hearing our answer, or if he should, yet New England had a God, who was able to save us, and did not use to forsake his servants, etc. So soon as he had set our men upon an island, in a deep snow, without fire, and only a sorry wigwam for their shelter, he carried his ship up close to La Tour's fort (supposing they would have yielded it up to him, for the friars and other their confederates whom the lady presently upon her arrival had sent away, had persuaded him that he might easily gain the place, La Tour being come into the Bay, and not above fifty men left in it, and little powder, and that decayed also;) but after they had moored their ship, and began to let fly at the fort with their ordnance, they within behaved themselves so well with their ordnance, that they tare his ship so as he was forced to warp her on shore behind a point of land, to save her from sinking, (for the wind coming easterly, they could not bring her forth,) and they killed (as one of his own men reported) twenty of his men, and wounded thirteen more.

The governor and assistants had used for ten or eleven years at least to appoint one to preach on the day of election, but about three or four years since the deputies challenged it as their right, and accordingly had twice made the choice, (the magistrates still professing it to be a mere intrusion, etc.,) and now at the last general court in October they had given order to call Mr. Norton to that service, (never acquainting the magistrates therewith,) and about some two months before the time, the governor and divers other of the magistrates (not knowing any thing of what the deputies had done) agreed upon Mr. Norris of Salem, and gave him notice of it. But at this meeting of the magistrates it grew a question, whether of these two should be employed, seeing both had been invited, and both were prepared. At last it was put to vote, and that determined it upon Mr. Norton. The reason was, the unwillingness of the magistrates to have any fresh occasion of contestation with the deputies. But some judged it a failing (especially in one or two who had already joined in calling Mr. Norris) and a betraying, or at least weakening the power of the magistrates, and a countenancing of an unjust usurpation. For the deputies could do no such act, as an act of court, without the concurrence of the magistrates; and out of court they had no power at all, (but only for regulating their own body,) and it was resolved and voted at last court, (according to the elders' advice,) that all occurrents out of court belong to the magistrates to take care of, being the standing council of the commonwealth.

One of our ships, which went to the Canaries with pipestaves in the beginning of November last, returned now, and brought wine, and sugar, and salt, and some tobacco, which she had at Barbadoes, in exchange for Africoes, which she carried from the Isle of Maio.[1] She brought us news, that a ship of ours of about 260 tons, set out from Cambridge before winter, was set upon, near the Canaries, by an Irish man-of-war,[2] which had seventy men and twenty pieces of ordnance, whereas ours had but fourteen pieces and not above thirty men, and the Irishman grappled with our ship, and boarded her, and fought with her,

[1] A man of Winthrop's generation took such slave trading as is here referred to, as the ordinary course of business. The Isla de Maio was one of the Cape Verde Islands.

[2] The harbors of Ireland, especially Old Kinsale, became in the Civil War refuges for the King's ships which are described as Irish.

side by side, near a whole day, but falling off, a shot of ours had taken off their steerage, so as they could not bring their ship to ours again, but we received a shot under water, which had near sunk our ship, but the Lord preserved her and our men, so as we had but two slain in all that time and some four wounded; but the damage of the ship and her merchandise was between 2 and 300 pounds.

We had tidings also of another of our ships of the like force, set out from Boston, which the Earl of Marlborough had lain in wait for at the Madeiras a good time, and with a ship of great force, but it pleased the Lord to send him away the very day before our ship arrived there.

The wars in England kept servants from coming to us, so as those we had could not be hired, when their times were out, but upon unreasonable terms, and we found it very difficult to pay their wages to their content, (for money was very scarce). I may upon this occasion report a passage between one of Rowley and his servant. The master, being forced to sell a pair of his oxen to pay his servant his wages, told his servant he could keep him no longer, not knowing how to pay him the next year. The servant answered, he would serve him for more of his cattle. But how shall I do (saith the master) when all my cattle are gone? The servant replied, you shall then serve me, and so you may have your cattle again.[1]

A village was erected near Lynn, and called Reading; another village erected between Salem and Gloucester, and called Manchester.

Among other benefactors to this colony, one Union Butcher, a clothier, near Cranbrook in Kent, did (for divers years together, in a private way) send over a good quantity of cloth, to be disposed of to some godly poor people.

The government of Plymouth sent one of their magistrates,

---

[1] This passage, perhaps, approached the humorous more nearly than anything else in the *Journal*. Winthrop, staid and aristocratic, writes in the margin opposite, "insolent."

Mr. Brown, to Aquiday Island to forbid Mr. Williams, etc., to exercise any of their pretended authority upon the Island, claiming it to be within their jurisdiction.[1]

Our court also sent to forbid them to exercise any authority within that part of our jurisdiction at Patuxent and Mishaomet; and although they had boasted to do great matters there by virtue of their charter, yet they dared not to attempt anything.

3. (*May*) 14.] The court of elections was held at Boston. Mr. Thomas Dudley was chosen governor, Mr. Winthrop, deputy governor again, and Mr. Endecott, serjeant major general. Mr. Israel Stoughton, having been in England the year before, and now gone again about his private occasions, was by vote left out, and Herbert Pelham, Esquire, chosen an assistant.

This court fell out a troublesome business, which took up much time. The town of Hingham, having one Emes their lieutenant seven or eight years, had lately chosen him to be their captain, and had presented him to the standing council for allowance; but before it was accomplished, the greater part of the town took some light occasion of offence against him, and chose one Allen to be their captain, and presented him to the magistrates (in the time of the last general court) to be allowed. But the magistrates, considering the injury that would hereby accrue to Emes, (who had been their chief commander so many years, and had deserved well in his place, and that Allen had no other skill, but what he learned from Emes,) refused to allow of Allen, but willed both sides to return home, and every officer to keep his place, until the court should take further order. Upon their return home, the messengers, who came for Allen, called a private meeting of those of their own party, and told them truly, what answer they received from the magistrates, and soon after they appointed a training day, (without their lieutenant's knowledge,) and being assembled,

---

[1] Savage's note may be quoted. "I rejoice in the defeat of this futile claim by Plymouth, and equally rejoice in the ill success of the attempt by our own people mentioned in the next paragraph."

the lieutenant hearing of it came to them, and would have exercised them, as he was wont to do, but those of the other party refused to follow him, except he would show them some order for it. He told them of the magistrates' order about it; the others replied, that authority had advised him to go home and lay down his place honorably. Another asked, what the magistrates had to do with them? Another, that it was but three or four of the magistrates, and if they had been all there, it had been nothing, for Mr. Allen had brought more for them from the deputies, than the lieutenant had from the magistrates. Another of them professeth he will die at the sword's point, if he might not have the choice of his own officers. Another (viz. the clerk of the band) stands up above the people and requires them to vote, whether they would bear them out in what was past and what was to come. This being assented unto, and the tumult continuing, one of the officers (he who had told them that authority had advised the lieutenant to go home and lay down his place) required Allen to take the captain's place; but he not then accepting it, they put it to the vote, whether he should be their captain. The vote passing for it, he then told the company, it was now past question, and thereupon Allen accepted it, and exercised the company two or three days, only about a third part of them followed the lieutenant. He, having denied in the open field, that authority had advised him to lay down his place, and putting (in some sort) the lie upon those who had so reported, was the next Lord's day called to answer it before the church, and he standing to maintain what he had said, five witnesses were produced to convince him. Some of them affirmed the words, the others explained their meaning to be, that one magistrate had so advised him. He denied both. Whereupon the pastor, one Mr. Hubbert,[1] (brother to three of the principal in this sedition,)

---

[1] Peter Hobart, Hubbert, or Hubbard, so strenuous in this tea-pot tempest in Hingham which became the occasion of such a difference between the magistrates and the democracy, was a scholar of Magdalene College, Cambridge. He

was very forward to have excommunicated the lieutenant presently, but, upon some opposition, it was put off to the next day. Thereupon the lieutenant and some three or four more of the chief men of the town inform four of the next magistrates of these proceedings, who forthwith met at Boston about it, (viz. the deputy governor, the serjeant major general, the secretary, and Mr. Hibbins). These, considering the case, sent warrant to the constable to attach some of the principal offenders (viz. three of the Hubbards and two more) to appear before them at Boston, to find sureties for their appearance at the next court, etc. Upon the day they came to Boston, but their said brother the minister came before them, and fell to expostulate with the said magistrates about the said cause, complaining against the complainants, as talebearers, etc., taking it very disdainfully that his brethren should be sent for by a constable, with other high speeches, which were so provoking, as some of the magistrates told him, that, were it not for respect to his ministry, they would commit him. When his brethren and the rest were come in, the matters of the information were laid to their charge, which they denied for the most part. So they were bound over (each for other) to the next court of assistants. After this five others were sent for by summons (these were only for speaking untruths of the magistrates in the church). They came before the deputy governor, when he was alone, and demanded the cause of their sending for, and to know their accusers. The deputy told them so much of the cause as he could remember, and referred them to the secretary for a copy, and for their accusers he told them they knew both the men and the matter, neither was a judge bound to let a criminal offender know his accusers before the day of trial, but only in his own discretion, least the accuser might be taken off or perverted, etc. Being required to give bond for

became minister of Hingham in 1635, where he remained nearly forty-five years. Five sons, four of them divines, were educated at Harvard. Few New England names have spread more widely or appear in more honorable connections.

their appearance, etc., they refused. The deputy labored to
let them see their error, and gave them time to consider of it.
About fourteen days after, seeing two of them in the court,
(which was kept by those four magistrates for smaller causes,)
the deputy required them again to enter bond for their
appearance, etc., and upon their second refusal committed
them it nhat open court.

The general court falling out before the court of assistants,
the Hubberts and the two which were committed, and others of
Hingham, about ninety, (whereof Mr. Hubbert their minister
was the first,) presented a petition to the general court, to this
effect, that whereas some of them had been bound over, and
others committed by some of the magistrates for words spoken
concerning the power of the general court, and their liberties,
and the liberties of the church, etc., they craved that the court
would hear the cause, etc. This was first presented to the
deputies, who sent it to the magistrates, desiring their concurrence with them, that the cause might be heard, etc. The
magistrates, marvelling that they would grant such a petition,
without desiring conference first with themselves, whom it so
much concerned, returned answer, that they were willing the
cause should be heard, so as the petitioners would name the
magistrates whom they intended, and the matters they would
lay to their charge, etc. Upon this the deputies demanded of
the petitioners' agents (who were then deputies of the court) to
have satisfaction in those points, thereupon they singled out
the deputy governor, and two of the petitioners undertook the
prosecution. Then the petition was returned again to the
magistrates for their consent, etc., who being desirous that
the deputies might take notice, how prejudicial to authority and
the honor of the court it would be to call a magistrate to
answer criminally in a cause, wherein nothing of that nature
could be laid to his charge, and that without any private examination preceding, did intimate so much to the deputies,
(though not directly, yet plainly enough,) showing them that

nothing criminal, etc. was laid to his charge, and that the things objected were the act of the court, etc., yet if they would needs have a hearing, they would join in it. And indeed it was the desire of the deputy, (knowing well how much himself and the other magistrates did suffer in the cause, through the slanderous reports wherewith the deputies and the country about had been possessed,) that the cause might receive a public hearing.

The day appointed being come, the court assembled in the meeting house at Boston. Divers of the elders were present, and a great assembly of people. The deputy governor, coming in with the rest of the magistrates, placed himself beneath within the bar, and so sate uncovered. Some question was in the court about his being in that place (for many both of the court and the assembly were grieved at it). But the deputy telling them, that, being criminally accused, he might not sit as a judge in that cause, and if he were upon the bench, it would be a great disadvantage to him, for he could not take that liberty to plead the cause, which he ought to be allowed at the bar, upon this the court was satisfied.

The petitioners having declared their grievances, etc., the deputy craved leave to make answer, which was to this effect, viz., that he accounted it no disgrace, but rather an honor put upon him, to be singled out from his brethren in the defence of a cause so just (as he hoped to make that appear) and of so public concernment. And although he might have pleaded to the petition, and so have demurred in law, upon three points, 1. In that there is nothing laid to his charge, that is either criminal or unjust; 2, if he had been mistaken either in the law or in the state of the case, yet whether it were such as a judge is to be called in question for as a delinquent, where it doth not appear to be wickedness or wilfulness; for in England many erroneous judgments are reversed, and errors in proceedings rectified, and yet the judges not called in question about them; 3, in that being thus singled out from three other of the magistrates, and to answer by himself for some things, which were the act of a court, he is deprived of the just means of his defence, for many things may be justified as done by four, which are not warrantable if done by one alone, and the records of a court are a full justification of any act, while such record stands in force. But he was willing to waive this plea, and to make answer to the particular charges, to the end that the truth of the case, and of all proceedings thereupon might appear to all men.

Hereupon the court proceeded to examine the whole cause. The deputy justified all the particulars laid to his charge, as that upon credible information of such a mutinous practice, and open disturbance of the peace, and slighting of authority, the offenders were sent for, the principal by warrant to the constable to bring them, and others by summons, and that some were bound over to the next court of assistants, and others that refused to be bound were committed; and all this according to the equity of laws here established, and the custom and laws of England, and our constant practice here these fifteen years. And for some speeches he was charged with as spoken to the delinquents, when they came before him at his house, when none were present with him but themselves, first, he appealed to the judgment of the court, whether delinquents may be received as competent witnesses against a magistrate in such a case; then, for the words themselves, some he justified, some he explained so as no advantage could be taken of them, as that he should say, that the magistrates could try some criminal causes without a jury, that he knew no law of God or man, which required a judge to make known to the party his accusers (or rather witnesses) before the cause came to hearing. But two of them charged him to have said, that it was against the law of God and man so to do, which had been absurd, for the deputy professed he knew no law against it, only a judge may sometimes, in discretion, conceal their names, etc., least they should be tampered with, or conveyed out of the way, etc.

Two of the magistrates and many of the deputies were of opinion that the magistrates exercised too much power, and that the people's liberty was thereby in danger; and other of the deputies (being about half) and all the rest of the magistrates were of a different judgment, and that authority was overmuch slighted, which, if not timely remedied, would endanger the commonwealth, and bring us to a mere democracy. By occasion of this difference, there was not so orderly carriage at the hearing, as was meet, each side striving unseasonably to enforce the evidence, and declaring their judgments thereupon, which should have been reserved to a more private debate, (as after it was,) so as the best part of two days was spent in this public agitation and examination of witnesses, etc. This being ended, a committee was chosen of magistrates and deputies, who stated the case, as it appeared upon the whole pleading and evidence, though it cost much time, and with great diffi· culty did the committee come to accord upon it.

The case being stated and agreed, the magistrates and deputies considered it apart, first the deputies, having spent a whole day, and not attaining to any issue, sent up to the magistrates to have their thoughts about it, who taking it into consideration, (the deputy always withdrawing when that matter came into debate,) agreed upon these four points chiefly; 1. That the petition was false and scandalous, 2. That those who were bound over, etc., and others that were parties to the disturbance at Hingham, were all offenders, though in different degrees, 3. That they and the petitioners were to be censured, 4. That the deputy governor ought to be acquit and righted, etc. This being sent down to the deputies, they spent divers days about it, and made two or three returns to the magistrates, and though they found the petition false and scandalous, and so voted it, yet they would not agree to any censure. The magistrates, on the other side, were resolved for censure, and for the deputy's full acquittal. The deputies being thus hard held to it, and growing weary of the court, for it began (3) (*May*) 14, and brake not up (save one week) till (5) (*July*) 5, were content they should pay the charges of the court. After, they were drawn to consent to some small fines, but in this they would have drawn in lieutenant Emes to have been fined deeply, he being neither plaintiff nor defendant, but an informer only, and had made good all the points of his information, and no offence found in him, other than that which was after adjudged worthy admonition only; and they would have imposed the charges of the court upon the whole trained band at Hingham, when it was apparent, that divers were innocent, and had no hand in any of these proceedings. The magistrates not consenting to so manifest injustice, they sent to the deputies to desire them to join with them in calling in the help of the elders, (for they were now assembled at Cambridge from all parts of the United Colonies, and divers of them were present when the cause was publicly heard, and declared themselves much grieved to see that the deputy governor should be called forth to answer as a delinquent in such a case as this was, and one of them, in the name of the rest, had written to him to that effect, fearing least he should apprehend over deeply of the injury, etc.) but the deputies would by no means consent thereto, for they knew that many of the elders understood the cause, and were more careful to uphold the honor and power of the magistrates than themselves well liked of, and many of them (at the request of the elder and others of the church of Hingham during this court) had been at Hingham, to see if they could settle peace in the church there, and found the elder and others the petitioners in great fault, etc. After this (upon motion of the deputies) it was agreed to refer the cause to arbitrators according to an order of court, when the magistrates and deputies cannot agree, etc. The magistrates named six of the elders of the next towns, and left it to them to choose any three or four of them, and required them to name six others. The deputies finding themselves now at the wall, and not daring to trust the elders with the cause, they sent to desire that six of themselves might come and confer with the magistrates, which being granted, they came, and at last came to this agreement, viz., the chief petitioners and the rest of the offenders were severally fined, (all their fines not amounting to 50 pounds,) the rest of the petitioners to bear equal share to 50 pounds more towards the charges of the court, (two of the principal offenders were the deputies of the town, Joshua Hubbert and Bozone Allen, the first was fined 20 pounds, and the other 5 pounds,) lieutenant Emes to be under admonition, the deputy governor to be legally and publicly acquit of all that was laid to his charge.

According to this agreement, (5) (*July*) 3, presently after the lecture the magistrates and deputies took their places in the meeting house, and the people being come together, and the deputy governor placing himself within the bar, as at the time of the hearing, etc., the governor read the sentence of the court, without speaking any more, for the deputies had (by importunity) obtained a promise of silence from the magistrates. Then was the deputy governor desired by the court to go up and take his place again upon the bench, which he did accordingly, and the court being about to arise, he desired leave for a little speech, which was to this effect.

I suppose something may be expected from me, upon this charge that is befallen me, which moves me to speak now to you; yet I intend not to intermeddle in the proceedings of the court, or with any of the persons concerned therein. Only I bless God, that I see an issue of this troublesome business. I also acknowledge the justice of the court, and, for mine own part, I am well satisfied, I was publicly charged, and I am publicly and legally acquitted, which is all I did expect or desire. And though this be sufficient for my justification before men, yet not so before the God, who hath seen so much amiss in my dispensations (and even in this affair) as calls me to be humble. For to be publicly and criminally charged in this court, is matter of humiliation, (and I desire to make a right use of it,) notwithstanding I be thus acquitted. If her father had spit in her face, (saith the Lord concerning Miriam,) should she not have been ashamed seven days? Shame had lien upon her, whatever the occasion had been. I am unwilling to stay you from your urgent affairs, yet give me leave (upon this special occasion) to speak a little more to this assembly.  It may be of some good use, to inform and rectify the judgments of some of the people, and may prevent such distempers as have arisen amongst us.  The great questions that have troubled the country, are about the authority of the magistrates and the liberty of the people. It is yourselves who have called us to this office, and being called by you, we have our authority from God, in way of an ordinance, such as hath the image of God eminently stamped upon it, the contempt and violation whereof hath been vindicated with examples of divine vengeance.  I entreat you to consider, that when you choose magistrates, you take them from among yourselves, men subject to like passions as you are.  Therefore when you see infirmities in us, you should reflect upon your own, and that would make you bear the more with us, and not be severe censurers of the failings of your magistrates, when you have continual experience of the like infirmities in yourselves and others.  We account him a good servant, who breaks not his covenant.  The covenant between you and us is the oath you have taken of us, which is to this purpose, that we shall govern you and judge your causes by the rules of God's laws and our own, according to our best skill.  When you agree with a workman to build you a ship or house, etc., he undertakes as well for his skill as for his faithfulness, for it is his profession, and you pay him for both.  But when you call one to be a magistrate, he doth not profess nor undertake to have sufficient skill for that office, nor can you furnish him with gifts, etc., therefore you must run the hazard of his skill and ability.  But if he fail in faithfulness, which by his oath he is bound unto, that he must answer for.  If it fall out that the case be clear to common apprehension, and the rule clear also, if he transgress here, the error is not in the skill, but in the evil of the will: it must be required of him.  But if the case be doubtful, or the rule doubtful, to men of such understanding and parts as your magistrates are, if your magistrates should err here, yourselves must bear it.

For the other point concerning liberty, I observe a great mistake in the country about that.  There is a twofold liberty, natural (I mean as our nature is now corrupt) and civil or federal.  The first is common to man with beasts and other creatures.  By this, man, as he stands in relation to man simply, hath liberty to do what he lists; it is a liberty to evil as well as to good.  This liberty is incompatible and inconsistent with authority, and cannot endure the least restraint of the most just authority. The exercise and maintaining of this liberty makes men grow more evil, and in time to be worse than brute beasts: omnes sumus licentia deteriores.  This is that great enemy of truth and peace, that wild beast, which all the ordinances of God are bent against, to restrain and subdue it. The other kind of liberty I call civil or federal, it may also be termed moral, in reference to the covenant between God and man, in the moral law, and the politic covenants and constitutions, amongst men themselves. This liberty is the proper end and object of authority, and cannot subsist without it; and it is a liberty to that only which is good, just, and honest. This liberty you are to stand for, with the hazard (not only of your goods, but) of your lives, if need be. Whatsoever crosseth this, is not authority, but a distemper thereof. This liberty is maintained and exercised in a way of subjection to authority; it is of the same kind of liberty wherewith Christ hath made us free. The woman's own choice makes such a man her husband; yet being so chosen, he is her lord, and she is to be subject to him, yet in a way of liberty, not of bondage; and a true wife accounts her subjection her honor and freedom, and would not think her condition safe and free, but in her subjection to her husband's authority. Such is the liberty of the church under the authority of Christ, her king and husband; his yoke is so easy and sweet to her as a bride's ornaments; and if through frowardness or wantonness, etc., she shake it off, at any time, she is at no rest in her spirit, until she take it up again; and whether her lord smiles upon her, and embraceth her in his arms, or whether he frowns, or rebukes, or smites her, she apprehends the sweetness of his love in all, and is refreshed, supported, and instructed by every such dispensation of his authority over her. On the other side, ye know who they are that complain of this yoke and say, let us break their bands, etc., we will not have this man to rule over us. Even so, brethren, it will be between you and your magistrates. If you stand for your natural corrupt liberties, and will do what is good in your own eyes, you will not endure the least weight of authority, but will murmur, and oppose, and be always striving to shake off that yoke; but if you will be satisfied to enjoy such civil and lawful liberties, such as Christ allows you, then will you quietly and cheerfully submit unto that authority which is set over you, in all the administrations of it, for your good. Wherein, if we fail at any time, we hope we shall be willing (by God's assistance) to hearken to good advice from any of you, or in any other way of God; so shall your liberties be preserved, in upholding the honor and power of authority amongst you.[1]

The deputy governor having ended his speech, the court arose, and the magistrates and deputies retired to attend their

---

[1] Winthrop's speech is fairminded and good tempered, though his soul was outraged at the democratic demands.

other affairs. Many things were observable in the agitation and proceedings about this case. It may be of use to leave a memorial of some of the most material, that our posterity and others may behold the workings of Satan to ruin the colonies and churches of Christ in New England, and into what distempers a wise and godly people may fall in times of temptation; and when such have entertained some false and plausible principles, what deformed superstructures they will raise thereupon, and with what unreasonable obstinacy they will maintain them.

Some of the deputies had seriously conceived, that the magistrates affected an arbitrary government, and that they had (or sought to have) an unlimited power to do what they pleased without control, and that, for this end, they did strive so much to keep their negative power in the general court. This caused them to interpret all the magistrates' actions and speeches (not complying exactly with their own principles) as tending that way, by which occasions their fears and jealousies increased daily. For prevention whereof they judged it not unlawful to use even extrema remedia, as if salus populi had been now the transcendent rule to walk by, and that magistracy must be no other, in effect, than a ministerial office, and all authority, both legislative, consultative, and judicial, must be exercised by the people in their body representative. Hereupon they labored, equis et velis, to take away the negative vote. Failing of that, they pleaded that the magistrates had no power out of the general court, but what must be derived from the general court; and so they would have put upon them commissions, for what was to be done in the vacancy of the general court, and some of themselves to be joined with the magistrates, and some of the magistrates left out. This not being yielded unto, recourse was had to the elders for advice, and the case stated, with incredible wariness; but the elders casting the cause against them, (as is before declared,) they yet believed, (or at least would that others should,) that the elders' advice was as much for them in their sense as for the magistrates, (and if it were, they had no cause to shun the advice of the elders, as they have seemed to do ever since). This project not prevailing, the next is, for such a body of laws, with prescript penalties in all cases, as nothing might be left to the discretion of the magistrates, (while in the mean time there is no fear of any danger in reserving a liberty for their own discretion in every case,) many laws are agreed upon, some are not assented unto by the magistrates not finding them just. Then is it given out, that the magistrates would have no laws, etc. This gave occasion to the deputy governor to write that treatise about arbitrary government, which he first tendered to the deputies in a model, and finding it approved by some, and silence in others, he drew it up more at large, and having advised with most of the magistrates and elders about it, he intended to have presented it orderly to the court. But to prevent that, the first day of the court, the deputies had gotten a copy, which was presently read amongst them as a dangerous libel of some unknown author, and a committee was presently appointed to examine it, many false and dangerous things were collected out of it, all agreed and voted by them, and sent up to the magistrates for their assent, not seeming all this time to take any notice of the author, nor once moving to have his answer about it, for they feared that his place in the council would have excused him from censure, as well as the like had done Mr. Saltonstall for his book against the standing council not long before. But if they could have prevailed to have had the book censured, this would have weakened his reputation with the people; and so if one of their opposite had been removed, it would somewhat have facilitated their way to what they intended; but this not succeeding as they expected, they kept it in deposito till some fitter season. In this time divers occasions falling out, wherein the magistrates had to do in the vacancy of the general court, as the French business, the seizure of the Bristol ship by Captain Stagg, and of the Dartmouth ship by ourselves, as is before related, and other affairs, they would still declare their judgments contrary to the magistrates' practice; and if the event did not answer the counsel, (though it had been interrupted by themselves or others,) there needed no other ground to condemn the counsel; all which tended still to weaken the authority of the magistrates, and their reputation with the people.

Then fell out the Hingham case, which they eagerly laid hold on, and pursued to the utmost, for they doubted not but they could now make it appear, either that the magistrates had abused their authority, or else that their authority was too great to consist with the people's liberty, and therefore ought to be reduced within narrower bounds.   In pursuit whereof it may be observed,

1. That a cause, orderly referred to a trial, at a court of assistants, should be taken into the general court, before it had received a due proceeding in the proper court; the like having never been done before, nor any law or order directing thereto, but rather the contrary.

2. That a scandalous petition against some of the magistrates should be received by the deputies, and the magistrates often pressed to consent to a judicial hearing, and to give way that the deputy governor should be called to answer thereupon, as a delinquent, before any examination were first privately had, about the justice of the cause.

3. That the testimony, in writing, of the three chiefest officers of the commonwealth (in a case properly committed to their trust) should be rejected, by a considerable part of the court, as a thing of no credit.

4. That the same part of the court should vote manifest contradictions, and require assent to both.

5. That being clearly convinced, that the petition was false and scandalous, and so voted, they should yet professedly refuse to assent to any due censure.

6. That they should receive the testimony of two of those

whom themselves judged delinquents and false accusers, and
thereupon judge him, the deputy governor, an offender in
words, against his own protestation, and other testimony concurring, and that in a matter of no moment, and against common reason, to be either spoken by him, or believed by others,
in such sense as they were charged upon him.

7. That a mutinous and seditious practice, carried on with
an high hand, to the open contempt of authority, attempting
to make division in the town, and a dangerous rent in the
highest court of the jurisdiction, should (by such a considerable
part of the same court, looked at by others as the choice of the
country for piety, prudence, and justice) be accounted as
worthy of no censure, and in the conclusion not valued at so
high a rate, as some offences have been of private concernment
arising of common infirmity.

8. That this practice should hold forth an apprehension,
that liberty and authority are incompatible, in some degrees;
so as no other way can be found to preserve the one, but by
abasing and abating the honor and power of the other.

9. That being entrusted with the care and means of the
country's prosperity, we should waste our time and their estates and our own (for the charges of this court came to 300
pounds) in such agitations as tend only to the discountenancing and interrupting the ordinary means of our welfare.

10. That while we sympathize with our native country in
their calamities, and confess our own compliance with them in
the provocations of God's wrath, (as in many days of humiliation, and one even in the time of this court,) we should be hasting by all our skill and power to bring the like miseries upon
ourselves.

11. That Bozon Allen, one of the deputies of Hingham, and
a delinquent in that common cause, should be publicly convict
of divers false and reproachful speeches published by him concerning the deputy governor, and the book he wrote about
arbitrary government, as that it was worse than Gorton's let-

ters, that it should be burnt under the gallows, that if some other of the magistrates had written it, it would have cost him his ears, if not his head, and other like speeches, and no censure set upon him for this, only he was fined 5 pounds among others, for their offences in general.

12. It is observable, that the deputies, being so divided, (for of thirty-three there was only the odd man who carried it in most of their votes,) remembered at length a law they had agreed to in such cases, viz., that in causes of judicature they would not proceed without taking an oath, etc., whereupon the most of them took it among themselves, (quaere, quo jure?) but five of them came to the magistrates, who administered the oath to them.

We had intelligence from Pascataquack of a French ship of 200 tons, full of men, which hovered up and down, and would not take harbor, though a pilot had been offered them by a fisher's boat of Isle of Shoals; whereupon all concluded it was Monsieur D'Aulnay lying in wait for La Tour, and the wind continuing easterly, we had intelligence from Plymouth, that she was imbayed near Sandwich among the Shoals. The court consulted what was to be done. Some advised to take no notice of her, lest, if we should send out to her, we should be necessitated (in common courtesy) to invite him to Boston, and so put ourselves to a needless charge and interruption in our business; for being but one ship, there was no fear of any danger, etc. But the major part prevailed to send out two shallops and the letter which we had ready to send to him; but before the shallops could get out, she was gone, and it was found after to be a fishing ship, which had lost her way, by contrary winds, etc.

I should have mentioned in the Hingham case, what care and pains many of the elders had taken to reconcile the differences which were grown in that church. Mr. Hubbert, the pastor there, being of a Presbyterial spirit, did manage all affairs without the church's advice, which divers of the congregation not liking of, they were divided in two parts. Lieutenant Emes, etc., having complained to the magistrates, as is before expressed, Mr. Hubbert, etc., would have cast him out of the church, pretending that he had told a lie, whereupon they procured the elders to write to the church, and so did some of the magistrates also, whereupon they stayed proceeding against the lieutenant for a day or two. But he and some twelve more of them, perceiving he was resolved to proceed, and finding no way of reconciliation, they withdrew from the church, and openly declared it in the congregation. This course the elders did not approve of. But being present in the court, when their petition against the deputy governor was heard, Mr. Hubbert, perceiving the cause was like to go against him and his party, desired the elders to go to Hingham to mediate a reconciliation (which he would never hearken to before, being earnestly sought by the other party, and offered by the elders) in the interim of the court's adjournment for one week. They readily accepted the motion, and went to Hingham, and spent two or three days there, and found the pastor and his party in great fault, but could not bring him to any acknowledgment. In their return by water, they were kept twenty-four hours in the boat, and were in great danger by occasion of a tempest which arose in the night; but the Lord preserved them.

This year the *Trial* of Boston arrived from London, and brought many useful commodities from thence and from Holland. She had been preserved in divers most desperate dangers, having been on ground upon the sands by Flushing, and again by Dover, and in great tempests; but the Lord delivered him beyond expectation. Here arrived about ten ships more, (one of our own called the *Endeavor* of Cambridge,) which brought store of linen, woollen, shoes, stockings, and other useful commodities, so as we had plenty of all things, and divers of the ships took pay in wheat, rye, peas, etc., so as there went out of the country this year about 20,000 bushels of corn. Yet it was feared no ships would have come to us, because we had suffered the Bristol and Dartmouth ships to be taken in our harbor.

The parliament also had made an ordinance to free all goods from custom, which came to New England, which caused the magistrates to dispense with an order, made the last general court, for all ships to pay sixpence the ton, which we freed all parliament ships from; and good reason, for by that order we might have gotten 20 or 30 pounds this year, and by the ordinance of parliament we saved 3 or 400 pounds.

When one of the ships came near Cape Ann, 20 (6) (*August* 20) 45, an hour and a half before night, there appeared to all the company a sun near the horizon, more bright than the true sun, (which was seen above it,) which continued near an hour, there being a small cloud between the true sun and that. This was affirmed by divers persons of credit, who were of this country and then in the ship. But it was not seen by any upon the shore. Captain Wall was master of the ship.

The merchants of Boston sent a pinnace the last winter to trade in Delaware Bay. She traded upon Maryland side, and had gotten a good parcel of beaver; at last the Indians came aboard, and while the English (who were about five and a boy) were trading with some of them, others drew out hatchets from under their coats, and killed the master and three others, and took the other and the boy, and carried them on shore, and rifled the pinnace of all her goods and sails, etc. Soon after, other Indians came upon these and slew the sachem, and took away all their goods they had stolen. There was one Redman suspected to have betrayed their pinnace, for he being linkister,[1] (because he could speak the language,) and being put out of that employment for his evil carriage, did bear ill will to the master, and the Indians spared him, and gave him a good part of the spoil, and he lived amongst them five or six weeks, till the Swedish governor procured other Indians to go fetch him and the boy to his fort, from whence they were

---

[1] Linkister, linguister, interpreter.

brought to Boston, and the said Redman was tried for his life, and being found guilty by the grand jury, was deferred his farther trial in expectation of more evidence to come from Delaware.

The governor, Mr. Endecott, having received a letter from Monsieur D'Aulnay in the spring, wherein he slighted us very much, and charged us with breach of covenant in entertaining La Tour, in sending home his lady, etc., we returned a sharp answer to him by Mr. Allen, declaring our innocency, in that we sent not the lady home, but she hired three London ships, etc., as is before related, page 208. When he had received this letter, he was in a great rage, and told Mr. Allen that he would return no answer; nor would he permit him to come within his fort, but lodged him in his gunner's house without the gate, and himself came daily, and dined and supped with him, but at last he wrote to our governor in very high language, requiring satisfaction for burning his mill, etc., and threatening revenge, etc. So the matter rested till the meeting of the commissioners in the seventh month next, and then their agreement to the peace was sent to him by a special messenger, Captain Robert Bridges, as is hereafter declared.

We understood for certain afterward that Monsieur La Tour's fort was taken by assault and scalado,[1] that Monsieur D'Aulnay lost in the attempt twelve men, and had many wounded, and that he had put to death all the men (both French and English) and had taken the lady, who died within three weeks after, and her little child and her gentlewoman were sent into France. La Tour valued his jewels, plate, household, ordnance, and other moveables, at 10,000 pounds. The more was his folly to leave so much substance in so great danger, when he might have brought the most of it to Boston, whereby he might have discharged his engagements of more than 2500 pounds to Major Edward Gibbons, (who by this loss was now quite undone,) and might have had somewhat

---

[1] Escalade.

to have maintained himself and his men; for want whereof
his servants were forced to go out of the country, some to the
Dutch, and others to France, and he himself to lie at other
men's charge. But in the spring he went to Newfoundland,
and there was courteously entertained by Sir David Kirk, the
governor, who promised him assistance, etc. But he returned
to Boston again by the vessel which carried him, and all the
next winter was entertained by Mr. Samuel Maverick at Nottles
Island.[1]

Some of our merchants of Boston and Charlestown sent
forth a ship and other vessels to Newfoundland upon a fishing
voyage. They went not to Ferryland, (where they might
have been in safety,) but to the Bay of Bulls, and when they
had near made their voyage, Captain Firnes's ships (being
of the king's party) came and took their ship and most of their
fish; so the men returned safe, but lost their voyage. Firnes
was hereby five ships strong, and so went to the Terceras,
and there fought with two ships of London and a Scotch ship,
who sunk two of Firnes's ships, and made him fly with the rest.

Captain Thomas Hawkins, a shipwright of London, who had
lived here divers years, had built at Boston a ship of 400
tons and upward, and had set her out with much strength
of ordnance, and ornament of carving, painting, etc., and called
her the *Seafort*, and the last 23 (9) (*November* 23) he set sail
from Boston, accompanied with another ship of London, Mr.
Kerman, master, laden with bolts, tobacco, etc. for Malago.
When they came near the coast of Spain, in the evening, some
of the company supposed they saw land, yet they sailed on all
the night, with a fair gale, and towards the morning they saw a
light or two, which they conceiving to have been in some ships,
either Turks or others, they prepared their ships and stood on
towards them. But some three hours before day [*blank*]

---

[1] La Tour later had better fortune. D'Aulnay dying in 1650, La Tour,
then a widower, married the widow of d'Aulnay. Hutchinson, *History of Massachusetts Bay*, I. 127, note.

(10 ber.) (*December*) both ships struck aground, and presently brake.  Nineteen were drowned, whereof Mr. Kerman was one, and one Mr. Thomas Coytmore of Charlestown (a right godly man, and an expert seaman) was another, and Mr. Pratt and his wife.  This man was above sixty years old, an experienced surgeon, who had lived in New England many years, and was of the first church at Cambridge in Mr. Hooker's time, and had good practice, and wanted nothing.  But he had been long discontented, because his employment was not so profitable to himself as he desired, and it is like he feared lest he should fall into want in his old age, and therefore he would needs go back into England, (for surgeons were then in great request there by occasion of the wars,) but God took him away childless.  The rest of the company (both women and children, who went passengers that way into England, choosing to go in that ship, because of her strength and conveniency, rather than in another ship, which went right for England, and arrived safe there) were all saved, upon pieces of the ships, and by the help of a rope which one of the seamen swam on shore with; and although the ships at first grounded two or three miles from the shore, yet (through the Lord's great mercy) they were heaved by the seas near to the dry land before they fell in pieces.  This was five miles from Cales.[1]  In the morning the poor people of the island came down, and pillaged all they could come by, yea they took away some pieces of plate, which the passengers had saved.  But when they came to the city, (naked and barefoot as they went frighted out of their cabins,) the Spaniards used them kindly, especially the women, and clothed them, and took them into their houses.  There was an English ship then in the roads, whereof one Mr. Mariot was master: he entertained as many as his ship could stow, and clothed many of them with his own clothes, (the Lord reward him).  The governor of the island gave Captain Hawkins 500 pounds for the wreck of his ship.

[1] Cadiz.

The same Captain Hawkins going for London, found much favor with his creditors and others his friends there, so as the next year they employed him to Malago, to meet a New England ship called [blank,] built at Cambridge, and freight for Malago with pipe staves, fish, and other commodities, which he was to freight thence with wine, etc., for London, but as she was on her voyage, (Captain Hawkins being in her, and twelve other ships in company) being come out of the Streight's mouth,[1] they were taken with such a violent tempest at south, as they were (five of them, whereof Captain Hawkins's ship was one) cast upon the same place at Cales, where his ship was wrecked the year before, and there all their ships were cast away, but all the men in Captain Hawkins's ship were saved, and most of the rest. This was 2 (12) 45.[2]

The scarcity of good ministers in England, and want of employment for our new graduates here, occasioned some of them to look abroad. Three honest young men, good scholars, and very hopeful, viz. a younger son of Mr. Higginson, to England, and so to Holland, and after to the East Indies, a younger son of Mr. Buckley, a Batchellor of Arts to England, and Mr. George Downing,[3] son of Mr. Emanuel Downing of Salem, Batchellor of Arts also, about twenty years of age, went in a ship to the West Indies to instruct the seamen. He went by Newfoundland, and so to Christophers, and Barbados, and

[1] Strait of Gibraltar. [2] February 2, 1645/6.
[3] Of these hopeful youths, George Downing later figured prominently upon the old-world stage. Quick, adroit, and indefatigable, he passed rapidly to the post of scoutmaster-general, serving the Commonwealth as chief of the intelligence department, and later as an instrument of Cromwell, in high diplomatic position. As unprincipled as able, he became the tool of Charles II. at the Restoration, and is charged with having given over to execution three regicides, his old associates, one of them the commander under whom he had served, the Colonel Okey mentioned above. As envoy to the Netherlands, he had much to do with bringing about the Second Dutch War and the acquisition of New Netherland. His defective character was recognized by his contemporaries. Pepys, who had a place under him, calls him "a perfidious rogue." (Diary, March 12, 1662.) He was Winthrop's nephew, the first son of Harvard to attain high distinction. For Downing's methods see Pepys, Diary, December 27, 1668.

Nevis, and being requested to preach in all these places, he gave such content, as he had large offers made to stay with them. But he continued in the ship to England, and being a very able scholar, and of a ready wit and fluent utterance, he was soon taken notice of, and called to be a preacher in Sir Thomas Fairfax his army, to Colonel Okye his regiment.

The inhabitants of Boston, Charlestown, Cambridge, Roxbury, and Dorchester, conceiving that the fortification at Castle Island (which by a late order of court was deserted) would be of great use for their defence against a foreign enemy, agreed among themselves (with leave of the court) to repair and fortify the same; and accordingly they chose a committee out of the several towns to raise means, and to get the work done. Whereupon the old earthwork was slighted, and a new work of pine trees, [blank] foot square, fourteen foot high, and [blank] foot thick, was reared, with four bulwarks, which cost in all [blank]. But finding the charge of the work and the maintenance of a garrison to be over heavy for them, they petitioned the general court in [blank] to afford assistance, which with much difficulty was at length obtained to this effect.

In the beginning of the winter a Portugal ship lying at Natascot, (now called Hull,) the seamen stole divers goats off the islands there. Complaint thereof being made to the governor and council, they gave warrant to one Mr. Smith, who then lay with his ship in the same place, to require the Portugal to give satisfaction, or else to bring his ship up to Boston. Mr. Smith (who was a member of the church of Boston) sent one Thomas Keyser his mate with his long boat well manned, to require satisfaction, who coming to the Portugal did not reason the case with him, nor give him any time to consider, but presently boarded him, and took possession of his ship, and brought her up, and his men fell to rifling his ship, as if she had been a prize. The Portugal being brought to the magistrates, and the theft proved, he was ordered to make double restitution, (as our manner was,) and the seamen were made to restore what they had taken out of the ship.    So the Portugal departed well satisfied.

The said Mr. James Smith with his mate Keyser were bound to Guinea to trade for negroes.    But when they arrived there, they met some Londoners, with whom they consorted, and the Londoners having been formerly injured by the natives (or at least pretending the same,) they invited them aboard one of their ships upon the Lord's day, and such as came they kept prisoners, then they landed men, and a murderer, and assaulted one of their towns and killed many of the people, but the country coming down, they were forced to retire without any booty, divers of their men being wounded with the negroes' arrows, and one killed.    Mr. Smith, having taken in wine at Madeiras, sailed to Barbados to put off his wine.    But being engaged there, and his wife being there also unprovided of maintenance, and his ship and cargo bound over to the said Keyser his mate and others of Boston who set out the ship, Keyser refused to let any of the wines go on shore, except he might have security for the proceeds to be returned on ship board.    So the ship lay a week in the roads, and then Keyser fearing that the master would use some means by other ships which rode there to deprive him of the cargo, told him plainly that if he would not come aboard, and return to Boston, (which was the last port they were bound to,) he would carry away the ship, and leave him behind, which accordingly he did; and arriving at Boston about midsummer, he repaired to the magistrates and told them how he was come away, and tendered the cargo to them, who finding that it was engaged to himself and others, and that there would be great loss in the wines if they were not presently disposed, delivered them to the merchants and himself, taking bond of them to be responsible to Mr. Smith, etc.    A short time after, Mr. Smith came, and brought his action against Keyser and the other mariners for bringing away the ship, and by a jury of seamen and

merchants recovered three or four times the value of what he
was damnified, and the mate Keyser to lose not only his wages,
but he and the rest of the merchants to lose the proceed or
interest agreed for their stock and adventure, which was forty
per cent. and all the mariners to lose their wages.   But divers
of the magistrates being unsatisfied with this verdict, (perceiving that the jury in their displeasure against Keyser, etc.,
did not only regard Smith's satisfaction for his damages, but
also the punishment of Keyser, etc.) the defendants at the next
court brought a review, and then another jury abated much of
the former damages; whereupon the plaintiff Smith preferred
a petition to the next general court.

For the matter of the negroes, whereof two were brought
home in the ship, and near one hundred slain by the confession
of some of the mariners, the magistrates took order to have
these two set at liberty, and to be sent home; but for the
slaughter committed, they were in great doubt what to do
in it, seeing it was in another country, and the Londoners
pretended a just revenge.   So they called the elders; and
desired their advice.[1]

Mr. Israel Stoughton, one of the magistrates, having been in
England about merchandize, and returned with good advantage, went for England again the last winter, with divers
other of our best military men, and entered into the parliament's service.   Mr. Stoughton was made lieutenant colonel
to colonel Rainsborow, Mr. Nehemiah Bourne, a ship carpenter,
was major of his regiment, and Mr. John Leverett, son of one
of the elders of the church of Boston, a captain of a foot company, and one William Hudson, ensign of the same company,
Lioll, surgeon of the Earl of Manchester's life guard.   These did
good service, and were well approved, but Mr. Stoughton
falling sick and dying at Lincoln, the rest all returned to their

---

[1] This compunction of the Massachusetts magistrates seems rather in advance
of the time.   The colony records for the date show their sentiment to have been
sustained by the community.

wives and families.   But three of them went to England again
about the end of this year, but came back again and settled
themselves here, all save the surgeon.[1]

The Narragansetts having begun war upon Uncus, the Mon-
heagan sachem, notwithstanding their covenant to the contrary
and divers messages sent to them from the commissioners to
require them to forbear, until a meeting might be had, and the
cause heard, it was thought fit by the general court in the
third month, that though the next meeting was in course to be
at New Haven in the beginning of September, yet in regard of
the danger Uncus was in, and our engagement to save him
harmless from any damage from Miantonomo his death, as
also in regard of the distressed condition of Monsieur La Tour,
(who earnestly petitioned the court for relief, etc.) the commissioners should be written to to meet at Boston in the 28 of the
fifth month, which was done accordingly.   The names of the
commissioners and all their proceedings are at large set down
in the books of their records, whereof every colony hath one.

At this general court, which continued from 14 (3), to 5 (5),[2]
the military officers prevailed with much importunity to have
the whole power of those affairs committed to them; which
was thought by divers of the court to be very unfit, and not
so safe in times of peace; but a great part of the court being
military officers, and others not willing to contend any further
about it, the order passed, the inconvenience whereof appeared
soon after, and will more in future time.

The taking of the Bristol ship in our harbor by Captain

[1] Of Stoughton, mention has already been made.   John Leverett, returning
from his English experiences, became a citizen of the first consequence, serving
as deputy, speaker, assistant, sergeant-major-general and governor.   He occupied the supreme office five years, from 1673, during which period came the terrible
Philip's War.   That was a crisis which required the heart and head of an Ironside,
and Leverett met the situation.

[2] May 14 to July 5.   The *Records of Massachusetts*, II. 112, for this court,
contain an order for a rate of £616.15.   It was assessed in the following proportions:  Boston, £100;  Ipswich, £61.10;  Charlestown, £55;  Salem, £45;  Cambridge, £45;  Dorchester, £43.17.6;  Watertown, £41.5;  Roxbury, £37.10;
Lynn, £25, etc.

Stagg occasioned much debate in the court. The deputies
drew up a bill to give protection to all ships in our harbor,
coming as friends. The magistrates forseeing that this might
put us upon a necessity of fight with some parliament ships,
(which we were very unwilling to be engaged in,) and so
might weaken that interest we had in the parliament, they
refused the bill; and so divers bills passed from one to the
other, before they could agree. At length (few of the magistrates being then in the court) a bill passed to that effect, but
not so full as was desired. But to strengthen the same, and to
secure all ships which should come as friends into our harbor,
commission was given to major Gibbons for Boston, and major
Sedgwick[1] for Charlestown to keep the peace in the said towns,
and not to permit any ships to fight in the harbor without
license from authority.

14. 5. (*July* 14.)] A new watch house set up on the fort hill
at Boston was smote with lightning, and the boards and timber
at one end of it torn in pieces, and many of the shingles of the
covering torn off.

25.] Monsieur La Tour having stayed here all the winter
and thus far of the summer, and having petitioned the court
for aid against Monsieur D'Aulnay, and finding no hope to
obtain help that way, took shipping in one of our vessels which
went on fishing to Newfoundland, hoping by means of Sir
David Kirk, governor there, and some friends he might procure in England to obtain aid from thence, intending for that
end to go from thence to England. Sir David entertained him
courteously, and promised to do much for him; but no means
of help appearing to answer his ends, he returned hither before
winter, Sir David giving him passage in a vessel of his which
came hither.

---

[1] Robert Sedgwick, having spent his younger manhood in Massachusetts, in
honorable positions, at length went to England into the ranks of Cromwell. He
was in the force sent by the Protector to the West Indies, and died there in 1656,
a major-general.

Captain Bayley being returned into England, and informing Alderman Barkly of the proceedings here against him and Mr. Barkly his brother in the business of the Lady La Tour, withal he carried a certificate of the proceedings of the court under the hands of divers persons of good credit here, who although they reported truth for the most part, yet not the whole truth, (being somewhat prejudiced in the case; they were called in question about it after, for the offence was great, and they had been censured for it, if proof could have been had for a legal conviction,) whereby the alderman was so incensed as he attached a ship of ours being then arrived at London; but being persuaded to release the ship, he attached two of New England, viz., Mr. Stephen Winthrop, who was recorder of the court when the cause was tried, and Captain Joseph Weld, who was one of the jury, so as they were forced to find sureties in a bond of 4000 pounds to answer him in the court of admiralty. But it pleased God to stir them up such friends, viz., Sir Henry Vane, (who had sometime lived at Boston, and though he might have taken occasion against us for some dishonor which he apprehended to have been unjustly put upon him here, yet both now and at other times he showed himself a true friend to New England, and a man of a noble and generous mind, etc.)[1] and some others by Mr. Peter's means, so as (although he spared for no costs) yet he was forced to give over his suit in the admiralty, and then procured out of Chancery a ne exeat regno against them. But the cause being heard there, and they discharged, he petitioned the lords of the parliament (pretending great injuries, which he was not able to prove) for letters of reprisal. After he had tried all means in vain, he was brought at length to sit down and lose his charges, and they theirs.

---

[1] An entry pleasant to read, giving proof of the magnanimity of Vane, who could do a service to a colony which had slighted him and cast out his friends,— and also of Winthrop, who could forget many occasions of offence to commend an old opponent.

1. (*March*) 5.] Many books coming out of England, some in defence of anabaptism and other errors, and for liberty of conscience as a shelter for their toleration, etc., others in maintenance of the Presbyterial government (agreed upon by the assembly of divines in England) against the congregational way, which was practised here, the elders of the churches through all the United Colonies agreed upon a meeting at Cambridge this day, where they conferred their councils and examined the writings which some of them had prepared in answer to the said books, which being agreed and perfected were sent over into England to be printed. The several answers were these; Mr. Hooker in answer to Mr. Rutterford the Scotch minister about Presbyterial government, (which being sent in the New Haven ship was lost). While Mr. Hooker lived, he could not be persuaded to let another copy go over, but after his death, a copy was sent, and returned in print (3) 48.[1]

A sad business fell out this year in Boston. One of the brethren of the church there, being in England in the parliament service about two years, had committed the care of his family and business to another of the same church, (a young man of good esteem for piety and sincerity, but his wife was in England,) who in time grew over familiar with his master's wife, (a young woman no member of the church,) so as she would be with him oft in his chamber, etc., and one night two of the servants, being up, perceived him to go up into their dame's chamber, which coming to the magistrates' knowledge, they were both sent for and examined, (but it was not discovered till about a quarter of a year after, her husband being then come home,) and confessed not only that he was in the chamber with her in such a suspicious manner, but also that he was in bed with her, but both denied any carnal knowledge; and being tried by a jury upon their lives by our law, which makes

---

[1] May, 1648. This was Hooker's famous *Survey of the Summe of Church Discipline* (London, 1648), the preface of which may be seen in *Old South Leaflets*, No. 55.

adultery death, the jury acquitted them of the adultery, but
found them guilty of adulterous behavior. This was much
against the minds of many, both of the magistrates and elders,
who judged them worthy of death; but the jury attending
what was spoken by others of the magistrates, 1. that seeing
the main evidence against them was their own confession of
being in bed together, their whole confession must be taken,
and not a part of it; 2. the law requires two witnesses, but here
was no witness at all, for although circumstances may amount
to a testimony against the person, where the fact is evident, yet
it is otherwise where no fact is apparent; 3. all that the evidence could evince was but suspicion of adultery, but neither
God's law nor ours doth make suspicion of adultery (though
never so strong) to be death; whereupon the case seeming
doubtful to the jury, they judged it safest in case of life to find
as they did.  So the court adjudged them to stand upon the
ladder at the place of execution with halters about their necks
one hour, and then to be whipped, or each of them to pay 20
pounds. The husband (although he condemned his wife's
immodest behavior, yet) was so confident of her innocency
in point of adultery, as he would have paid 20 pounds rather
than she should have been whipped; but their estate being
but mean, she chose rather to submit to the rest of her punishment than that her husband should suffer so much for her
folly.  So he received her again, and they lived lovingly
together.  All that she had to say for herself upon her trial was
the same which she had revealed to her husband as soon as he
came home, before the matter had been discovered, viz. that he
did indeed come into bed to her, which so soon as she perceived, she used the best arguments she could to dissuade him
from so foul a sin, so as he lay still, and did not touch her, but
went away again as he came; and the reason why she did not
cry out, was because he had been very faithful and helpful to
her in her husband's absence, which made her very unwilling to
bring him to punishment or disgrace.

This punishment of standing upon the gallows was not so well approved by some of the magistrates; because the law of God appoints in case of whipping, that they should not exceed forty stripes, and the reason given is, lest thy brother should seem despised in thine eyes, and why this reason should not hold in all cases and punishments not capital doth not appear.

29. 8. (*October* 29.)][1] The wind E. N. E. with rain, so great a tempest as it drave three ships upon the shore, and did very much harm besides in bilging boats, and breaking down wharfs; and the night after for the space of two hours the tempest arose again at S. with more wind and rain than before. In which tempest one of our vessels coming from Bermuda had two men fetched overboard with the sea, and the vessel was in great danger of being foundered.

At the general court held at Boston the first of this month, there was a petition preferred by divers merchants and others about two laws, the one forbidding the entertaining of any strangers above three weeks, except such as should be allowed by two magistrates, etc., (this was made in Mrs. Hutchinson's time;) the other for banishing anabaptists, made the last year. The petitioners complained to the court of the offence taken thereat by many godly in England, and that some churches there did thereupon profess to deny to hold communion with such of our churches as should resort thither. Whereupon they entreated the court that they would please to take the said laws into further consideration, and to provide as far as they might for the indemnity of such of ours as were to go into England. Many of the court well inclined for these and other considerations to have had the execution of those laws to have been suspended for a season. But many of the elders, hearing of it, went first to the deputies and after to the magistrates, and laying before them what advantage it would give to the anabaptists, (who began to increase very fast through the country

---

1 Here, and in several subsequent places, the numeral for the month is placed last, contrary to the practice followed by the writer up to this point.

here, and much more in England, where they had gathered divers churches and taught openly, and had published a confession of their faith,) entreated that the law might continue still in force, and the execution of it not suspended, though they disliked not that all lenity and patience should be used for convincing and reclaiming such erroneous persons. Whereupon the court refused to make any farther order about the petition. See 60 a counter petition.[1]

There came hither to Boston at the same time out of England one Captain Partridge, who had served the parliament, but in the ship he broached and zealously maintained divers points of antinomianism and familism, for which he was called before the magistrates and charged with the said opinions, to which he refused to give any answer. But before he departed, he was willing to confer with Mr. Cotton, which accordingly he did, and Mr. Cotton reported to the magistrates, that he found him corrupt in his judgment, but ignorant of those points which he had maintained, so as he perceived he had been but lately taken with them, and that upon argument he was come off from some of the worst of them, and he had good hope to reclaim him wholly; but some of the magistrates requiring a present renouncing of all under his hand, he the said captain was not willing to that before he were clearly convinced of his error in them. It was moved by some of the magistrates, in regard he had made so hopeful a beginning, and that winter was now at hand, and it would be very hard to expose his wife and family to such hardships, etc., to permit him to stay here till the spring, but the major part (by one or two) voting the contrary, he was forced to depart, and so went to Rhode Island. This strictness was offensive to many, though approved of by others. But sure the rule of hospitality to strangers, and of seeking to pluck out of the fire such as there may be hope of to be reduced out of error and the snare of the devil, do seem to require more moderation and indulgence of human in-

[1] See *post*, p. 271.

firmity where there appears not obstinacy against the clear truth.

This year about twenty families (most of them of the church of Braintree) petitioned the court for allowance to begin a plantation at the place where Gorton and his company had erected three or four small houses upon the land of Pumham, the Indian sachem by Narragansett, who had submitted himself and country to this jurisdiction. The court readily granted their petition, promising all encouragement, etc., (for it was of great concernment to all the English in these parts, that a strong plantation should be there as a bulwark, etc. against the Narragansetts). But Mr. John Browne, one of the magistrates of Plymouth, and then one of their commissioners for the United Colonies, dwelling at Rehoboth, and intending to drive a trade with the Indians in those parts, meeting with some of ours when they went to view the place and to take the bounds of it, forbade them in the name of the government of Plymouth to proceed in the said plantation, telling them that it belonged to Plymouth, and that it should be restored to the right owners, (meaning Gorton and his company). Whereupon the planters (not willing to run any hazard of contention for place in a country where there was room enough) gave over their purpose, and disposed themselves otherwise; some removed more southward, and others staid where they were. This practice of Mr. Browne being complained of to the governor of the Massachusetts, Mr. Dudley, he informed the magistrates of Plymouth thereof by letter, who returned answer, that Mr. Browne had no order from their court to forbid the proceedings, etc., for they should have been glad to have had the place planted by us, though the right of it were (as they conceived) in themselves, and for that end referred themselves to an order of the commissioners, wherein liberty is given to the Massachusetts to take course with Gorton and the lands they had possessed, etc., and therein is a proviso, that it should not prejudice the right of Plymouth, etc. But they took not the rest of the order, wherein it follows, that all such lands of English or Indians, as had submitted themselves to the government of the Massachusetts, should not be comprised in that proviso. Now this land where the plantation should have been erected was part of Pumham's land. And our general court wrote to the governor and council of Plymouth to the same effect, with desire to have their further answer about the same, and for satisfaction about Mr. Browne's carriage herein. The governor and three magistrates returned answer, that Mr. Browne had commission in general to forbid any to plant upon their jurisdiction within the Narragansett river without their leave, which, if any of ours would seek, they might have. But the case being after put to the commissioners for explanation of their said order, they resolved for the Massachusetts.

8. (*October.*)] A church was gathered at Haverhill upon the north side of Merrimack, and Mr. John Ward chosen and ordained pastor. About the same time a church was also gathered at Andover upon the south side of Merrimack, and Mr. Woodbridge ordained pastor.[1]

5. 9. (*November* 5.)] A church was gathered at Reading, and Mr. Greene ordained pastor. He was a very godly man, and died (8) (*October*) 48.

The village at Jeffry's creek was named Manchester, and the people there (not being yet in church state) had procured Mr. Smith (sometimes pastor of the church of Plymouth) to preach to them.

At the last general court it was ordered, that divers farmers belonging to Ipswich and Salem (but so far distant from either town as they could not duly repair to the public ordinances there) should erect a village and have liberty to gather a church. This was much opposed by those of the town of Ipswich, plead-

[1] John Woodbridge was a son-in-law of Governor Dudley. After a term at Andover, he returned to England, becoming there minister at Andover in Wiltshire. Driven thence in 1662, in the general expulsion of the non-conformists, he came back to America.

ing their interest in the land, etc.  But it was answered, that, when the land was granted to the town, it was not intended only for the benefit of the near inhabitants, or for the maintenance of the officers of that one church only, but of all the inhabitants and of any other church which should be there gathered; and a principal motive which led the court to grant them and other towns such vast bounds was, that (when the towns should be increased by their children and servants growing up, etc.) they might have place to erect villages, where they might be planted, and so the land improved to the more common benefit.

15. 10. (*December* 15.)] There appeared about noon, upon the north side of the sun, a great part of a circle like a rainbow, with the horns reversed, and upon each side of the sun, east and west, a bright light.  And about a month after were seen three suns, about the sun-setting; and about a month after that two suns at sun-rising, the one continued close to the horizon, while the other (which was the true sun) arose about half an hour. This was the earliest and sharpest winter we had since we arrived in the country, and it was as vehement cold to the southward as here.  Divers of our ships were put from their anchors with the ice and driven on shore 25 (10) (*December* 25), and one ketch carried out to sea, and wrecked upon Lovell's Island. At New Haven a ship bound for England was forced to be cut out of the ice three miles.  And in Virginia the ships were frozen up six weeks.

# 1646

At Ipswich there was a calf brought forth with one head, and three mouths, three noses, and six eyes. What these prodigies portended the Lord only knows, which in his due time he will manifest.

There was beside so sudden a thaw in the spring, (the snow lying very deep,) and much rain withal, that it bare down the bridge at Hartford upon Connecticut, and brake down divers mills to the southward about New Haven, and did much other harm.

This winter also the Swedes' fort upon Delaware river and all the buildings in it were burnt down, and all their powder and goods blown up. It happened in the night, through the negligence of a servant who fell on sleep leaving a candle burning. Some houses at Hartford, and a barn with corn, were burnt also; and two houses at Hingham in the Massachusetts.

1646. 26. (1.) (*March* 26.)] The governor and council met at Boston to take order about a rescue which they were informed of to have been committed at Hingham upon the marshal, when he went to levy the fines imposed upon Mr. Hubberd their pastor and many others who joined with him in the petition against the magistrates, etc., and having taken the information of the marshal and others, they sent out summons for their appearance at another day, at which time Mr. Hubberd came not, nor sent any excuse, though it was proved that he was at home, and that the summons was left at his house. Whereupon he was sent for by attachment directed to the constable, who brought him at the day of the return. And being then charged with joining in the said rescue by animating the offenders, and discouraging the officer, questioning the authority of his warrant because it was not in the king's name, and standing upon his allegiance to the crown of England, and exemption from such laws as were not agreeable to the laws of England, saying to the marshal that he could never know wherefore he was fined, except it were for petitioning, and if they were so waspish that they might not be petitioned, he knew not what to say to it, etc.  All the answer he would give was, that if he had broken any wholesome law not repugnant to the laws of England, he was ready to submit to censure. So he was bound over to the next court of assistants.

The court being at Boston, Mr. Hubberd appeared, and the marshal's information and other concurrent testimony being read to him, and his answer demanded, he desired to know in what state he stood, and what offence he should be charged with, or what wholesome law of the land, not repugnant to the law of England, he had broken.  The court told him, that the matters he was charged with amounted to a seditious practice and derogation and contempt of authority.  He still pressed to know what law, etc.  He was told that the oath which he had taken was a law to him; and beside the law of God which we were to judge by in case of a defect of an express law.  He said that the law of God admitted various interpretations, etc. Then he desired to see his accusers.  Upon that the marshal was called, who justified his information.  Then he desired to be tried by a jury, and to have the witnesses produced viva voce.  The secretary told him that two were present, and the third was sworn to his examination, (but in that he was mistaken, for he had not been sworn,) but to satisfy him, he was sent for and sworn in court.  The matters testified against him were his speeches to the marshal before thirty persons, against our authority and government, etc.  1. That we were but as a corporation in England; 2. That by our patent (as he understood it) we could not put any man to death, nor do divers other things which we did; 3. That he knew not wherefore

the general court had fined them, except it were for petitioning, and if they were so waspish (or captious) as they might
not be petitioned, etc., and other speeches tending to disparage
our authority and proceedings. Accordingly a bill was drawn
up, etc., and the jury found that he seemed to be ill affected
to this government, and that his speeches tended to sedition
and contempt of authority. Whereupon the whole court
(except Mr. Bellingham, who judged him to deserve no censure,
and desired in open court to have his dissent recorded) adjudged him to pay 20 pounds fine, and to be bound to his
good behavior, till the next court of assistants, and then farther
if the court should see cause. At this sentence his spirit rose,
and he would know what the good behavior was, and desired
the names of the jury, and a copy of all the proceedings, which
was granted him, and so he was dismissed at present.

The contention continuing between Mr. Cleves, deputy president of Ligonia[1] for Mr. Rigby, and Mr. Jocelin and other
commissioners of Sir Ferdinando Gorge, they both wrote letters
to the governor and council of the Massachusetts, complaining
of injuries from each other, and Mr. Cleves desiring aid for
his defence against open force threatened by the other part;
the governor and magistrates returned answer to them severally, to this effect, to persuade them both to continue in peace,
and to forbear all violent courses until some London ships
should arrive here, by which it was expected that order would
come from the commissioners for the colonies, etc., to settle
their differences. These letters prevailed so far with them, as
they agreed to refer the cause to the determination of the court
of assistants at Boston, which was to be held 3 (4) (*June* 3),
next. For Mr. Rigby came Mr. Cleves and Mr. Tucker; for the
province of Maine came Mr. Jocelin and Mr. Roberts. The
court appointed them a day for hearing their cause, and caused
a special jury to be empannelled. Mr. Cleves was plaintiff,
and delivered in a declaration in writing. The defendants

[1] This was the Plough Patent, often referred to.

(though they had a copy thereof before) pleaded to it by word only. Some of the magistrates advised not to intermeddle in it, seeing it was not within our jurisdiction, and that the agents had no commission to bind the interest of the gentlemen in England. Others (and the most) thought fit to give them a trial, both for that it was a usual practice in Europe for two states being at odds to make a third judge between them, and though the principal parties could not be bound by any sentence of this court, (for having no jurisdiction, we had no coercion, and therefore whatever we should conclude was but advice,) yet it might settle peace for the present, etc. Upon a full hearing, both parties failed in their proof. The plaintiff could not prove the place in question to be within his patent, nor could derive a good title of the patent itself to Mr. Rigby, (there being six or eight patentees, and the assignment only from two of them). Also the defendant had no patent of the province, but only a copy thereof attested by witnesses, which was not pleadable in law. Which so perplexed the jury, as they could find for neither, but gave in a non liquet. And because the parties would have it tried by a jury, the magistrates forbore to deal any further in it. Only they persuaded the parties to live in peace, etc., till the matter might be determined by authority out of England.

This spring was more early and seasonable than many before it, yet many were taken with a malignant fever, whereof some died in five or six days, but if they escaped the eighth they recovered; and divers of the churches sought the Lord by public humiliation, and the Lord was entreated, so as about the middle of the third month it ceased. It swept away some precious ones amongst us, especially one Mr. John Oliver, a gracious young man, not full thirty years of age, an expert soldier, an excellent surveyor of land, and one who, for the sweetness of his disposition and usefulness through a public spirit, was generally beloved, and greatly lamented. For some few years past he had given up himself to the ministry of the gospel, and was become very hopeful that way, (being a good scholar and of able gifts otherwise, and had exercised publicly for two years).

There fell out also a loathsome disease at Boston, which raised a scandal upon the town and country, though without just cause. One of the town [*blank*] having gone cooper in a ship into [*blank*], at his return his wife was infected with lues venerea, which appeared thus: being delivered of a child, and nothing then appearing, but the midwife, a skilful woman, finding her body as sound as any other, after her delivery, she had a sore breast, whereupon divers neighbors resorting to her, some of them drew her breast, and others suffered their children to draw her, and others let her child suck them, (no such disease being suspected by any,) by occasion whereof about sixteen persons, men, women, and children, were infected, whereby it came at length to be discovered by such in the town as had skill in physic and surgery, but there was not any in the country who had been practised in that cure. But (see the good providence of God) at that very season there came by accident a young surgeon out of the West Indies, who had had experience of the right way of the cure of that disease. He took them in hand, and through the Lord's blessing recovered them all [*blank*] in a short time. And it was observed that although many did eat and drink and lodge in bed with those who were infected and had sores, etc., yet none took it of them, but by copulation or sucking. It was very doubtful how this disease came at first. The magistrates examined the husband and wife, but could find no dishonesty in either, nor any probable occasion how they should take it by any other, (and the husband was found to be free of it). So as it was concluded by some, that the woman was infected by the mixture of so many spirits of men and women as drew her breast, (for thence it began). But this is a question to be decided by physicians.

6. 3. (*May* 6.)] The court of elections was at Boston. Mr. Norris of Salem preached. Mr. Winthrop was chosen governor,

Mr. Dudley, (the last governor,) deputy governor, Mr. Endecott, serjeant major general, and he and Mr. Pelham, commissioners for the United Colonies.  The magistrates and
deputies had formerly chosen the commissioners, but the freemen, looking at them as general officers, would now choose them
themselves, and the rather because some of the deputies had
formerly been chosen to that office, which gave offence to our
confederates and to many among ourselves.  This court lasted
near three weeks, and was carried on with much peace and
good correspondency; and when the business was near ended,
the magistrates and deputies met, and concluded what remained, and so departed in much love.  The several committees for laws made return of their commissions, and brought
in many laws which were read over, and some of them scanned,
but finding much difficulty in digesting and agreeing them, and
the court having much other business, another committee was
chosen out of several parts of the jurisdiction in the vacancy of
the court, which was adjourned to 7 (8,) (*October* 7), to extract
out of the whole such as should be thought fit to be established,
and so to reduce them into one volume, to agree with such as
were already in force, etc.

The last year the court had imposed ten shillings upon
every butt of sack, etc., to be landed in our jurisdiction, and
this spring there came in four ships with sack, and landed
about 800 butts, but the merchants being much offended at the
impost, (having no intelligence of it before, for indeed there had
not been a due course taken to give notice thereof to foreign
parts,) after much debate, etc., the court remitted the one half
thereof for the present.  See after, four leaves.

Captain Bridges was sent by the commissioners the last year
to Monsieur D'Aulnay with the articles of peace ratified by
them, and with order to demand his confirmation of them
under his hand, wherein also was expressed our readiness that
all injuries, etc., of either part might be heard and composed in
due time and place, and the peace to be kept at the same time,

so as he would subscribe the same. Monsieur D'Aulnay entertained our messenger with all state and courtesy that he possibly could; but refused to subscribe the articles, until differences
were composed, and accordingly wrote back, that he perceived
our drift was to gain time, etc., whereas if our messenger had
been furnished with power to have treated with him, and conclude about the differences, he doubted not but all had been
agreed; for we should find, that it was more his honor which
he stood upon, than his benefit, therefore he would sit still till
the spring, expecting our answer herein, and would attempt
nothing against us until he heard from us.

The general court, taking this answer into consideration,
(and there not being opportunity for the commissioners to
meet in season, only they had been certified by letters of
Monsieur D'Aulnay's propositions, etc., and consented to a
course for hearing, etc.,) agreed to send the deputy governor,
Mr. Dudley, Mr. Hawthorne, and Major Denison,[1] with full
power to treat and determine, etc., and wrote a letter to him to
that end, (assenting to his desire for the place, viz. Penobscot
which they call Pentagoet) and referring the time also to him,
so it were in September. Some thought it would be dishonorable for us to go to him, and therefore would have had the
place to have been Pemaquid. But others were of a different
judgment, 1. for that he was lieutenant general to a great
prince; 2. being a man of a generous disposition, and valuing
his reputation above his profit, it was considered, that it would
be much to our advantage to treat with him in his own house.
This being agreed, a private committee was chosen to draw up
instructions, which were not to be imparted to the court, in
regard of secresy, (for we had found that D'Aulnay had intelligence of all our proceedings,) and the same committee had
orders to provide all things for the commissioners' voyage, and

[1] Daniel Dennison attained later to great distinctions, serving many years
as assistant and sergeant-major-general commanding the troops. He died in
1682.

to draw up their commission, etc., and it was ordered, that if the deputy governor (in regard of his age, being above 70) should not be fit for the voyage, then Mr. Bradstreet should supply his place.

One Mr. William Vassall, sometimes one of the assistants of the Massachusetts, but now of Scituate in Plymouth jurisdiction, a man of a busy and factious spirit, and always opposite to the civil governments of this country and the way of our churches, had practised with such as were not members of our churches to take some course, first by petitioning the courts of the Massachusetts and of Plymouth, and (if that succeeded not) then to the parliament of England, that the distinctions which were maintained here, both in civil and church estate, might be taken away, and that we might be wholly governed by the laws of England; and accordingly a petition was drawn up to the parliament, pretending that they being freeborn subjects of England, were denied the liberty of subjects, both in church and commonwealth, themselves and their children debarred from the seals of the covenant, except they would submit to such a way of entrance and church covenant, as their consciences could not admit, and take such a civil oath as would not stand with their oath of allegiance, or else they must be deprived of all power and interest in civil affairs, and were subjected to an arbitrary government and extrajudicial proceedings, etc.   And now at this court at Boston a petition to the same effect, much enlarged, was delivered in to the deputies under the hands of Doctor Childe, Mr. Thomas Fowle, Mr. Samuel Maverick, Mr. Thomas Burton, Mr. John Smith, Mr. David Yale, and Mr. John Dand, in the name of themselves and many others in the country, whereto they pressed to have present answer.   But the court being then near at an end, and the matter being very weighty, they referred the further consideration thereof to the next session. And whereas a law was drawn up, and ready to pass, for allowing non-freemen equal power with the freemen in all town affairs, and to some freemen of such estate, etc., their votes in election of magistrates, it was thought fit to defer this also to the next session.[1]

4. (*June.*)]  The Narragansetts having broken their covenants with us in three days of payment, so as there was now due to us above 1300 fathom of wampom, they now sent us to Boston to the value of 100 fathom, (the most in old kettles,) excusing themselves by their poverty and by the Nianticks and others failing to contribute their parts.  But the commissioners (who were then two of them at Boston) refused to accept so small a sum, and rebuking them sharply for breaking their covenants both in their payments [and] other acts, told them that if they were forced to fetch the rest, they could as well fetch this.  So they sold their kettles to a brazier in Boston, and left the pay in his hands for us, if we would accept it, when they should bring the rest.

One Captain Cromwell (about ten years since a common seaman in the Massachusetts) had been out with Captain Jackson in a man of war by commission from the Earl of Warwick divers years, and having a commission of deputation from his said captain, had taken four or five Spanish vessels, and in some of them great riches, and being bound hither with three ships, and about eighty men, (they were frigates of cedar wood of about sixty and eighty tons,) by a strong northwest wind they were forced into Plymouth, (divine providence so directing for the comfort and help of that town, which was now almost deserted,) where they continued about fourteen days or more, and spent liberally and gave freely to many of the poorer sort.[2] It fell out, while they were there, that a desperate drunken fellow, one Voysye, (who had been in continual quarrels all the voyage,) on being reproved by his captain, offered to draw his

---

[1] An effort for freedom, brave and well-justified.  The theocracy gave abundant occasion for such a petition.  Several of the men who presented it we know to have been most respectable.

[2] The episode is narrated by Bradford, on almost the last page of his history.

rapier at him, whereupon the captain took it from him, and giving him some blows with it, as it was in the scabbard, he threw it away; Voysye gate it again, and came up to his captain, who taking it from him again, and throwing it away, when he could not make him to leave his weapon, nor forbear his insolent behavior, he gave him a blow on the forehead with the hilt of it, which made a small wound, which the captain would presently to have been searched and dressed, but Voysye refused, and the next day went into the field to fight with another of his fellows, but their weapons being taken from them, no hurt was done; and the next day after, his wound putrifying immediately, he died.   It was then the general court at Plymouth, and a jury being empannelled, they found that he died of the wound received from the captain, where-upon the captain was sent for on shore.   He offered to put himself upon trial, so as he might not be imprisoned, and that he might be tried by a council of war, both which were granted him, and one of Plymouth, one of their chief men, but no magistrate, undertook for him, body for body, and some of the magistrates and other military officers were chosen a coun-cil of war, who, upon the evidence, and sight of his commission, by which he had power of martial law, etc., acquitted him. The trained band accompanied the body to the grave, and the captain gave every one of them an eln of black taffeta for a mourning robe.   After this he came 10 (4,) (*June* 10) with his three ships to Boston, and presented the governor with a sedan, which (as he said) was sent by the viceroy of Mex-ico to his sister.   It was a very fair one, and could not be less worth than 50 pounds.   He and all his men had much money, and great store of plate and jewels of great value; yet he took up his lodging in a poor thatched house, and when he was offered the best in the town, his answer was, that in his mean estate that poor man entertained him, when others would not, and therefore he would not leave him now, when he might do him good.   He was ripped out of his mother's belly, and never sucked, nor saw father nor mother, nor they him.

At the last general court a bill was presented by some of the elders for a synod to be held in the end of the summer.  The magistrates passed it, but the deputies sending some of themselves to confer with the magistrates about it, their objections were these, first, because therein civil authority did require the churches to send their messengers to it, and divers among them were not satisfied of any such power given by Christ to the civil magistrate over the churches in such cases; secondly, whereas the main end of the synod was propounded to be, an agreement upon one uniform practice in all the churches, the same to be commended to the general court, etc., this seemed to give power either to the synod or the court to compel the churches to practise what should so be established.  To these it was answered, 1. that the civil magistrate had power upon just occasion to require the churches to send their messengers to advise in such ecclesiastical matters, either of doctrine or discipline, as the magistrate was bound by God to maintain the churches in purity and truth in (which was assented unto;) 2. that the end of the synod was not to proceed by way of power, but only of counsel from the word of God, and the court was at liberty either to establish or disannul such agreement of the synod, as they should see cause, which could put no more power into the court's hands than it had by the word of God and our own Laws and Liberties established in that case.  Whereupon it was ordered, that howsoever the civil magistrate had authority to call a synod when they saw it needful, yet in tender respect of such as were not yet fully satisfied in that point, the ensuing synod should be convened by way of motion only to the churches, and not by any words of command.[1] . . . .

A petition was presented to the court under many hands for the continuance of the two laws against anabaptists and other

[1] The careful avoidance of the Presbyterian way will be noticed here.

heretics, which was done in reference to a petition presented at the former court concerning the same laws.[1]

A plantation was this year begun at Pequod river by Mr. John Winthrop, junr., Mr. Thomas Peter, a minister, (brother to Mr. Peter of Salem,) and this court power was given to them two for ordering and governing the plantation till further order, etc., although it was uncertain whether it would fall within our jurisdiction or not, because they of Connecticut challenged it by virtue of a patent from the king, which was never showed us, so it was done de bene esse, quousque, etc., for it mattered not much to which jurisdiction it did belong, seeing the confederation made all as one; but it was of great concernment to have it planted, to be a curb to the Indians, etc.

Monsieur La Tour being returned from Newfoundland in a pinnace of Sir David Kirk, was (by some merchants of Boston) set forth in the same pinnace to the eastward with trading commodities to the value of 400 pounds. When he came at Cape Sable, (which was in the heart of winter,) he conspired with the master (being a stranger) and his own Frenchmen, being five, to go away with the vessel, and so forced out the other five English, (himself shooting one of them in the face with a pistol,) who, through special providence, having wandered up and down fifteen days, found some Indians who gave them a shallop, and victuals, and an Indian pilot. So they arrived safe at Boston in the third month. Whereby it appeared (as the scripture saith) that there is no confidence in an unfaithful or carnal man. Though tied with many strong bonds of courtesy, etc., he turned pirate, etc.

Mr. Lamberton, Mr. Grigson, and divers other godly persons, men and women, went from New Haven in the eleventh month last (*January*) in a ship of 80 tons, laden with wheat for

---

[1] A petition of a nature contrary to that mentioned a few pages back, and one which had more favor with the court. The *Records of Massachusetts*, II. 141, record a sharp rebuff to the liberals from the General Court.

London; but the ship was never heard of after. The loss was very great, to the value of some 1000 pounds; but the loss of the persons was very deplorable.

Monsieur D'Aulnay, having received our letter, returned answer, that he saw now that we seriously desired peace, which he (for his part) did also, and that he accounted himself so highly honored, that we would send such principal men of ours home to him, etc., that he desired this favor of us, that he might spare us that labor, for which purpose he would send two or three of his to us to Boston about the end of August, to treat and determine, etc. Upon receipt of this letter, the governor thought it expedient to call the general court (if it were but for one day) to have considered of commissioners to treat with his here, for he conceived that those who were invited to treat at Penobscot had not power to treat at home, and besides the court had declared their mind not to have chosen all these three, if they had been to have treated at home. But some other of the magistrates differing, he deferred it, and the harvest coming on, it was thought better to let it alone.

One Smith of Watertown had a son about five years old, who fell into the river near the mill gate, and was carried by the stream under the wheel, and taken up on the other side, without any harm. One of the boards of the wheel was fallen off, and it seems (by special providence) he was carried through under that gap, for otherwise if an eel pass through, it is cut asunder. The miller perceived his wheel to check on the sudden, which made him look out, and so he found the child sitting up to the waist in the shallow water beneath the mill.

5. (*July.*)] Three of our elders, viz., Mr. Mather, Mr. Allen and Mr. Eliot, took with them an interpreter, and went to the place where Cutshamekin, the Indian sachem [*blank*].

A daughter of Mrs. Hutchinson was carried away by the Indians near the Dutch, when her mother and others were killed by them; and upon the peace concluded between the

Dutch and the same Indians, she was returned to the Dutch governor, who restored her to her friends here.   She was about eight years old, when she was taken, and continued with them about four years, and she had forgot her own language, and all her friends, and was loath to have come from the Indians.[1]

Great harm was done in corn (especially wheat and barley) in this month by a caterpillar, like a black worm about an inch and a half long.   They eat up first the blades of the stalk, then they eat up the tassels, whereupon the ear withered.   It was believed by divers good observers, that they fell in a great thunder shower, for divers yards and other bare places, where not one of them was to be seen an hour before, were presently after the shower almost covered with them, besides grass places where they were not so easily discerned.   They did the most harm in the southern parts, as Rhode Island, etc., and in the eastern parts in their Indian corn.   In divers places the churches kept a day of humiliation, and presently after the caterpillars vanished away.[2]

The court had made an order in (8) (*October*) last, for ten shillings to be paid upon every butt of Spanish wine landed, etc., and now this spring arrived divers English ships, which brought about 800 butts; but having lost much by leakage, and coming to a bad market, they were very unwilling to pay the impost, and refused to give in an invoice of such wines as they had landed, whereupon they were forfeited by the order.   But upon their petition the general court remitted the forfeiture and half the impost, (in regard the order was made so lately as they could not have notice of it in those parts from whence the wines came,) but this notwithstanding, they would not submit to the order, so as the auditor who had the charge of receiving the said impost was forced to break open the cellar doors where their wines lay, and took out of the best wines for the impost,

---

[1] She became reconciled, married in 1651 John Cole, and left descendants.

[2] To one who examines the manuscript, the success of the transcription here will seem remarkable.   No page better illustrates Savage's painstaking accuracy.

which by the order he might do.   But this also they took as a
great injury, because their best wines being gone, the sale of
the rest was much hindered, and they threatened to get recompense some other way.

The merchants of New Haven had purchased some land of
the Indians about thirty miles to the northwest of them upon
Pautucket river, and had set up a trading house.[1]   The Dutch
governor made a protest against it, and sent it to Mr. Eaton,
claiming the place to be theirs, and within ten Dutch miles of
Fort Orange.   Mr. Eaton answered the protest, acknowledging
no right in the Dutch, but alleging their purchase and offering
to refer the cause, etc.   The Dutch governor by letter complained of it to the governor of Massachusetts, and also of Mr.
Whiting for saying that the English were fools in suffering
the Dutch in the centre, etc.   The governor of Massachusetts
informed Mr. Eaton hereof, (the commissioners being then to
meet at New Haven,) and tendered it to their consideration,
if it would not be expedient to call Mr. Whiting (then a magistrate at Hartford) to give account of these speeches, seeing the
Dutch would expect satisfaction, etc.

When the time of the synod drew near, it was propounded
to the churches.   The order was sent to the churches within
this jurisdiction; and to the churches in other jurisdictions a
letter was sent withal.

All the churches in this jurisdiction sent their messengers,
except Boston, Salem, Hingham, Concord [blank].   Concord
would have sent, if their elder had been able to come, or if
they had had any other whom they had judged fit, etc.   Boston and Salem took offence at the order of court, 1. Because
by a grant in the Liberties the elders had liberty to assemble
without the compliance of the civil authority, 2. It was
reported, that this motion came originally from some of the
elders, and not from the court, 3. In the order was expressed,
that what the major part of the assembly should agree upon

[1] Probably at the junction of the Naugatuck with the Housatonic.

should be presented to the court, that they might give such allowance to it as should be meet, hence was inferred that this synod was appointed by the elders, to the intent to make ecclesiastical laws to bind the churches, and to have the sanction of the civil authority put upon them, whereby men should be forced under penalty to submit to them, whereupon they concluded that they should betray the liberty of the churches, if they should consent to such a synod. The principal men who raised these objections were some of Boston, who came lately from England, where such a vast liberty was allowed, and sought for by all that went under the name of Independents, not only the anabaptists, antinomians, familists, seekers, etc., but even the most godly and orthodox, as Mr. Goodwin, Mr. Nye, Mr. Burrows, etc., who in the assembly there had stood in opposition to the presbytery, and also the greater part of the house of commons, who by their commissioners had sent order to all English plantations in the West Indies and Summers Islands, that all men should enjoy their liberty of conscience, and had by letters intimated the same to us. To these did some others of the church of Boston adhere, but not above thirty or forty in all.[1]

1. To the particular objections, it was thus answered, viz., to the first, that that liberty was granted only for a help in case of extremity, if, in time to come, the civil authority should either grow opposite to the churches, or neglect the care of them, and not with any intent to practise the same, while the civil authority were nursing fathers to the churches. For the second, that it was not for the churches to inquire, what or who gave the court occasion to call the synod, but if they thought fit to desire the churches to afford them help of council in any matters which concerned religion and conscience, it was the churches' duty to yield it to them; for so far as it concerns their command or request it is an ordinance of man,

---

[1] The tolerant spirit of their brethren in England, the Independents, was becoming a trial to the New Englanders.

which we are to submit unto for the Lord's sake, without troubling ourselves with the occasion or success. Ex malis moribus bonae leges: the laws are not the worse by being occasioned by evil men and evil manners. 3. Where the order speaks of the major part of the assembly, it speaks in its own language, and according to the court's practice, where the act of the major part is the act of the court; but it never intended thereby to restrain or direct the synod in the manner of their proceeding, nor to hinder them but that they might first acquaint the churches with their conclusions, and have their assent to them before they did present them to the court, for that is their care; the court's care was only to provide for their own cognizance. And for that inference which is drawn from that clause, that the court might give them such allowance as should be meet, it is without rule, and against the rule of charity, to infer from thence any such sanction of the court as is supposed. For if they say only they will give them such allowance as is meet, it cannot be inferred, that they will put any such sanction or stamp of authority upon them, as should be unmeet.

Two Lord's days the agitation was in Boston, and no conclusion made, by reason of the opposite party. So the elders sate down much grieved in spirit, yet told the congregation, that they thought it their duty to go notwithstanding, not as sent by the church, but as specially called by the order of court.

The assembly or synod being met at Cambridge, 1 (7) (*September* 1), they wrote letters to the elders and brethren of the church of Boston, inviting them and pressing them also by arguments to send their elders and other messengers. Upon this, the ruling elders, being at home, assembled so many of the church, as they could upon the sudden, but the greater part being from home, and divers of those who were met still opposing, nothing could be done.

The next day was Boston lecture, to which most of the synod repaired, and Mr. Norton, teacher of the church of Ipswich, being procured to supply the place, took his text suitable to the occasion, viz., of Moses and Aaron meeting in the mount and kissing each other, where he laid down the nature and power of the synod, as only consultative, decisive, and declarative, not coactive, etc.  He showed also the power of the civil magistrate in calling such assemblies, and the duty of the churches in yielding obedience to the same.  He showed also the great offence and scandal which would be given in refusing, etc.  The next Lord's day the matter was moved again, in three propositions; 1. Whether the church would hold communion with the other churches, etc., and desired them to express it by holding up their hands, which most of the church did, but some of the opposite party resisted and gave this reason, that though they did assent to the proposition, yet they could not vote it, because they knew not what would be inferred upon it; upon this the second proposition was mentioned, viz., whether they would exercise this communion in sending messengers to the synod, and if not, then the third proposition was, whether the church would then go themselves.

Exception was taken at this way of doing a church act by the major part, which had not been our practice in former times. To this it was answered, that in some cases (as the choice of officers, etc.) it is needful to have every man's consent but in other cases, as admission of a member, etc., it was sufficient, if the major part assented; and for this practice of proceeding by erection of hands that in [2] Cor. [viii. 19] was alleged, where the Greek word $\chi\epsilon\iota\rho o[\tau o\nu\eta\theta\epsilon\iota s]$ signifies the same.  And in the present case, it was necessary, because the order of court, and the letters of the synod to us, required (both in duty and civility) that the church should return answer, which the minor part could not do, therefore the major part (of necessity) must.

Then it was moved by some, that the third proposition might rather be intended and the church agree to go to the synod, rather than to send.  To this it was answered, 1. That it would not be convenient nor of good report, to go in a singular way; 2. It would savor of disorder and tumult; 3. It might produce an impossibility, for if one man's conscience should bind him to attend, so might another man's, and then as well might every man's, and if all (or but the major part of our church) should go thither, it were almost impossible any business could proceed in due order. In the end it was agreed by vote of the major part, that the elders and three of the brethren should be sent as messengers, etc.

The synod brake up and was adjourned to 8 (4) (*June* 8), having continued but about fourteen days, in regard of winter drawing on, and few of the elders of other colonies were present.

Gorton and two others of his company, viz., John Greene and Randall Holden, going into England, complained to the commissioners for Plantations, etc., against us, etc., who gave order, that some of ours then in England should be summoned to answer their petition; whereupon some appeared, but they having no instructions about the case, and the writings sent over to Mr. Welde the year before being either lost or forgotten, so as a full answer could not be given in the particular, and the petitioners being favored by some of the commissioners, partly for private respects, and partly for their adhering to some of their corrupt tenets, and generally out of their dislike of us for our late law for banishing anabaptists, they seemed to be much offended with us for our rigorous proceeding (as they called it) against them, and thereupon (without sending to us to hear our answer, etc.) they gave them this order following:—

> By the governor in chief Lord high admiral and. commissioners appointed by parliament for the English plantations in America.
>
> Whereas we have thought fit to give an order for Mr. Samuel Gorton, Mr. Randall Holden, Mr. John Greene, and others, late inhabitants of a tract of land called the Narragansett Bay, near the Massachusetts Bay in New England, to return with freedom to the said tract of land, and there to inhabit and

abide without interruption, these are therefore to pray and require you, and all others whom this may concern, to permit and suffer the said Samuel Gorton, etc., with their company, goods and necessaries carried with them out of England, to land at any port in New England, where the ship wherein they do embark themselves shall arrive, and from thence to pass, without any of your lets or molestations, through any part of the continent of America, within your jurisdiction, to the said tract of land called Narragansett Bay, or any part thereof, they carrying themselves without offence, and paying according to the custom of the country, and their contract, for all things they shall make use of in their way, for victuals, carriage, or other accommodation.  Hereof you may not fail; and this shall be your warrant.  Dated at Westminster this 15 of May.

To the governor and assistants of the English plantation in the Massachusetts Bay in New England, and to all other governors and other inhabitants of New England, and all others whom this may concern.

NOTTINGHAM,
FRA. DACRE,
FER. RIGBY,
COR. HOLLAND,
SAM. VASSALL,
GEO. FENWICK,
FRAN. ALLEIN,
WM. PUREFOY,
GEO. SNELLING.[1]

13. (7.) (*September* 13.)]  Randall Holden arrived here in a London ship, Captain Wall master, and sent this order to the governor to desire leave to land, etc.  Accordingly the governor answered, that he could not give him leave of himself, nor dispense with an order of the general court; but the council were to meet within two or three days, and he would impart it unto them, etc., and in the mean time he would not seek after him, etc.

The council being met, they were of different judgments in the case, so as they agreed to take the advice of such of the elders as were then met at the lecture at Boston (being about

[1] The rift opening here between the Congregationalists of England and America was indeed serious.  It is indicated in the margin of the manuscript that the document bore the seal of the Earl of Warwick as governor and admiral.

ten). The elders also differed, some were very earnest for his commitment till the general court, etc. But the greater part, both of magistrates and elders, thought it better to give so much respect to the protection which the parliament had given him, (and whereupon he adventured his life, etc.,) as to suffer him to pass quietly away, and when the general court should be assembled, (which would be within a month,) then to consider further about their repossessing the land they claimed.

20. (7.) (*September* 20.)] Being the Lord's day, and the people ready to go to the assembly after dinner, Monsieur Marie and Monsieur Louis, with Monsieur D'Aulnay his secretary, arrived at Boston in a small pinnace, and major Gibbons sent two of his chief officers to meet them at the water side, who conducted them to their lodgings sine strepitu. The public worship being ended, the governor repaired home, and sent major Gibbons, with other gentlemen, with a guard of musketeers to attend them to the governor's house, who, meeting them without his door, carried them into his house, where they were entertained with wine and sweetmeats, and after a while he accompanied them to their lodgings (being the house of major Gibbons, where they were entertained that night). The next morning they repaired to the governor, and delivered him their commission, which was in form of a letter directed to the governor and magistrates. It was open, but had a seal only let into the paper with a label. Their diet was provided at the ordinary, where the magistrates use to diet in court times; and the governor accompanied them always at meals. Their manner was to repair to the governor's house every morning about eight of the clock, who accompanied them to the place of meeting; and at night either himself or some of the commissioners accompanied them to their lodging. It was the third day at noon before our commissioners could come together. When they were met, they propounded great injuries and damages, sustained by Captain Hawkins and our men, in assistance of La Tour. and would have engaged our govern-

ment therein. We denied that we had any hand, either by
commission or permission, in that action. We only gave way
to La Tour to hire assistance to conduct his ship home, according to the request made to us in the commission of the vice
admiral of France. And for that which was done by our men
beyond our commission, we showed Monsieur D'Aulnay's letter
to our governor, by Captain Bayley, wherein he writes, that
the king of France had laid all the blame upon the vice admiral,
and commanded him not to break with us, upon that occasion.
We also alleged the peace formerly concluded without any
reservation of those things. They replied, that howsoever the
king of France had remitted his own interest, yet he had not
nor intended to deprive Monsieur D'Aulnay of his private satisfaction. Here they did stick two days. Their commissioners
alleged damages to the value of 8000 pounds, but did not stand
upon the value. They would have accepted of very small
satisfaction, if we would have acknowledged any guilt in our
government. In the end they came to this conclusion: we
accepted their commissioner's answer, in satisfaction of those
things we had charged upon Monsieur D'Aulnay, and they
accepted our answer for clearing our government of what he
had charged upon us; and because we could not free Captain
Hawkins and the other voluntaries of what they had done, we
were to send a small present to Monsieur D'Aulnay in satisfaction of that, and so all injuries and demands to be remitted,
and so a final peace to be concluded. Accordingly we sent
Monsieur D'Aulnay by his commissioners a very fair new
sedan, (worth forty or fifty pounds where it was made, but of
no use to us,) sent by the viceroy of Mexico to a lady his sister,
and taken in the West Indies by Captain Cromwell, and by
him given to our governor.[1] This the commissioners very well
accepted; and so the agreement being signed in several instru-
ments, by the commissioners of both parts, on 28 day of the
same month, they took leave and departed to their pinnace, the

---

[1] See *ante*, p. 273.

governor and our commissioners accompanying them to their boat, attended with a guard of musketeers, and gave them five guns from Boston, three from Charlestown, and five from Castle Island, and we sent them aboard a quarter cask of sack and some mutton. They answered all our salutations with such small pieces as they had, and so set sail, major Sedgwick and some other gentlemen accompanying them as far as Castle Island. The Lord's day they were here, the governor, acquainting them with our manner, that all men either come to our public meetings, or keep themselves quiet in their houses, and finding that the place where they lodged would not be convenient for them that day, invited them home to his house, where they continued private all that day until sunset, and made use of such books, Latin and French, as he had, and the liberty of a private walk in his garden, and so gave no offence, etc. The two first days after their arrival their pinnace kept up her flag in the main top, which gave offence both to the Londoners who rode in the harbor and also to our own people, whereupon Monsieur Marie was put in mind of it. At first he excused it by a general custom for the king's ships, both French, English, and Dutch, etc., to use it in all places; but being now under our government, if we would so command, he would cause [it] to be taken down. We desired him not [to] put us to that, but seeing he knew our minds he would do it of himself. Whereupon he gave order to have it taken down.

There fell a sad affliction upon the country this year, though it more particularly concerned New Haven and those parts. A small ship of about 100 tons set out from New Haven in the middle of the eleventh month last (the harbor there being so frozen, as they were forced to hew her through the ice near three miles). She was laden with pease and some wheat, all in bulk, with about 200 West India hides, and store of beaver, and plate, so as it was estimated in all at 5000 pounds. There were in her about seventy persons, whereof divers were of very precious account, as Mr. Grigson, one of their magistrates, the wife of Mr. Goodyear, another of their magistrates, (a right godly woman,) Captain Turner, Mr. Lamberton, master of the ship, and some seven or eight others, members of the church there. The ship never went voyage before, and was very crank-sided, so as it was conceived, she was overset in a great tempest, which happened soon after she put to sea, for she was never heard of after.

7. (*September*.)] Some few families being gone to the new plantation at Pequod,[1] some of them kept in the Indians' wigwams there, while their own houses were building. Some of these Indians, accompanied with some English, went to hunt deer, Unkas, the Moheagen sachem, pretending they had hunted in his limits, came with 300 men, and set upon them, and beat some of the Indians, and took away some of their goods, putting them by force out of their wigwams, where the English kept. Complaint being made hereof to the commissioners, (who were then met at New Haven,) they sent for Unkas, and charged him with this outrage, etc. He confessed he had done very ill, and said, he thought he was mad; so he promised to go to the English there, and acknowledge his offence, and make full satisfaction, and for time to come, would live peaceably with them, etc.

The merchants of New Haven had set up a trading house upon a small river some thirty miles up into the country, and some fifty miles from fort Orange. The Dutch governor hearing thereof, sent a protest there against it, claiming the place to be in New Netherland. Mr. Eaton returned answer by the same messenger.

A woman of the church of Weymouth being cast out for some distempered speeches, by a major party, (the ruling elder and a minor party being unsatisfied therein,) her husband complained to the synod, which being then ready to break up, could do nothing in it, but only acquainted the pastor therewith privately. Whereupon complaint was made to the elders of the neighboring churches, and request made to them to

[1] The Thames River.

come to Weymouth and to mediate a reconciliation. The elders acquainted their churches with it. Some scrupled the warrantableness of the course, seeing the major party of the church did not send to the churches for advice. It was answered, that it was not to be expected, that the major party would complain of their own act, and if the minor party, or the party grieved, should not be heard, then God should have left no means of redress in such a case, which could not be. Some of the churches approved their going; the rest permitted it. So they went, and the church of Weymouth, having notice before hand, gave them a meeting, and first demanded, whether they were sent by their churches or not. Being certified, as before, they objected this, that except they had been sent by their churches, they should never know when they had done, for others might come still, and require like satisfaction, etc. It was answered, the like objection would lie, if the churches had sent, for other churches might yet have required, etc., but they came not in way of authority, but only of brotherly communion, and therefore impose nothing upon them, but only to give their advice as occasion should require. This and some other scruples being removed, the church consented to have the cause heard, and opened from the beginning, whereupon some failing was found in both parties, the woman had not given so full satisfaction as she ought to have done, and the major party of the church had proceeded too hastily against a considerable party of the dissenting brethren, whereupon the woman who had offended was convinced of her failing, and bewailed it with many tears, the major party also acknowledged their error, and gave the elders thanks for their care and pains.

7. (*September*.)] One William Waldron, a member of the church of Dover upon Pascataquack, (received into the church in the corrupt beginning of it,) a man given to drunkenness and contention, being after cast out, and upon some formal repentance received in again, being also a good clerk, and a subtle man, was made their recorder, and also recorder of the

province of Maine under Sir Ferdinando Gorge, and returning from Saco about the end of September alone, passing over a small river at Kennebunk, was there drowned, and his body not found until near a month after.

(8.) (*October*) 17.]   A ship of 300 tons, built at Boston, was this day launched.

(9.) (*November*) 4.]   The general court (being adjourned from (8) began again, and that night was a most dreadful tempest at northeast with wind and rain, in which the lady Moodye her house at Salem, being but one story in height, and a flat roof with a brick chimney in the midst, had the roof taken off in two parts (with the top of the chimney) and carried six or seven rods off.   Also one Cross of Connecticut had his pinnace cast away in Narragansett Bay, but the men and goods saved.   Mr. Haines, etc., taken in this tempest half way from Connecticut, and by providence brought casually in the night to an empty wigwam, where they found fire kindled, and room for themselves and horses, else had perished.

This court the business of Gorton, etc., and of the petitioners, Dr. Child, etc., were taken into consideration, and it was thought needful to send some able man into England, with commission and instructions, to satisfy the commissioners for plantations about those complaints; and because it was a matter of so great and general concernment, such of the elders as could be had were sent for, to have their advice in the matter. Mr. Hubbard of Hingham came with the rest, but the court being informed that he had an hand in a petition, which Mr. Vassall carried into England against the country in general, the governor propounded, that if any elder present had any such hand, etc., he would withdraw himself.   Mr. Hubbard sitting still a good space, and no man speaking, one of the deputies informed the court, that Mr. Hubbard was the man suspected, whereupon he arose, and said, that he knew nothing of any such petition.   The governor replied, that seeing he was now named, he must needs deliver his mind about him, which

was, that although they had no proof present about the
matter of the petition, and therefore his denial was a sufficient
clearing, etc., yet in regard he had so much opposed authority,
and offered such contempt to it, as for which he had been
lately bound to his good behavior, he thought he would
(in discretion) withdraw himself, etc., whereupon he went out.
Then the governor put the court in mind of a great miscarriage, in that our secretest counsels were presently known
abroad, which could not be but by some among ourselves, and
desired them to look at it as a matter of great unfaithfulness,
and that our present consultations might be kept in the breast
of the court, and not be divulged abroad, as others had been.

Then it was propounded to consideration, in what relation
we stood to the state of England; whether our government was
founded upon our charter, or not; if so, then what subjection
we owed to that state. The magistrates delivered their minds
first, that the elders might have the better light for their advice.
All agreed that our charter was the foundation of our government, and thereupon some thought, that we were so subordi-
nate to the parliament, as they might countermand our orders
and judgments, etc., and therefore advised, that we should petition the parliament for enlargement of power, etc. Others
conceived otherwise, and that though we owed allegiance and
subjection to them, as we had always professed, and by a copy
of a petition which we presented to the lords of the privy
council when they sent for our charter anno [blank] then read
in the court, did appear, yet by our charter we had absolute
power of government; for thereby we have power to make
laws, to erect all sorts of magistracy, to correct, punish, pardon,
govern, and rule the people absolutely, which word implies two
things, 1. a perfection of parts, so as we are thereby furnished
with all parts of government, 2. it implies a self-sufficiency,
quoad subjectam materiam, and ergo should not need the help
of any superior power, either general governor, or, etc., to
complete our government; yet we did owe allegiance and sub-

jection, 1. because our commonwealth was founded upon the power of that state, and so had been always carried on, 2. in regard of the tenure of our lands, of the manor of East Greenwich, 3. we depended upon them for protection, etc., 4. for advice and counsel, when in great occasions we should crave it, 5. in the continuance of naturalization and free liegeance of ourselves and our posterity.   Yet we might be still independent in respect of government, as Normandy, Gascoyne, etc., were, though they had dependence upon the crown of France, and the kings of England did homage, etc., yet in point of government they were not dependent upon France.  So likewise Burgundy, Flanders, etc.  So the Hanse Towns in Germany, which have dependence upon the empire, etc.  And such as are subject to the imperial chamber, in some great and general causes, they had their deputies there, and so were parties to all orders there.[1]

And for that motion of petitioning, etc., it was answered, 1. that if we receive a new charter, that will be (ipso facto) a surrender of the old, 2. the parliament can grant none now, but by way of ordinance, and it may be questioned, whether the king will give his royal assent, considering how he hath taken displeasure against us, 3. if we take a charter from the parliament, we can expect no other than such as they have granted to us at Narragansett, and to others in other places, wherein they reserve a supreme power in all things.

The court having delivered their opinions, the elders desired time of consideration, and the next day they presented their advice, which was delivered by Mr. Allen, pastor of the church in Dedham, in divers articles, which (upon request) they delivered in writing as followeth.  But first I should have mentioned the order of the commissioners, sent to us in the

[1] These early discussions of the proper relation of a dependency to the mother state are interesting.  The ideas from which came the American Revolution are plainly seen, and also those from which was evolved the present English colonial policy.

behalf of Gorton, which, together with their petition and declaration, were sent over to us by the commissioners.    The order
was in these words.


After our hearty commendations, we being specially entrusted by
both houses of parliament with ordering the affairs and government
of the English plantations in America, have some months since received
a complaint from Mr. Gorton and Mr. Holden, in the name of themselves
and divers others English, who have transported themselves into New
England, and now are or lately were inhabitants of a tract of land called
by the name of the Narragansett Bay, (a copy of which complaint the
inclosed petition and narrative will represent to your knowledge,) we
could not forthwith proceed to a full hearing and determination of the
matter, it not appearing unto us, that you were acquainted with the
particular charge, or that you had furnished any person with power to
make defence in your behalf, nor could we conveniently respite some kind
of resolution therein without a great prejudice to the petitioners, who
would have lain under much inconvenience, if we had detained them
from their families till all the formality and circumstances of proceeding
(necessary at this distance) had regularly prepared the cause for a hearing.
We shall therefore let you know in the first place, that our present resolution is not grounded upon an admittance of the truth of what is charged,
we knowing well how much God hath honored your government, and
believing that your spirits and affairs are acted by principles of justice,
prudence and zeal to God, and therefore cannot easily receive any evil
impressions concerning your proceedings.    In the next place, you may
take notice, that we found the petitioners' aim and desire, in the result of
it, was not so much a reparation for what past, as a settling their habita-
tion for the future under that government by a charter of civil incorporation which was heretofore granted them by ourselves.    We find withal
that the tract of land, called the Narragansett Bay, (concerning which
the question is arisen,) was divers years since inhabited by those of Providence, Portsmouth, and Newport, who are interested in the complaint, and
that the same is wholly without the bounds of the Massachusetts patent
granted by his majesty.    We have considered that they be English, and
that the forcing of them to find out new places of residence will be very
chargeable, difficult, and uncertain.

And therefore upon the whole matter do hereby pray and require
you to permit and suffer the petitioners and all the late inhabitants of
Narragansett Bay, with their families and such as shall hereafter join

with them, freely and quietly to live and plant upon Shawomett and such other parts of the said tract of land within the bounds mentioned in our said charter, on which they have formerly planted and lived, without extending your jurisdiction to any part thereof, or otherwise disquieting them in their consciences or civil peace, or interrupting them in their possession until such time as we shall have received your answer to their claim in point of title, and you shall thereupon have received our further order therein.

And in case any others, since the petitioners' address to England, have taken possession of any part of the lands heretofore enjoyed by the petitioners or any their associates, you are to cause them which are newly possessed, as aforesaid, to be removed, that this order may be fully performed. And till our further order neither the petitioners are to enlarge their plantations, nor are any others to be suffered to intrude upon any part of the Narragansett Bay.

And if they shall be found hereafter to abuse this favor by any act tending to disturb your right, we shall express a due sense thereof, so as to testify a care of your honor, protection, and encouragement.

In order to the effecting of this resolution, we do also require, that you do suffer the said Mr. Gorton, Mr. Holden, Mr. Greene, and their company, with their goods and necessaries, to pass through any part of that territory which is under your jurisdiction, toward the said tract of land, without molestation, they demeaning themselves civilly, any former sentence of expulsion or otherwise notwithstanding.

We shall only add that to these orders of ours we shall expect a conformity, not only from yourselves, but from all other governors and plantations in New England whom it may concern. And so commending you to God's gracious protection, we rest, your very loving friends.

From the governor in chief, Lord Admiral and Commissioners for foreign Plantations, sitting at Westminster, 15 May, 1646.

WARWICK, Governor and Admi. Jud.
NORTHUMBERLAND,
PEMBROKE AND MONTGOMERY,
NOTTINGHAM,
MANCHESTER,
FRA. DACRE,
SAM. VASSALL,
CORN. HOLLAND,
WM. WALLER,
WM. PUREFOY,
DENNIS BOND,
GEO. SNELLING,
BEN. RUDYER.

Upon this order one question was, whether we should give the commissioners their title, least thereby we should acknowledge all that power they claimed in our jurisdiction as well as in other plantations, which had not so large a charter as we. It was considered withal, that whatever answer or remonstrance we presented to them, if their stile were not observed, it was doubted they would not receive it.

The advice of the elders was as follows.

Concerning the question of our dependence upon England, we conceive,

1. That as we stand in near relation, so also in dependence upon that state, in divers respects, viz. 1. We have received the power of our government and other privileges, derived from thence by our charter. 2. We owe allegiance and fidelity to that state. 3. Erecting such a government as the patent prescribes and subjecting ourselves to the laws here ordained by that government, we therein yield subjection to the state of England. 4. We owe unto that state the fifth part of gold and silver ore that shall, etc. 5. We depend upon the state of England for protection and immunities of Englishmen, as free denization, etc.

2. We conceive, that in point of government we have granted by patent such full and ample power of choosing all officers that shall command and rule over us, of making all laws and rules of our obedience, and of a full and final determination of all cases in the administration of justice, that no appeals or other ways of interrupting our proceedings do lie against us.

3. Concerning our way of answering complaints against us in England, we conceive, that it doth not well suit with us, nor are we directly called thereto, to profess and plead our right and power, further than in a way of justification of our proceedings questioned, from the words of the patent. In which agitations and the issues thereof our agents shall discern the mind of the parliament towards us, which if it be propense and favorable, there may be a fit season to procure such countenance of our proceedings, and confirmation of our just power, as may prevent such unjust complaints and interruptions, as now disturb our administrations. But if the parliament should be less inclinable to us, we must wait upon providence for the preservation of our just liberties.

4. Furthermore we do not clearly discern, but that we may give the Earl of Warwick and the rest such titles as the parliament hath given them, without subjecting to them in point of our government.

5. Lastly we conceive that as the hazardous state of England, the case of the church of Bermuda, and so this weighty case of our liberties do call the churches to a solemn seeking of the Lord for the upholding of our state and disappointment of our adversaries.

The court had made choice of Mr. Edward Winslow, (one of the magistrates of Plymouth,) as a fit man to be employed in our present affairs in England, both in regard of his abilities of presence, speech, courage, and understanding, as also being well known to the commissioners, having suffered a few years before divers months imprisonment, by means of the last arch prelate, in the cause of New England. But it was now moved by one of the elders, to send one of our own magistrates and one of our elders. The motion and the reasons of it were well apprehended, so as the governor and Mr. Norton, teacher of the church in Ipswich, were named, and in a manner agreed upon; but upon second thoughts it was let fall, chiefly for these two reasons, 1. it was feared, in regard that Mr. Peter had written to the governor to come over and assist in the parliament's cause, etc., that if he were there, he would be called into the parliament, and so detained, 2. many were upon the wing, and his departure would occasion more new thoughts and apprehensions, etc. 3. it was feared what changes his absence might produce, etc.

The governor was very averse to a voyage into England, yet he declared himself ready to accept the service, if he should be called to it, though he were then fifty-nine years of age, wanting one month; but he was very glad when he saw the mind of the Lord to be otherwise.

The court conferred with the elders about the petition of Dr. Child, etc., also, for it had given great offence to many godly in the country, both elders and others, and some answers had been made to it, and presented to the court, out of which one entire answer had been framed, in way of declaration of the court's apprehension thereof, not by way of answer, because it was adjudged a contempt, which declaration was after pub-

lished.  The elders declared their opinion about it, but gave
no advice for censure, etc., leaving that to the court.

There was a ship then ready to set sail for England, wherein
Mr. Fowle (one of the petitioners) was to go, etc.  The court
therefore sent for him, and required an account of him about
it, before his departure, and also Mr. John Smith of Rhode
Island, being then in town, and they were both required to find
sureties to be responsal, etc., whereupon they were troubled,
and desired they might answer presently, in regard they were
to depart, taking exception also, that the rest of the petitioners
were not called as well as they.  Whereupon Dr. Child, etc.,
were sent for, and all appeared, save Mr. Maverick; and the
Dr. (being the chief speaker) demanded what should be laid to
their charge, seeing it was no offence to prefer a petition, etc.
It was answered, that they were not questioned for petitioning,
but for such miscarriages, etc., as appeared in their petition
and remonstrance.  The Doctor replied, desiring that they
might know their charge.  The court answered, they should
have it in due time; it was not ready at present, nor had they
called them then, had it not been, that some of them were
upon their departure, and therefore the court required sureties
for their forth coming, etc.  The Doctor, etc., still demanded
what offence they had committed, for which they should find
sureties, etc.  Upon this pressing, one clause in their petition
was read to them, which was this, our brethren of England's
just indignation against us, so as they fly from us as from a
pest, etc., whereby they lay a great scandal upon the country,
etc.  This was so clear as they could not evade it, but quarrelled
with the court, with high terms.  The Doctor said, they did
beneath themselves in petitioning to us, etc., and in conclusion
appealed to the commissioners in England.  The governor told
them, he would admit no appeal, nor was it allowed by our
charter, but by this it appeared what their aim was in their
petition; they complained of fear of perpetual slavery, etc.,
but their intent was, to make us slaves to them and such as

themselves were, and that by the parliament and commissioners, (meaning, by threatening us with their authority, or calum-
niating us to them, etc.). For ourselves, it was well known,
we did ever honor the parliament, and were ready to perform
all due obedience, etc., to them according to our charter, etc.
The court let them know, that they did take notice of their
contemptuous speeches and behavior, as should further
appear in due time. In conclusion Mr. Fowle and Mr. Smith
were committed to the marshal for want of sureties, and the
rest were enjoined to attend the court when they should be
called. So they were dismissed, and Mr. Fowle, etc. found
sureties before night, and were set at liberty.

A committee was appointed to examine the petition, and
out of it to draw a charge, which was done, as followeth:

The court doth charge Dr. Child, etc., with divers false and scandalous
passages in a certain paper, entitled a remonstrance and petition (exhibited by them to this court in the third month last) against the churches
of Christ and the civil government here established, derogating from the
honor and authority of the same, and tending to sedition, as in the particulars following will appear:

1. They take upon them to defame our government, and to control
both the wisdom of the state of England in the frame of our charter, and
also the wisdom and integrity of this court, in charging our government
to be an ill-compacted vessel.

2. They lay open the afflictions, which God hath pleased to exercise
us with, and that to the worst appearance, and impute it to the evil of
our government.

3. They charge us with manifest injury to a great part of the people
here, persuading them, that the liberties and privileges in our charter
belong to all freeborn Englishmen, inhabitants here; whereas they are
granted only to such as the governor and company shall think fit to
receive into that fellowship.

4. They closely insinuate into the minds of the people, that those
now in authority do intend to exercise unwarranted dominion and an
arbitrary government, such as is abominable to the parliament and that
party in England, thereby to make them slaves; and (to hide themselves) they pretend it to be the jealousies of others, and (which

tends to stir up commotion) they foretel them of intolerable bondage to ensue.

5. They go about to weaken the authority of our laws, and the reverence and esteem of them, and consequently their obedience to them, by persuading the people, that partly through want of the body of English laws, and partly through the insufficiency or ill frame of those we have, they can expect no sure enjoyment of their lives and liberties under them.

6. They falsely charge us with denying liberty of votes in such cases where we allow them, as in choice of military officers, which is common to the non-freemen with such as are free.

7. Their speeches tend to sedition, by insinuating into the people's minds, that there are many thousands secretly discontented at the government, etc., whereby those who indeed were so might be emboldened to discover themselves, and to attempt some innovation, in confidence of so many thousands to join with them, and so to kindle a great flame, the foretelling whereof is a chief means to kindle it.

8. They raise a false report and foul slander upon the discipline of our churches, and upon the civil government, by inferring that the frame and dispensation thereof are such, as godly, sober, peaceable, etc., men cannot live here like Christians, which they seem to conclude from hence, that they desire liberty to remove where they may live like Christians.

9. They do (in effect) charge this government with tyranny, in impressing their persons into the wars, committing them to prison, fining, rating, etc., and all unjustly and illegally.

10. They falsely charge and slander the people of God, in affirming that Christian vigilancy is no way exercised towards such as are not in church fellowship, whereas themselves know, and have had experience to the contrary. And if they had discerned any such failing, they ought first to have complained of it in private to the elders, or brethren of such churches where they have been so neglected, which (we may well think) they have not done, nor had any just cause thereof.

11. Having thrown all this dirt and shame upon our churches and government, etc., they endeavor to set it on, that it might stick fast, so as all men might undoubtedly be persuaded of the reality thereof, by proclaiming it in their conclusion, that our own brethren in England have just indignation against us for the same, which they labor to confirm by the effect thereof, viz. that for these evils amongst us, these our own brethren do fly from us as from a pest.

12. Lastly, that it may yet more clearly appear, that these evils and obliquities, which they charge upon our government, are not the mere jealousies of others, but their own apprehensions, (or pretences rather,)

they have publicly declared their disaffection thereto, in that, being called
by the court to render account of their misapprehensions and evil expressions in the premises, they refused to answer; but, by appealing from this
government, they disclaimed the jurisdiction thereof, before they knew
whether the court would give any sentence against them, or not.

Their petition being read, and this charge laid upon them,
in the open court, before a great assembly, they desired time to
make answer to it, which was granted.  And giving the court
notice that their answer was ready, they assembled again, and
before all the people caused their answer to be read, which was
large, and to little purpose, and the court replied to the particulars extempore, as they were read.  The substance both of
the answer and reply was, as followeth, with some little addition, which for want of time was then omitted.

Answer.  To the first they answer, that they termed these
plantations an ill-compacted vessel, 1. comparatively, in respect of our native country, 2. in regard of the paucity of
people, scattered, etc., 3. for diversity of judgments amongst
us, many being for presbyterial government, according to the
reformation in England, others opposing it; some freemen,
others not.  Differences there are also about bounds of colonies, patents, privileges, etc.

Reply.  To this was replied, 1. that the being of a thing,
talis, etc., lies in the perfection of parts, not degrees; a child of
a year old is as truly a man, and as well compact, as one of
sixty; a ship of forty tons may be as well compact a vessel,
as the *Royal Sovereign*.  And for the differences which are
amongst us, (through the Lord's mercy,) they are not either in
number or degree suitable to those in England, nor do they concern our esse or non esse; and those which are, are raised by
such discontented and unquiet spirits as these petitioners.

To the second they answer negatively, which needed no
reply, it being evident in their petition, that (though they speak
of our sins in general, yet) they chiefly impute them to our evil
government, etc.

Answer.  To the third, they deny the charge, but grant that the governor and company may have some peculiar privileges, as other corporations of England have, which corporation privileges, made for the most part for advancing mechanical professions, in some places are much slighted by the English gentry, unless in London and some great cities, because free-born privileges are far greater and more honorable, etc.

Reply.  To this it was replied, that we could not but take this as a scorn and slighting of us, (according to their former carriage,) allowing us no more than any ordinary corporation, and such privileges only as belong to mechanic men; but for greater and more gentile privileges, (as they term them,) those they would share in; and (which they impudently deny against the plain words of their petition) they would have all freeborn English to have as much right to them as the governor and company.

Answer.  To the fourth they answer as in their petition, and a reason they give of their fear of arbitrary government is, that some speeches and papers have been spread abroad for maintenance thereof, etc., and that a body of English laws have not been here established, nor any other not repugnant thereto.

Reply.  To this it was replied, 1. that the constant care and pains the court hath taken for establishing a body of laws, and that which hath been effected herein beyond any other plantation, will sufficiently clear our government from being arbitrary, and our intentions from any such disposition, 2. for the laws of England (though by our charter we are not bound to them, yet) our fundamentals are framed according to them, as will appear by our declaration, which is to be published upon this occasion, and the government of England itself is more arbitrary in their chancery and other courts than ours is, 3. because they would make men believe, that the want of the laws of England was such a grievance to them, they were pressed to show, what laws of England they wanted, and it was offered them, (before all the assembly, who were desired to bear witness of it,) that if they could produce any one law of England, the want whereof was a just grievance to them, the court would quit the cause, whereupon one of them instanced in a law used in London, (where he had been a citizen,) but that was easily taken away, by showing that that was only a bye-law, or peculiar custom of the city, and none of the common or general laws of England.

Answer. They answer negatively to the fifth, alleging that they only commend the laws of England as those they are best accustomed unto, etc., and therein they impudently and falsely affirm, that we are obliged to those laws by our general charter and oath of allegiance, and that without those laws, or others no way repugnant to them, they could not clearly see a certainty of enjoying their lives, liberties, and estates, etc., according to their due natural rights, as freeborn English, etc.

Reply. To this it was replied, that they charge us with breach of our charter and of our oaths of allegiance, whereas our allegiance binds us not to the laws of England any longer than while we live in England, for the laws of the parliament of England reach no further, nor do the king's writs under the great seal go any further; what the orders of state may, belongs not in us to determine. And whereas they seem to admit of laws not repugnant, etc., if by repugnant they mean, as the word truly imports, and as by the charter must needs be intended, they have no cause to complain, for we have no laws diametrically opposite to those of England, for then they must be contrary to the law of God and of right reason, which the learned in those laws have anciently and still do hold forth as the fundamental basis of their laws, and that if any thing hath been otherwise established, it was an error, and not a law, being against the intent of the law-makers, however it may bear the form of a law (in regard of the stamp of authority set upon it) until it be revoked.

Answer. To the sixth they confess, that non-freemen have a vote in choice of military officers, but they justify their assertion, in regard they must first take an oath of fidelity, which, they say, is not (as they conceive) warranted by our charter, and seems not to concur with the oath of allegiance and the later covenants, but detracts from our native country and laws, so as they cannot take it, etc.

Reply. This needs no reply. An absolute denial, and a denial sub modo are not the same.

Answer. To the seventh they answer negatively only, which their petition will sufficiently clear, for (reply) the inference is so plain, as is obvious to any reasonable understanding.

Answer and reply. The like for the eighth.

Answer. To the ninth they confess the words in their petition, viz., that divers of the English subjects have been impressed for the wars, that rates are many and grievous, but charge them not with tyranny, or injustice, or illegal proceeding.

Reply. See what a manifest contradiction they have run themselves into. They complain of these impresses and rates as an unsupportable grievance, and yet neither tyrannical, unjust, nor illegal; so as we must then conclude (as the very truth is indeed) that the exercise of lawful authority, justice and law, are a grievance to these men, if it come not in their own way.

Answer. To the tenth, they would shift off that slander upon our churches and brethren, by this distinction of Christian vigilancy, properly and improperly so called; properly is in three respects, 1. of the church covenant, 2. of the term, brethren, 3. church censure. And all other Christian vigilancy they account improper; and so this is not to be intended or comprised in this proposition, viz., Christian vigilancy is no way exercised towards non-members.

Reply. This is so gross a fallacy, as needs no skill to discover it.

Answer. To the eleventh they answer by confessing the

words, save that they say, they spake of their brethren, not our
brethren. Reply. Who they challenge for their brethren pecul-
iarly we know not, for all such there as in judgment of charity
go for true Christians in England, we do and have always
accounted brethren, and in a common sense all of that nation
we have accounted brethren; and further they justify that
speech, that they have just indignation against us, etc., for
three reasons, 1. for not establishing the laws of England, 2.
not admitting them to civil liberties, 3. not admitting them to
the sacraments; and yet they dare affirm that they do not
charge this upon the court, etc.   They also justify that speech,
of flying from us as from a pest, by the like speeches some of
them have heard from godly men in England, and by so many
going from us, and so few coming to us.   But admit all this to
be true, yet what calling have these men to publish this to our
reproach?   And beside they know well, that as some speak
evil of us, because we conform not to their opinions, in allowing liberty to every erroneous judgment, so there are many, no
less godly and judicious, who do approve our practice, and continue their good affection to us.

   Answer.   To the twelfth (professing their ignorance of the
meaning of the word, obliquities, to which was replied, that
then they did not know rather what rectum was, for whatsoever is not rectum is obliquum) they make an apology for their
appeal, as conceiving it lawful to appeal to the parliament, to
which they were necessitated, some of them being hindered
from their necessary occasions, and accounting it no offence to
petition, etc., nor had the parliament ever censured any for the
like, etc.   And if this will not satisfy the court, etc., some few
queries to the parliament (the best arbiters in these cases) will
(we hope) end all controversies, etc., concluding that they hope
we will censure all things candidly and in the best sense.

   To which it was replied, that appeals did not lie from us, by
our charter; and to appeal, before any sentence, was to dis-
claim our jurisdiction, etc.

I should also have noted the Doctor's logic, who undertook to prove, that we were subject to the laws of England. His argument was this, every corporation of England is subject to the laws of England; but this was a corporation of England, ergo, etc.

To which it was answered, 1. that there is a difference between subjection to the laws in general, as all that dwell in England are, and subjection to some laws of state, proper to foreign plantations, 2. we must distinguish between corporations within England and corporations of but not within England; the first are subject to the laws of England in general, yet not to every general law, as the city of London and other corporations have divers customs and by-laws differing from the common and statute laws of England. Again, though plantations be bodies corporate, (and so is every city and commonwealth,) yet they are also above the rank of an ordinary corporation. If one of London should say before the mayor and aldermen, or before the common council, you are but a corporation, this would be taken as a contempt. And among the Romans, Grecians, and other nations, colonies have been esteemed other than towns, yea than many cities, for they have been the foundations of great commonwealths. And it was a fruit of much pride and folly in these petitioners to despise the day of small things.

These petitioners persisting thus obstinately and proudly in their evil practice, the court proceeded to consider of their censure, and agreed, that the Doctor (in regard he had no cause to complain, and yet was a leader to the rest, and had carried himself proudly, etc., in the court) should be fined fifty pounds, Mr. Smith (being also a stranger) forty pounds, Mr. Maverick (because he had not as yet appealed) ten pounds, and the other four thirty pounds each.[1] So being again called before the

---

[1] The modern reader will not sympathize with this narrow action of the theocracy. "Surprise almost equals our indignation at this exorbitant imposition, for in this very year Fowle was associated with Winthrop as one of the selectmen of

court, they were exhorted to consider better of their proceedings, and take knowledge of their miscarriage, which was great, and that they had transgressed the rule of the Apostle [*blank*], study to be quiet and to meddle with your own business. They were put in mind also of that sin of Corah, etc., and of the near resemblance between theirs and that; they only told Moses and Aaron, that they took too much upon them, seeing all were the Lord's people, etc., so these say, that the magistrates and freemen take too much upon them, seeing all the people are Englishmen, etc., and others are wise, holy, etc. They were offered also, if they would ingenuously acknowledge their miscarriage, etc., it should be freely remitted. But they remaining obstinate, the court declared their sentence, as is before expressed.

Upon which they all appealed to the parliament, etc., and tendered their appeal in writing. The court received the paper; but refused to accept it, or to read it in the court.

Three of the magistrates, viz., Mr. Bellingham, Mr. Saltonstall, and Mr. Bradstreet dissented, and desired to be entered contradicentes in all the proceedings (only Mr. Bradstreet went home before the sentence). Two or three of the deputies did the like. So the court was dissolved.[1]

Dr. Child prepared now in all haste to go for England in the ship which was to go about a week after, to prosecute their appeal, and to get a petition from the non-freemen to the parlia-

---

Boston, and Maverick was so much interested in the great work of fortifying Castle Island, that he advanced a large part of the outlay, and the metropolis engaged to save him harmless to a certain extent. Union of the good spirit of the civilians, that dreaded all appeals to England for correction of any error in our administration, with the evil spirit of the clergy, that would enforce uniformity in ceremonies and belief, produced the effect of preventing many from coming to Massachusetts, and drove away many who had already established here their domestic altars. All these petitioners, but Maverick, left the country, I believe. He had long experience enough of the habits of our rulers to know, that their intolerance sometimes yielded to interest, and that humanity often overpowered the perversity of their zeal for God's house, by which they might seem to be eaten up." (Savage.)

[1] One reads gladly of the dissent of these important men.

ment, and many high and menacing words were given forth by
them against us, which gave occasion to the governor and
council (so many of them as were then assembled to hold the
court of assistants) to consider what was fit to be done. Neither
thought they fit to impart their counsel to such of the magistrates as had declared their dissent; but the rest of them agreed
to stay the Doctor for his fine, and to search his trunk and Mr.
Dand's study, but spake not of it till the evening before the
Doctor was to depart. Then it was propounded in council,
and Mr. Bellingham dissented, as before, (yet the day before
he moved for stopping the Doctor, which was conceived to be to
feel if there were any such intention,) and presently went aside,
and spake privately with one, who we were sure would prevent
our purpose, if it were possible. Whereupon (whereas we had
agreed to defer it till he had been on shipboard) now perceiving
our counsel was discovered, we sent the officers presently to
fetch the Doctor, and to search his study and Dand's both at
one instant, which was done accordingly, and the Doctor was
brought, and his trunk, that was to be carried on shipboard
(but there was nothing in that, which concerned the business).
But at Dand's they found Mr. Smith, who catched up some
papers, and when the officer took them from him, he brake
out into these speeches, viz. we hope shortly we shall have
commission to search the governor's closet. There were
found the copies of two petitions and twenty-three queries,
which were to be sent to England to the commissioners for
plantations. The one from Dr. Child and the other six petitioners, wherein they declare, how they had formerly petitioned
our general court, and had been fined for the same, and forced
to appeal, and that the ministers of our churches did revile
them, etc., as far as the wit or malice of man could, etc., and
that they meddled in civil affairs beyond their calling, and were
masters rather than ministers, and ofttimes judges, and that
they had stirred up the magistrates against them, and that a
day of humiliation was appointed, wherein they were to pray

against them, etc. Then they mention (as passing by them)
what affronts, jeers, and despiteful speeches were cast upon
them by some of the court, etc. Then they petition, 1. for
settled churches according to the reformation of England, 2.
that the laws of England may be established here, and that
arbitrary power may be banished, 3. for liberties for English
freeholders here as in England, etc., 4. that a general governor
or some honorable commissioners be appointed for settling, etc.,
5. that the oath of allegiance may be commanded to be taken
by all, and other covenants which the parliament shall think
most convenient, to be as a touchstone to try our affections to
the state of England and true restored protestant religion, 6.
to resolve their queries, etc., 7. to take into consideration their
remonstrance and petition exhibited to the general court.

Their queries were chiefly about the validity of our patent,
and how it might be forfeited, and whether such and such acts
or speeches in the pulpits or in the court, etc., were not high
treason; concerning the power of our court and laws in divers
particular cases; and whether they may be hindered by the
order of this court from settling in a church way according to
the reformation of England, etc.

The other petition was from some non-freemen (pretending
to be in the name, and upon the sighs and tears of many
thousands). In the preamble they show how they were driven
out of their native country by the tyranny of the bishops, etc.
Then they petition for liberty of conscience, etc., and for a
general governor, etc. They sent their agents up and down
the country to get hands to this petition. But of the many
thousands they spake of, we could hear but of twenty-five to
the chief petition, and those were (for the most part) either
young men who came over servants, and never had any show
of religion in them, or fishermen of Marblehead, profane
persons, divers of them brought the last year from Newfoundland to fish a season, and so to return again; others were
such as were drawn in by their relations, men of no reason

neither, as a barber of Boston, who, being demanded by the
governor, what moved him to set his hand, made answer, that
the gentlemen were his customers, etc.; and these are the men,
who must be held forth to the parliament, as driven out of England by the bishops, etc., and whose tears and sighs must move
compassion.[1]

Dr. Child, being upon this apprehended and brought before
the governor and council, fell into a great passion, and gave
big words, but being told, that they considered he was a person
of quality, and therefore he should be used with such respect
as was meet to be showed to a gentleman and a scholar, but if
he would behave himself no better, he should be committed to
the common prison and clapped in irons, upon this he grew
more calm; so he was committed to the marshal, with Smith
and Dand, for two or three days, till the ships were gone.   For
he was very much troubled to be hindered from his voyage, and
offered to pay his fine; but that would not be accepted for his
discharge, seeing we had now new matter and worse against
him (for the writings were of his hand).   Yet, upon tender of
sufficient bail, he was set at liberty, but confined to his house,
and to appear at the next court of assistants.   His confinement
he took grievously, but he could not help it.   The other two
were committed to prison, yet lodged in the keeper's house,
and had what diet they pleased, and none of their friends forbidden to come to them.   There was also one Thomas Joy, a
young fellow, a carpenter, whom they had employed to get
hands to the petition; he began to be very busy, and would
know of the marshal, when he went to search Dand's study, if
his warrant were in the king's name, etc.   He was laid hold
on, and kept in irons about four or five days, and then he humbled himself, confessed what he knew, and blamed himself for
meddling in matters belonging not to him, and blessed God
for these irons upon his legs, hoping they should do him good

[1] The great risks for those who gave their names will explain the small number
of signers

while he lived. So he was let out upon reasonable bail. But Smith and Dand would not be examined, and therefore were not bailed; but their offence being in nature capital, etc., bail might be refused in that regard.

For their trial at the general court in (4) 47 (*June*, 1647), and the sentence against them, etc., it is set down at large in the records of that court, with their petitions and queries intended for England, and all proceedings. Mr. Dand not being able to pay his fine of two hundred pounds, nor willing to acknowledge his offence, was kept in prison; but at the general court (3) 48 (*May*, 1648), upon his humble submission, he was freely discharged.[1]

Mr. Winslow being now to go for England, etc., the court was troubled how to furnish him with money or beaver, (for there was nothing in the treasury, the country being in debt one thousand pounds, and what comes in by levies is corn or cattle,) but the Lord stirred up the hearts of some few persons to lend one hundred pounds, to be repaid by the next levy. Next we went in hand to draw up his commission and instructions, and a remonstrance and a petition to the commissioners in England, which were as follows:

To the right honorable Robert, Earl of Warwick, governor in chief, lord admiral, and other the lords and gentlemen, commissioners for foreign plantations, the humble remonstrance and petition of the governor and company of the Massachusetts Bay in New England in America.

In way of answer to the petition and declaration of Samuel Gorton, etc.

Whereas by virtue of his majesty's charter, granted to your petitioners

---

[1] Dr. Robert Child, whose boldness was met by such severe checks, was a young man well trained and connected, the reputed holder of a degree in medicine from the University of Padua, in Italy. Thomas Joy, a man of humbler station, but perhaps no less courageous and self-sacrificing, was the ancestor of an important Boston family. The recalcitrants appear to have believed that a subversion of the existing colonial government would be an easy matter; notice Smith's remark above. Winthrop and his party plainly appreciated their danger, and sent their best man, Edward Winslow, to present to the powers in England their carefully worded statement.

in the fourth year of his highness's reign, we were incorporated into a body
politic with divers liberties and privileges extending to that part of New
England where we now inhabit, we do acknowledge (as we have always
done, and as in duty we are bound) that, although we are removed out of
our native country, yet we still have dependence upon that state, and owe
allegiance and subjection thereunto, according to our charter, and accordingly we have mourned and rejoiced therewith, and have held friends
and enemies in common with it, in all the changes which have befallen
it.  Our care and endeavor also hath been to frame our government and
administrations to the fundamental rules thereof, so far as the different
condition of this place and people, and the best light we have from the
word of God, will allow.  And whereas, by order from your honors, dated
May 15, 1646, we find that your honors have still that good opinion of
us, as not to credit what hath been informed against us before we be
heard, we render humble thanks to your honors for the same;  yet foras-
much as our answer to the information of the said Gorton, etc., is expected, and something also required of us, which (in all humble submission) we conceive may be prejudicial to the liberties granted us by the
said charter, and to our well being in this remote part of the world, (under
the comfort whereof, through the blessing of the Lord, his majesty's
favor, and the special care and bounty of the high court of parliament,
we have lived in peace and prosperity these seventeen years,) our humble
petition (in the first place) is, that our present and future conformity to
your orders and directions may be accepted with a salvo jure, that when
times may be changed, (for all things here below are subject to vanity,)
and other princes or parliaments may arise, the generations succeeding
may not have cause to lament, and say, England sent our fathers forth
with happy liberties, which they enjoyed many years, notwithstanding
all the enmity and opposition of the prelacy, and other potent adversaries,
how came we then to lose them, under the favor and protection of that
state, in such a season, when England itself recovered its own?  In freto
viximus, in portu morimur.  But we confide in your honors' justice,
wisdom, and goodness, that our posterity shall have cause to rejoice under
the fruit and shelter thereof, as ourselves and many others do;  and
therefore we are bold to represent to your honors our apprehensions,
whereupon we have thus presumed to petition you in this behalf.

It appears to us, by the said order, that we are conceived, 1. to have
transgressed our limits, by sending soldiers to fetch in Gorton, etc., out
of Shaomett in the Narragansett Bay, 2. that we have either exceeded or
abused our authority, in banishing them out of our jurisdiction, when
they were in our power.  For the first we humbly crave (for your better

satisfaction) that your honors will be pleased to peruse what we have delivered to the care of Mr. Edward Winslow, our agent or commissioner, (whom we have sent on purpose to attend your honors,) concerning our proceedings in that affair and the grounds thereof, which are truly and faithfully reported, and the letters of the said Gorton and his company, and other letters concerning them, faithfully copied out (not verbatim only, but even literatim, according to their own bad English). The originals we have by us, and had sent them, but for casualty of the seas. Thereby it will appear what the men are, and how unworthy your favor. Thereby also will appear the wrongs and provocations we received from them, and our long patience towards them, till they became our professed enemies, wrought us disturbance, and attempted our ruin. In which case, our charter (as we conceive) gives us full power to deal with them as enemies by force of arms, they being then in such place where we could have no right from them by civil justice; which the commissioners for the United Colonies finding, and the necessity of calling them to account, left the business [to us] to do.

For the other particular in your honor's order, viz., the banishment of Gorton, etc., as we are assured, upon good grounds, that our sentence upon them was less than their deserving, so (as we conceive) we had sufficient authority, by our charter, to inflict the same, having full and absolute power and authority to punish, pardon, rule, govern, etc., granted us therein.

Now, by occasion of the said order, those of Gorton's company begin to lift up their heads and speak their pleasures of us, threatening the poor Indians also, who (to avoid their tyranny) had submitted themselves and their lands under our protection and government; and divers other sachems, following their example, have done the like, and some of them brought (by the labor of one of our elders, Mr. John Eliot, who hath obtained to preach to them in their own language) to good forwardness in embracing the gospel of God in Christ Jesus. All which hopeful beginnings are like to be dashed, if Gorton, etc., shall be countenanced and upheld against them and us, which also will endanger our peace here at home. For some among ourselves (men of unquiet spirits, affecting rule and innovation) have taken boldness to prefer scandalous and seditious petitions for such liberties as neither our charter, nor reason or religion will allow; and being called before us in open court to give account of their miscarriage therein, they have threatened us with your honor's authority, and (before they knew whether we would proceed to any sentence against them, or not) have refused to answer, but appealed to your honors. The copy of their petition, and our declaration thereupon, our said commissioner hath ready to present to you, when your leisure shall permit to hear them. Their appeals we have not admitted, being assured, that they cannot stand with the liberty and power granted us by our charter, nor will be allowed by your honors, who well know it would be destructive to all government, both in the honor and also in the power of it, if it should be in the liberty of delinquents to evade the sentence of justice, and force us, by appeal, to follow them into England, where the evidence and circumstances of facts cannot be so clearly held forth as in their proper place; besides the insupportable charges we must be at in the prosecution thereof. These considerations are not new to your honors and the high court of parliament, the records whereof bear witness of the wisdom and faithfulness of our ancestors in that great council, who, in those times of darkness, when they acknowledged a supremacy in the bishops of Rome in all causes ecclesiastical, yet would not allow appeals to Rome, etc., to remove causes out of the courts in England.

Beside, (though we shall readily admit, that the wisdom and experience of that great council, and of your honors, as a part thereof, are far more able to prescribe rules of government, and to judge of causes, than such poor rustics as a wilderness can breed up, yet,) considering the vast distance between England and these parts, (which usually abates the virtue of the strongest influences,) your counsels and judgments could neither be so well grounded, nor so seasonably applied, as might either be so useful to us, or so safe for yourselves, in your discharge, in the great day of account, for any miscarriage which might befal us, while we depended upon your counsel and help, which could not seasonably be administered to us. Whereas if any such should befal us, when we have the government in our own hands, the state of England shall not answer for it. In consideration of the premises, our humble petition to your honors (in the next place) is, that you will be pleased to continue your favorable aspect upon these poor infant plantations, that we may still rejoice and bless our God under your shadow, and be there still nourished (tanquam calore et rore coelesti;) and while God owns us for a people of his, he will own our poor prayers for you, and your goodness towards us, for an abundant recompense. And this in special, if you shall please to pass by any failings you may have observed in our course, to confirm our liberties, granted to us by charter, by leaving delinquents to our just proceedings, and discountenancing our enemies and disturbers of our peace, or such as molest our people there, upon pretence of injustice. Thus craving pardon, if we have presumed too far upon your honors' patience, and expecting a gracious testimony of your wonted favor by this our agent, which shall further oblige us and our posterity in all humble and faithful service to the high court of parliament and to your honors, we continue our earnest prayers for your prosperity forever.

By order of the general court.

(10) (*December*) 46.                    INCREASE NOWELL, *Secretary.*

JOHN WINTHROP, *Governor.*

*The copy of the commission to Mr. Winslow.*

Mattachusetts in New England in America.

Whereas Samuel Gorton, John Greene, and Randall Holden, by petition and declaration exhibited to the right honorable the Earl of Warwick, governor in chief, and commissioners for foreign plantations, as members of the high court of parliament, have charged divers false and scandalous matters against us, whereof their honors have been pleased to give us notice, and do expect our answer for clearing the same, we therefore the governor and company of the Mattachusetts aforesaid, assembled in our general court, being careful to give all due respect to his lordship and the honorable commissioners, and having good assurance of the wisdom and faithfulness of you, our worthy and loving friend, Mr. Edward Winslow, do hereby give power and commission to you to appear befo·e his lordship and commissioners, and presenting our most humble duty and service to their honors, for us and in our name to exhibit our humble remonstrance and petition, in way of answer to the said false and unjust charge of the said Gorton, etc., and by the same and other writings and instructions delivered to you under the hand of Mr. Increase Nowell our secretary, to inform their honors of the truth and reason of all our proceedings with the said Gorton, etc., so as our innocency and the justice of our proceedings may appear to their honors' satisfaction. And if any other complaints, in any kind, have been, or shall be, made against us before the said commissioners, or before the high court of parliament, you have hereby like power and commission to answer on our behalf according to your instructions. And we humbly crave of the high court of parliament and of the honorable commissioners, that they will vouchsafe our said commissioner free liberty of seasonable access, as occasion shall require, and a favorable hearing, with such credit to such writings as he shall present in our name, under the hand of our said secretary, as if we had presented them in person, upon that faith and credit, which we would not wittingly violate, for all worldly advantages; and that our said commissioner may find such speed and despatch, and may be under such safe protection, in his stay and return, as that honorable court useth to afford to their humble subjects and servants in like cases.  In testimony hereof we have caused our common seal to be hereunto affixed, dated this 4 (10) 1646.

By order of the court.

INCREASE NOWELL, *Secretary.*

JOHN WINTHROP, *Governor.*

Mr. Winslow his instructions were of two sorts; the one (which he might publish, etc.) were only directions, according to his commission, and remonstrance and other writings delivered him.  The other were more secret, which were these following.

If you shall be demanded about these particulars:—

Obj. 1.  Why we make not out our process in the king's name?  you shall answer:—

1.  That we should thereby waive the power of our government granted to us, for we claim not as by commission, but by a free donation of absolute government, 2. for avoiding appeals, etc.

Obj. 2.  That our government is arbitrary.

Answer.  We have four or five hundred express laws, as near the laws of England as may be; and yearly we make more, and where we have no law, we judge by the word of God, as near as we can.

Obj. 3.  About enlarging our limits, etc.

Answer.  Such Indians as are willing to come under our government, we know no reason to refuse.  Some Indians we have subdued by just war, as the Pequids.  Some English also, having purchased lands of the Indians, have submitted to our government.

Obj. 4.  About our subjection to England.

Answer 1.  We are to pay the one fifth part of ore of gold and silver.

2.  In being faithful and firm to the state of England, endeavoring to walk with God in upholding his truth, etc., and praying for it.

3.  In framing our government according to our patent, so near as we may.

Obj. 5.  About exercising admiral jurisdiction.

Answer 1.  We are not restrained by our charter.

2.  We have power given us to rule, punish, pardon, etc., in all cases, ergo in maritime.

3.  We have power granted us to defend ourselves and offend our

enemies, as well by sea as by land, ergo we must needs have power to judge of such cases.

4. Without this, neither our own people nor strangers could have justice from us in such cases.

Obj. 6. About our independency upon that state.

Answer. Our dependency is in these points: 1. we have received our government and other privileges by our charter, 2. we owe allegiance and fidelity to that state, 3. in erecting a government here accordingly and subjecting thereto, we therein yield subjection to that state, 4. in rendering the one fifth part of ore, etc., 5. we depend upon that state for protection, and immunities as freeborn Englishmen.

Obj. 7. Seeing we hold of East Greenwich, etc., why every freeholder of forty shillings per annum have not votes in elections, etc., as in England.

Answer. Our charter gives that liberty expressly to the freemen only.

Obj. 8. By your charter, such as we transport are to live under his majesty's allegiance.

Answer. So they all do, and so intended, so far as we know.

Obj. 9. About a general governor.

Answer 1. Our charter gives us absolute power of government.

2. On the terms above specified, we conceive, the patent hath no such thing in it, neither expressed, nor implied.

3. We had not transported ourselves and families upon such terms.

4. Other plantations have been undertaken at the charge of others in England, and the planters have their dependence upon the companies there, and those planters go and come chiefly for matter of profit; but we came to abide here, and to plant the gospel, and people the country, and herein God hath marvellously blessed us.

# 1647

(1.) (*March.*)] At the court of assistants, three or four were sent for, who had been very active about the petition to the commissioners in procuring hands to it, (it being thought fit to pass by such as being drawn in had only subscribed the petition,) especially Mr. Samuel Maverick and Mr. Clerk of Salem, the keeper of the ordinary there and a church member. These having taken an oath of fidelity to the government, and enjoying all liberties of freemen, their offence was far the greater. So they were bound over to answer it at the next general court.

Mr. Smith and Mr. Dand (giving security to pay their fines, assessed upon the former petition, within two months) were bailed to the general court.

Dr. Child also was offered his liberty, upon bail to the general court, and to be confined to Boston; but he chose rather to go to prison, and so he was committed.

The reason of referring these and others to the general court was, both in regard the cause was of so great concernment, as the very life and foundation of our government, and also because the general court had cognizance thereof already upon the first petition.[1]

Mr. Burton, one of the petitioners, being in the town

---

[1] The record here concluded, deserves careful reading. The heads in New England proceed warily. In disturbed England, whether the King or Parliament was to prevail, and what was to be the situation, was involved in doubt. Behind the shield of their charter they determined, if they could, to establish a large degree of independence, but it must be noted that independence at this time was coupled with ecclesiastical domination and general loss of liberty, whereas dependence would bring to the colonies the far freer atmosphere of England. For severe contemporary criticism of the petition Winslow was to present, see Edward Johnson, *Wonder-Working Providence*, book III., chap. III.

meeting, when the court's declaration was read, was much moved, and spake in high language, and would needs have a copy of it, which so soon as he had, he went with it (as was undoubtedly believed) to Dr. Child, and in the way fell down, and lay there in the cold near half an hour, till company was gotten to carry him home in a chair, and after he continued in great pain, and lame divers months.

It is observable that this man had gathered some providences about such as were against them, as that Mr. Winslow's horse died, as he came riding to Boston; that his brother's son (a child of eight years old) had killed his own sister (being ten years of age) with his father's piece, etc., and his great trouble was, least this providence which now befel him, should be imputed to their cause.

There fell out at this time a very sad occasion. A merchant of Plymouth in England, (whose father had been mayor there,) called [blank] Martin, being fallen into decay, came to Casco Bay, and after some time, having occasion to return into England, he left behind him two daughters, (very proper maidens and of modest behavior,) but took not that course for their safe bestowing in his absence, as the care and wisdom of a father should have done, so as the eldest of them, called Mary, twenty-two years of age, being in [the] house with one Mr. Mitton, a married man of Casco, within one quarter of a year, he was taken with her, and soliciting her chastity, obtained his desire, and having divers times committed sin with her, in the space of three months, she then removed to Boston, and put herself in service to Mrs. Bourne; and finding herself to be with child, and not able to bear the shame of it, she concealed it, and though divers did suspect it, and some told her mistress their fears, yet her behavior was so modest, and so faithful she was in her service, as her mistress would not give ear to any such report, but blamed such as told her of it. But, her time being come, she was delivered of a woman child in a back room by herself upon the 13 (10) (*December* 13) in the night, and the child was born alive, but she kneeled upon the head of it, till she thought it had been dead, and having laid it by, the child, being strong, recovered, and cried again.  Then she took it again, and used violence to it till it was quite dead.  Then she put it into her chest, and having cleansed the room, she went to bed, and arose again the next day about noon, and went about her business, and so continued till the nineteenth day, that her master and mistress went on shipboard to go for England. They being gone, and she removed to another house, a midwife in the town, having formerly suspected her, and now coming to her again, found she had been delivered of a child, which, upon examination, she confessed, but said it was still-born, and so she put it into the fire.  But, search being made, it was found in her chest, and when she was brought before the jury, they caused her to touch the face of it, whereupon the blood came fresh into it.[1]  Whereupon she confessed the whole truth, and a surgeon, being called to search the body of the child, found a fracture in the skull.  Before she was condemned, she confessed, that she had prostituted her body to another also, one Sears.  She behaved herself very penitently while she was in prison, and at her death, 18 (1,) (*March* 18) complaining much of the hardness of her heart.  She confessed, that the first and second time she committed fornication, she prayed for pardon, and promised to commit it no more; and the third time she prayed God, that if she did fall into it again, he would make her an example, and therein she justified God, as she did in the rest.  Yet all the comfort God would afford her, was only trust (as she said) in his mercy through Christ.  After she was turned off and had hung a space, she spake, and asked what they did mean to do.  Then some stepped up, and turned the knot of the rope backward, and then she soon died.

Mention was made before of some beginning to instruct the

[1] In this pitiful tale appears, as in a previous case, a very old and wide-spread superstition.

Indians, etc. Mr. John Eliot, teacher of the church of Roxbury, found such encouragement, as he took great pains to get their language, and in a few months could speak of the things of God to their understanding; and God prospered his endeavors, so as he kept a constant lecture to them in two places, one week at the wigwam of one Wabon, a new sachem near Watertown mill, and the other the next week in the wigwam of Cutshamekin near Dorchester mill. And for the furtherance of the work of God, divers of the English resorted to his lecture, and the governor and other of the magistrates and elders sometimes; and the Indians began to repair thither from other parts. His manner of proceeding was thus; he would persuade one of the other elders or some magistrate to begin the exercise with prayer in English; then he took a text, and read it first in the Indian language, and after in English; then he preached to them in Indian about an hour; (but first I should have spoke of the catechising their children, who were soon brought to answer him some short questions, whereupon he gave each of them an apple or a cake) then he demanded of some of the chiefs, if they understood him; if they answered, yea, then he asked of them if they had any questions to propound. And they had usually two or three or more questions, which he did resolve. At one time (when the governor was there and about two hundred people, Indian and English, in one wigwam of Cutshamekin's) an old man asked him, if God would receive such an old man as he was; to whom he answered by opening the parable of the workmen that were hired into the vineyard; and when he had opened it, he asked the old man, if he did believe it, who answered he did, and was ready to weep. A second question was, what was the reason, that when all Englishmen did know God, yet some of them were poor. His answer was, 1. that God knows it is better for his children to be good than to be rich; he knows withal, that if some of them had riches, they would abuse them, and wax proud and wanton, etc.. therefore he gives them no more riches than may be needful for them, that they may be kept from pride, etc., to depend upon him, 2. he would hereby have men know, that he hath better blessings to bestow upon good men than riches, etc., and that their best portion is in heaven, etc. A third question was, if a man had two wives, (which was ordinary with them,) seeing he must put away one, which he should put away. To this it was answered, that by the law of God the first is the true wife, and the other is no wife; but if such a case fell out, they should then repair to the magistrates, and they would direct them what to do, for it might be, that the first wife might be an adulteress, etc., and then she was to be put away. When all their questions were resolved, he concluded with prayer in the Indian language.

The Indians were usually very attentive, and kept their children so quiet as caused no disturbance. Some of them began to be seriously affected, and to understand the things of God, and they were generally ready to reform whatsoever they were told to be against the word of God, as their sorcery, (which they call powwowing,) their whoredoms, etc., idleness, etc. The Indians grew very inquisitive after knowledge both in things divine and also human, so as one of them, meeting with an honest plain Englishman, would needs know of him, what were the first beginnings (which we call principles) of a commonwealth. The Englishman, being far short in the knowledge of such matters, yet ashamed that an Indian should find an Englishman ignorant of any thing, bethought himself what answer to give him, at last resolved upon this, viz. that the first principle of a commonwealth was salt, for (saith he) by means of salt we can keep our flesh and fish, to have it ready when we need it, whereas you lose much for want of it, and are sometimes ready to starve. A second principle is iron, for thereby we fell trees, build houses, till our land, etc. A third is, ships, by which we carry forth such commodities as we have to spare, and fetch in such as we need, as cloth, wine, etc. Alas! (saith the Indian) then I fear, we shall never be a commonwealth, for we can neither make salt, nor iron, nor ships.[1]

It pleased God so to prosper our fishing this season, as that at Marblehead only they had taken by the midst of the (11) month (*January*) about four thousand pounds worth of fish.

(10.) (*December.*)][2] But the Lord was still pleased to afflict us in our shipping, for Major Gibbons and Captain Leverett having sent a new ship of about one hundred tons to Virginia, and having there freighted her with tobacco, going out of the river, by a sudden storm was forced on shore from her anchor, and much of the goods spoiled, to the loss (as was estimated) of above two thousand pounds.

I must here observe a special providence of God, pointing out his displeasure against some profane persons, who took part with Dr. Child, etc., against the government and churches here. The court had appointed a general fast, to seek God (as for some other occasions, so) in the trouble which threatened us by the petitioners, etc. The pastor of Hingham, and others of his church (being of their party) made light of it, and some said they would not fast against Dr. Child and against themselves; and there were two of them (one Pitt and Johnson)

---

[1] The apostleship of John Eliot will always be held one of the most creditable episodes of our early history. Winthrop's picture of his labors may be easily filled out, for Eliot's worth has always been recognized and celebrated by all New England histories from William Hubbard and Cotton Mather to Palfrey and Edward Everett Hale. See also his life by Francis in Sparks's *American Biography*, first series. His great distinction was his labor among the Indians, crowned by his colossal work, the translation of the Bible into Indian (Cambridge, 1662, second edition, 1680). *The Christian Commonwealth*, which he wrote in 1660, was not approved, and he, although so much respected, was called sharply to account for it. With that curious facility in retraction which one notices in characters high and low, in John Cotton as well as John Underhill, he recanted and was restored to favor. He had a savage animosity to the sin of wearing wigs, sympathizing here with Cotton Mather, who writes, "for men to wear their hair with luxurious, delicate, feminine prolixity, or to disfigure themselves with hair which was not of their own, but above all for ministers of the gospel to ruffle it in excesses of this kind," was an enormous sin. Eliot's prejudice against tobacco was equally strong. In the list of our old worthies, he is as brave and persistent as any, and especially marked by amiability among men so often repulsively harsh.         [2] 1646.

who, having a great raft of masts and planks (worth forty or fifty pounds) to tow to Boston, would needs set forth about noon the day before (it being impossible they could get to Boston before the fast;) but when they came at Castle Island, there arose such a tempest, as carried away their raft, and forced them to cut their mast to save their lives. Some of their masts and planks they recovered after, where it had been cast on shore; but when they came with it to the Castle, they were forced back again, and were so oft put back with contrary winds, etc., as it was above a month before they could bring all the remainder to Boston.

Prescott, another favorer of the petitioners, lost a horse and his lading in Sudbury river; and a week after, his wife and children, being upon another horse, were hardly saved from drowning.

A woman of Charlestown having two daughters, aged under fourteen, sent them to the tide-mill near by with a little corn. They delivered their corn at the mill, and returning back (they dwelt towards Cambridge) they were not seen till three months after, supposed to be carried away by the tide, which was then above the marsh. This was 13 (11) (*January* 13).

(1.) (*March.*)] In the midst of this month a small pinnace was set out for Barbados with [*blank*] persons and store of provisions. It was her first voyage, and 2 (3) (*May* 2) after she was put on shore at Scituate, the goods in her, but not a man, nor any of their clothes.

The merchants of Boston had set forth a small ship to trade about the Gulf of Canada, and they had certificate under the public seal to that end. They set sail from Boston the midst of the (1) month (*March*), and by tempest were forced into an harbor near Cape Sable, and having lost their boat, and forced to let slip their cables, were driven on ground, and having staid there about four days, Mr. D'Aulney having intelligence of them, sent eighteen men by land, who finding eleven of ours on shore, without weapons, surprised them, and after the ship,

having but six men in her; and being carried to Port Royal, he
examined them upon oath, whether they had traded, which
they had not done, only the merchant had received two beaver
skins, given him by the sachem; for which, (notwithstanding
he allowed their commission,) after he had kept them three
weeks prisoners, he kept their ship and goods to the value
of one thousand pounds, and sent them home in two shallops,
meanly provided, and without any lead [?], etc. This is more
fully set down after, fol. 99.

One [*blank*] of Windsor arraigned and executed at Hartford
for a witch.[1]

1647. 30 (3.) (*May* 30.)] In the evening there was heard
the report as of a great piece of ordnance. It was heard all over
the Bay, and all along to Yarmouth, etc., and there it seemed
as if it had been to the southward of them.

26.] The court of elections was at Boston. Great laboring
there had been by the friends of the petitioners to have one
chosen governor, who favored their cause, and some new magistrates to have been chosen of their side; but the mind of the
country appeared clearly, for the old governor was chosen
again, with two or three hundred votes more than any other,
and no one new magistrate was chosen but only captain Robert
Bridges.

Captain Welde of Roxbury being dead, the young men of
the town agreed together to choose one George Denison,[2] a
young soldier come lately out of the wars in England, which
the ancient and chief men of the town understanding, they
came together at the time appointed, and chose one Mr.
Prichard, a godly man and one of the chief in the town, passing
by their lieutenant, fearing least the young Denison would

---

[1] Savage noted this as the first instance in New England of the witchcraft
delusion. The case is not mentioned by other historians.

[2] George Dennison had imbibed in Cromwell's army, ideas and a spirit
which did not commend him to the Roxbury brethren, whose minister had been
the strict Thomas Welde, but he was a brave and active soldier, as was proved
in Philip's War.

have carried it from him, whereupon much discontent and murmuring arose in the town. The young men were over strongly bent to have their will, although their election was void in law, (George Denison not being then a freeman,) and the ancient men over-voted them above twenty, and the lieutenant was discontented because he was neglected, etc. The cause coming to the court, and all parties being heard, Mr. Prichard was allowed, and the young men were pacified, and the lieutenant.

4 (4.) (*June* 4.)] Canonicus, the great sachem of Narragansett, died, a very old man.[1]

8. (4.) (*June* 8.)] The synod began again at Cambridge. The next day Mr. Ezekiel Rogers of Rowley preached in the forenoon, and the magistrates and deputies were present, and in the afternoon Mr. Eliot preached to the Indians in their own language before all the assembly. Mr. Rogers in his sermon took occasion to speak of the petitioners, (then in question before the court,) and exhorted the court to do justice upon them, yet with desire of favor to such as had been drawn in, etc., and should submit. He reproved also the practice of private members making speeches in the church assemblies to the disturbance and hindrance of the ordinances, also the call for the reviving the ancient practice in England of children asking their parents' blessing upon their knees, etc. Also he reproved the great oppression in the country, etc., and other things amiss, as long hair, etc. Divers were offended at his zeal in some of these passages. Mr. Bradford, the governor of Plymouth, was there as a messenger of the church of Plymouth. But the sickness (mentioned here in the next leaf) prevailed so as divers of the members of the synod were taken with it, whereupon they were forced to break up on the sudden.

The success of Mr. Eliot's labors in preaching to the Indians

[1] A faithful friend of the English who merited from the governor some appreciative words.

appears in a small book set forth by Mr. Shepherd and by other observations in the country.[1]

1646. 19, (1.) (*March* 19.)] One captain Dobson in a ship of eighty tons, double manned and fitted for a man of war, was set forth from Boston to trade to the eastward. Their testimonial was for the gulf of Canada. But being taken with foul weather, and having lost their boat, they put into harbor at Cape Sable, and there shooting off five or six pieces of ordnance, the Indians came aboard them, and traded some skins; and withal Mr. D'Aulney had notice, and presently sent away twenty men over land, (being about thirty miles from Port Royal,) who lurking in the woods for their advantage, providence offered them a very fair one. For the ship, having bought a shallop of the Indians, and being under sail, in the mouth of the harbor, the wind came about southerly with such violence, as forced them to an anchor; and having lost all their anchors, they were forced on shore, yet without danger of shipwreck. Whereupon the master and merchant and most of the company went on shore (leaving but six men aboard) and carried no weapons with them, which the French perceiving, they came upon them and bound them, and carried the master to the ship's side, who commanded the men aboard to yield up the ship. The French being possessed of the ship, carried her to Port Royal, and left some of their company to conduct the rest by land. When they came there, they were all imprisoned, and examined apart upon oath, and having confessed that they had traded, etc., the ship and cargo (being worth in all one thousand pounds) was kept as confiscated, and the men were put into two old shallops and sent home, and arrived at Boston 6 (3) (*May* 6) 47. The merchants complained to the court for

---

[1] The reference is to Rev. Thomas Shepard's *The Day-Breaking if not the Sun-Rising of the Gospell with the Indians in New England* (London, 1647), reprinted in 1865, and in *Old South Leaflets*, no. 143, or to his *The Clear Sun-Shine of the Gospel breaking forth upon the Indians in New England* (1648), reprinted 1834, 1865; and perhaps also to a preceding anonymous tract, *New England's First Fruits* (London, 1643), reprinted 1865.

redress, and offered to set forth a good ship, to deal with some
of D'Aulney's vessels, but the court thought it not safe nor
expedient for us to begin a war with the French; nor could we
charge any manifest wrong upon D'Aulney, seeing we had told
him, that if ours did trade within his liberties, they should do it
at their own peril. And though we judged it an injury to
restrain the natives and others from trading, etc., (they being
a free people,) yet, it being a common practice of all civil
nations, his seizure of our ship would be accounted lawful, and
our letters of reprisal unjust. And besides there appeared an
over-ruling providence in it, otherwise he could not have seized
a ship so well fitted, nor could wise men have lost her so foolishly.

At Concord a bullock was killed which had in his maw a
ten shilling piece of English gold, and yet it could not be
known that any had lost it.

A barn at Salem was set on fire with lightning, and all the
corn and hay consumed suddenly. It fell upon the thatch in
the breadth of a sheet, in the view of people.

(4.) (*June.*)] An epidemical sickness was through the
country among Indians and English, French and Dutch. It
took them like a cold, and a light fever with it. Such as bled or
used cooling drinks died; those who took comfortable things,
for most part recovered, and that in few days. Wherein a
special providence of God appeared, for not a family, nor but
few persons escaping it, had it brought all so weak as it did
some, and continued so long, our hay and corn had been lost
for want of help; but such was the mercy of God to his people,
as few died, not above forty or fifty in the Massachusetts, and
near as many at Connecticut. But that which made the stroke
more sensible and grievous, both to them and to all the country,
was the death of that faithful servant of the Lord, Mr. Thomas
Hooker, pastor of the church in Hartford, who, for piety, prudence, wisdom, zeal, learning, and what else might make him
serviceable in the place and time he lived in, might be com-

pared with men of greatest note; and he shall need no other praise: the fruits of his labors in both Englands shall preserve an honorable and happy remembrance of him forever.[1]

14, (4.) (*June* 14.)] In this sickness the governor's wife, daughter of Sir John Tindal, Knight, left this world for a better, being about fifty-six years of age: a woman of singular virtue, prudence, modesty, and piety, and specially beloved and honored of all the country.[2]

The meeting of the commissioners of the colonies should, in course, have been at Plymouth in the sixth month next, but upon special occasion of the Indians there was a meeting appointed at Boston [*blank*] which continued to the 17 (6) (*August* 17) next. The chief occasion was, that Ninicraft,[3] the sachem of Niantick, had professed his desire to be reconciled to the English, etc., and that many Indians would complain of Uncas and his brother their falsehood and cruelty, etc., if they might come to Boston to be heard there.

The general court made an order, that all elections of governor, etc., should be by papers delivered in to the deputies before the court, as it was before permitted. This was disliked by the freemen, and divers of the new towns petitioned for the repeal of it, as an infringement of their liberties; for when they consented to send their deputies with full power, etc., they reserved to themselves matter of election, as appears by the record of the court [*blank*]. Upon these petitions the said order was repealed, and it was referred to the next court

[1] The judgment of posterity bears out this warm contemporary tribute. In courage, humanity and wisdom the founder of Connecticut stands among the best men of his time.

[2] The virtues of Margaret Winthrop, the governor's third wife, are richly attested. She received the esteem of all, and her husband's affection was profound. Her letters still extant (see R. C. Winthrop, *Life of John Winthrop*) while over-unctuous with the inevitable effusive piety of the age, at the same time show the helpful, sweet-hearted woman. She has been made in our own day the subject of an attractive memoir by Mrs. Earle.

[3] Often spelt Ninigret, reported to have saved on one occasion the life of John Winthrop, jr., whose descendants possess a portrait of the sachem.

of elections to consider of a meet way for ordering elections. to the satisfaction of the petitioners and the rest of the free-men.  But that court being full of business, and breaking up suddenly, it was put off farther.

In the depth of winter, in a very tempestuous night, the fort at Saybrook was set on fire, and all the buildings within the pal-isado, with all the goods, etc., were burnt down, captain Mason, his wife, and children, hardly saved.  The loss was estimated at one thousand pounds, and not known how the fire came.

Captain Bridges house at Lynn burnt down 27 (2) 48.[1]

At Newfoundland, towards the end of the fishing season, there was a great hiracano in the night, which caused a great wreck of ships and boats, and much fish blown off the shore into the sea.  Some small vessels we had there, but through mercy none of them miscarried.

The United Colonies having made strict orders to restrain all trade of powder and guns to the Indians, by occasion whereof the greatest part of the beaver trade was drawn to the French and Dutch, by whom the Indians were constantly furnished with those things, though they also made profession of like restraint, but connived at the practice, so as our means of returns for English commodities were grown very short, it pleased the Lord to open to us a trade with Barbados and other Islands in the West Indies, which as it proved gainful, so the commodities we had in exchange there for our cattle and provisions, as sugar, cotton, tobacco, and indigo, were a good help to discharge our engagements in England.  And this summer there was so great a drouth, as their potatoes and corn, etc., were burnt up; and divers London ships which rode there were so short of provisions as, if our vessels had not supplied them, they could not have returned home; which was an ob-servable providence, that whereas many of the London seamen were wont to despise New England as a poor, barren country, should now be relieved by our plenty.

[1] April 27, 1648.

After the great dearth of victuals in these islands followed presently a great mortality, (whether it were the plague, or pestilent fever, it killed in three days,) that in Barbados there died six thousand, and in Christophers, of English and French, near as many, and in other islands proportionable. The report of this coming to us, by a vessel which came from Fayal, the court published an order, that all vessels, which should come from the West Indies, should stay at the castle, and not come on shore, nor put any goods on shore, without license of three of the council, on pain of one hundred pounds, nor any to go aboard, etc., except they continued there, etc., on like penalty. The like order was sent to Salem and other haven towns.[1]

But one goodman Dell of Boston, coming from Christophers in a small pinnace, and being put in to Gloucester, and there forbidden to land, and informed of the order of court, yet coming into the Bay, and being hailed by the Castle boat, and after by the captain of the Castle, denied that he came from the West Indies, and having taken in three fishermen (whom the captain knew) who joined with him in the same lie, they were let pass, and so came on shore at Boston, before it was known. But such of the council as were near assembled the next day, and sent for some of the company, and upon examination finding that the sickness had been ceased at Christophers three months before they came forth, so as there could be no danger of infection in their persons, they gave them liberty to continue on shore; but for cotton and such goods as might retain the infection, they ordered them to be laid in an house remote, and for Dell, he was bound over to the next court to answer his contempt.

About fourteen days after a ship came from Malago, which had staid nine days at Barbados. She was stopped at the Castle. The captain brought the master and two others to Boston (which he ought not to have done). Four magistrates

---

[1] An early instance of quarantine in English America.

examined them upon oath, and finding they were all well, save
two, (who had the flux,) and no goods from Barbados but
three bags of cotton, which were ordered to be landed, etc., at
an island, the ship was suffered to come up, but none to come
on shore for a week after, etc.

4. (6). (*August* 4.)] There was a great marriage to be sol-
emnized at Boston. The bridegroom being of Hingham, Mr.
Hubbard's church, he was procured to preach, and came to
Boston to that end. But the magistrates, hearing of it, sent
to him to forbear. The reasons were, 1. for that his spirit
had been discovered to be averse to our ecclesiastical and civil
government, and he was a bold man, and would speak his mind,
2. we were not willing to bring in the English custom of ministers performing the solemnity of marriage, which sermons at
such times might induce, but if any ministers were present, and
would bestow a word of exhortation, etc., it was permitted.

The new governor of the Dutch, called Peter Stevesant,
being arrived at the Monados,[1] sent his secretary to Boston with
letters to the governor, with tender of all courtesy and good
correspondency, but withal taking notice of the differences between them and Connecticut, and offering to have them referred
to friends here, not to determine, but to prepare for a hearing
and determination in Europe; in which letter he lays claim to
all between Connecticut and Delaware. The commissioners
being assembled at Boston, the governor acquainted them
with the letter; and it was put to consideration what answer
to return. Some advised, that seeing he made profession of
much good will and desire of all neighborly correspondency,
we should seek to gain upon him by courtesy, and therefore to
accept his offer, and to tender him a visit at his own home, or
a meeting at any of our towns where he should choose. But
the commissioners of those parts thought otherwise, supposing
it would be more to their advantage to stand upon terms of
distance, etc. And answer was returned accordingly, only tak-

[1] Petrus Stuyvesant arrived at Manhattan in May, 1647.

ing notice of his offer, and showing our readiness to give him a meeting in time and place convenient. So matters continued as they were.

26. (7). (*September* 26.)] But it appeared, that a Dutch ship from Holland, being in the harbor at New Haven, (where they had traded about a month,) was surprised by the Dutch governor and carried to the Monhados. The manner was thus: The merchants of New Haven had bought a ship at the Monhados, which was to be delivered at New Haven. In her the Dutch governor put a company of soldiers, who, being under decks when the ship came into New Haven, took their opportunity afterward, upon the Lord's day, to seize the Dutch ship, and having the wind fair, carried her away. The governor of New Haven complained of the injury to the Dutch governor, and made a protest, etc. The Dutch governor justified the act by examples of the like in Europe, etc., but especially by claiming the place and so all along the seacoast to Cape Codd. He pretended to seize the ship as forfeit to the West India Company, by trading in their limits without leave or recognition. It fell out at the same time, that three of the Dutch governor's servants fled from him and came to New Haven, and being pursued, were there apprehended and put in prison. The Dutch governor writes to have them delivered to him, but directs his letter to New Haven in New Netherlands. Upon this the governor of New Haven refused to deliver them, and writes back to the Dutch, maintaining their right to the place, both by patent from King James, and also by purchase from the natives, and by quiet possession and improvement many years. He wrote also to the governor of the Massachusetts, acquainting him with all that had passed, and desired advice. These letters coming to Boston about the time of the general court, he acquainted the court with them, and a letter was drawn and sent (as from the court) to this purpose, to the Dutch governor, viz. that we were very sorry for the difference which was fallen out between him and our confederates of

New Haven; that we might not withhold assistance from them, in case of any injurious violence offered to them; that we accounted their title to the place they possessed to be as good as the Dutch had to the Monhados; that we would willingly interpose for a friendly reconciliation; and that we would write to New Haven to persuade the delivery of the fugitives, etc. We wrote also to the governor of New Haven to the same purpose, intimating to him that at our request he might deliver the fugitives without prejudice to their right or reputation. But this notwithstanding, they detained the fugitives still, nor would send our letter to the Dutch governor; whereupon he made proclamation of free liberty for all servants, etc., of New Haven within his jurisdiction, and wrote to the governor of the Massachusetts, blaming the practice in the general, but excusing it in his particular case, as being enforced thereto, etc. This course not prevailing, about the end of winter he wrote privately to the fugitives, and the minister of their church wrote also, whereby he gave such assurance to the fugitives, both of pardon of what was passed, and satisfaction otherwise, as they made an escape and returned home. So that it then appeared, that the advice sent from Boston had been better to have been put in practice in season, than their own judgment, in pursuit whereof this reproach and damage befel them.

(1.) (*March.*)] After this the Dutch governor writes to our governor in Dutch, complaining of injuries from the governor of New Haven, (calling him the pretended governor, etc.,) particularly for wronging his reputation by slanderous reports, and proffers to refer all differences (as formerly he had done) to the two governors of the Massachusetts and Plymouth, Mr. Winthrop and Mr. Bradford, by name, and professing all good neighborhood to all the rest of the colonies, with some kind of retractation of his former claim to New Haven, etc., as if all claim by word or writing, protests, etc., were of no value, so long as there is no invasion by force.

The governor of New Haven, Mr. Theophilus Eaton, he

writes also about the same time, complaining of the Dutch governor, and informing of Indian intelligence of the Dutch his animating the natives to war upon the English, and of the excessive customs and other ill usage of our vessels arriving there, propounding withal a prohibition of all trade with the Dutch until satisfaction were given.  These letters being imparted 15 (1) (*March* 15) to the general court at Boston, they thought the matter more weighty and general to the concernment of all the country, than that any thing should then be determined about it, and more fit for the commissioners first to consider of, etc., and returned answer to New Haven accordingly.  See after 115.[1]

About this time we had intelligence of an observable hand of God against the Dutch at New Netherlands, which though it were sadly to be lamented in regard of the calamity, yet there appeared in it so much of God in favor of his poor people here, and displeasure towards such as have opposed and injured them, as is not to be passed by without due observation and acknowledgment.  The late governor, Mr. William Kieft, (a sober and prudent man,) though he abstained from outward force, yet had continually molested the colonies of Hartford and New Haven, and used menacings and protests against them, upon all occasions, and had burnt down a trading house which New Haven had built upon Delaware river, and went for Holland in a ship of 400 tons, well manned and richly laden, to the value (as was supposed) of twenty thousand pounds, and carried away with him two of our people under censure, (the one condemned for rape,) though we pursued them, etc.   But in their passage in the (8th) month (*October*), the ship, mistaking the channel, was carried into Severn, and cast away upon the coast of Wales near Swansey, the governor and eighty other persons drowned, and some twenty saved.

Complaint had been made to the commissioners of the colonies, at their last meeting, by Pumham and Sacononoco,

---

[1] P. 342 of this edition.

against the Gortonists (who were now returned to Shaomett, and had named it Warwick) for eating up all their corn with their cattle, etc.  It was left to our commissioners, who wrote to some in those parts to view the damages, and require satisfaction.  But Mr. Coggeshall (who died soon after) and other of their magistrates of Rhode Island, came to Shaomett, and gave the praisers a warrant under their hands and one of their seals, forbidding them or any other to intermeddle, etc., pretending it to be within their jurisdiction, whereupon the men returned, and did nothing.  And upon another warrant from the president, in the name of the commissioners, there was nothing done neither; so as the poor Indians were in danger to be starved, etc.  Upon their farther complaints to us, the general court in the (1) month (*March*) sent three messengers to demand satisfaction for the Indians, and for other wrongs to some English there, and to command them to depart the place, as belonging to us, etc.  They used our messengers with more respect than formerly, but gave no satisfaction, bearing themselves upon their charter, etc.  We could do no more at present, but we procured the Indians some corn in the mean time.

In the agitation of this matter in the general court, some moved to have an order (upon refusal of satisfaction, etc.) to send forces presently against them; but others thought better to forbear any resolution until the return of our messengers, and the rather because we expected our agent out of England shortly, by whom we should know more of the success of our petition to the parliament, etc., it being very probable, that their charter would be called in, as illegal, etc., and this counsel prevailed.

It may be now seasonable to set down what success it pleased the Lord to give Mr. Winslow, our agent, with the parliament.

Mr. Winslow set sail from Boston about the middle of 10ber. (*December*), 1646, and carried such commissions, instructions, etc., as are before mentioned.  Upon his arrival in England,

and delivery of his letters to the Earl of Warwick, Sir Henry
Vane, etc., from the governor, he had a day appointed for
audience before the committee, and Gorton and other of his
company appeared also to justify their petition and information, which they had formerly exhibited against the court, etc.,
for making war upon them, and keeping them prisoners, etc.
But after that our agent had showed the two letters they wrote
to us from Shaomett, and the testimony of the court, and some
of the elders, concerning their blasphemous heresies and other
miscarriages, it pleased the Lord to bring about the hearts of
the committees, so as they discerned of Gorton, etc., what they
were and of the justice of our proceedings against them; only
they were not satisfied in this, that they were not within our
jurisdiction, etc., to which our agent pleaded two things, 1. that
they were within the jurisdiction of Plymouth or Connecticut,
and so the orders of the commissioners of the United Colonies
had left them to us, 2. the Indians (upon whose lands they
dwelt) had subjected themselves and their land to our government.    Whereupon the committee made this order following,
which they directed in form of a letter to Massachusetts,
Plymouth, and Connecticut, (one to each) viz.

After our hearty commendations.

In our late letter of 25 May, etc., we imparted how far we had proceeded upon the petition of Mr. Gorton and Mr. Holden, etc.  We did
by our said letter declare our tenderness of your just privileges, and of
preserving entire the authority and jurisdiction of the several governments
in New England, whereof we shall still express our continued care.  We
have since that taken further consideration of the petition, and spent
some time in hearing both parties, concerning the bounds of those patents
under which yourselves and the other governments do claim, to the end
we might receive satisfaction, whether Shaomett and the rest of the tract
of land, pretended to by the petitioners, be actually included within any
of your limits.  In which point (being matter of fact) we could not, at
this distance, give a resolution, and therefore leave that matter to be
examined and determined upon the place, if there shall be occasion, for
that the boundaries will be there best known and distinguished.  And if

it shall appear, that the said tract is within the limits of any of the New
England patents, we shall leave the same, and the inhabitants thereof
to the proper jurisdiction of that government under which they fall.
Nevertheless, for that the petitioners have transplanted their families
thither, and there settled their residences at a great charge, we commend
it to the government, within whose jurisdiction they shall appear to be,
(as our only desire at present in this matter,) not only not to remove them
from their plantations, but also to encourage them, with protection and
assistance, in all fit ways; provided that they demean themselves peaceably, and not endanger any of the English colonies by a prejudicial correspondency with the Indians, or otherwise, wherein if they shall be found
faulty, we leave them to be proceeded with according to justice.  To
this purpose we have also written our letters of this tenor to the governments of New Plymouth and Connecticut, hoping that a friendly compliance will engage these persons to an inoffensive order and conformity,
and so become an act of greater conquest, honor, and contentment to you
all, than the scattering or reducing of them by an hand of power.  And
so, not doubting of your concurrence with this desire, as there shall be
occasion, we commend you to the grace of Christ, resting

Your very affectionate friends,

From  the  Committee,       WARWICK, Gov'r. and Admiral,
etc. 22 of July, 1647.        PEMBROKE AND MONTGOMERY,
                             MANCHESTER,
                             ARTH. HESELRIGE,
                             JOHN ROLLE,
                             HEN. MILDMAY,
                             GEO. FENWICK,
                             WM. PUREFOY,
                             RICH. SALWAY,
                             MILES CORBET,
                             COR. HOLLAND,
                             GEO. SNELLING.

The first letter from the committee after Mr. Winslow had
delivered our petition and remonstrance, which should have
been inserted before the former.

After our hearty commendations, etc.

By our letter of May 15, 1646, we communicated to you our reception
of a complaint from Mr. Gorton and Mr. Holden, etc., touching some

proceedings tried against them by your government. We also imparted to you our resolutions (grounded upon certain reasons set forth in our said letter) for their residing upon Shaomett, and the other parts of that tract of land, which is mentioned in a charter of civil incorporation heretofore granted them by us, praying and requiring you to permit the same accordingly, without extending your jurisdiction to any part thereof, or disquieting them in their civil peace, or otherwise interrupting them in their possession, until we should receive your answer to the same in point of title, and thereupon give further order. We have since received a petition and remonstrance from you by your commissioner, Mr. Winslow, and though we have not yet entered into a particular consideration of the matter, yet we do, in the general, take notice of your respect, as well to the parliament's authority, as your own just privileges, and find cause to be further confirmed in our former opinion and knowledge of your prudence and faithfulness to God and his cause. And perceiving by your petition, that some persons do take advantage, from our said letter, to decline and question your jurisdiction, and to pretend a general liberty to appeal hither, upon their being called in question before you for matters proper to your cognizance, we thought it necessary (for preventing of further inconveniences in this kind) hereby to declare, that we intended not thereby to encourage any appeals from your justice, nor to restrain the bounds of your jurisdiction to a narrower compass than is held forth by your letters patent, but to leave you with all that freedom and latitude that may, in any respect, be duly claimed by you; knowing that the limiting of you in that kind may be very prejudicial (if not destructive) to the government and public peace of the colony. For your further satisfaction wherein, you may remember, that our said resolution took rise from an admittance, that the Narragansett Bay (the thing in question) was wholly without the bounds of your patent, the examination whereof will, in the next place, come before us. In the mean time we have received advertisement, that the place is within the patent of New Plymouth, and that the grounds of your proceedings against the complainants was a joint authority from the four governments of Massachusetts, Plymouth, Connecticut, and New Haven, which if it falls in upon proof, will much alter the state of the question.

And whereas our said direction extended not only to yourselves, but also to all the other governments and plantations in New England, whom it might concern, we declare, that we intended thereby no prejudice to any of their just rights, nor the countenancing of any practice to violate them; and that we shall for the future be very ready to give our encouragement and assistance in all your endeavors for settling of your peace and

government, and the advancement of the gospel of Jesus Christ, to whose
blessing we commend your persons and affairs.

Your very loving friends,

From the committee of Lords and     WARWICK, Gov'r. and Admiral,
Commons, etc., 25 May, 1647.     BAS. DENBIGH,
    EDW. MANCHESTER,
    WM. SAY AND SEALE,
    FR. DACRE,
    WM. WALLER,
    ARTHUR HESELRIGE,
    MILES CORBET,
    FR. ALLEN,
    WM. PUREFOY,
    GEO. FENWICK,
    COR. HOLLAND.

The committee having thus declared themselves to have an
honorable regard of us and care to promote the welfare of the
four United Colonies and other English plantations to the eastward, (for they had confirmed Mr. Rigby his patent of Ligonia,
and by their favorable interpretation of it had brought it to the
sea-side, whereas the words of the grant laid it twenty miles
short, and had put Sir Ferdinando Gorge out of all as far as
Saco,) our agent proceeded to have the charter (which they had
lately granted to those of Rhode Island and Providence) to
be called in, as lying within the patent of Plymouth or Connecticut.[1]

[1] The colony had reason to be satisfied with the work of Winslow. Ligonia
was the Plough Patent, of the fortunes of which we have several times read.
Though Gorton and his followers were dispossessed at Warwick, we are not to
understand from the misleading language of the paragraph that Providence and
Newport were disturbed.

# 1648

1648.   10, (3.) (*May* 10.)]   The court of elections was at Boston.   Mr. Symmes, pastor of Charlestown, preached.   Mr. Winthrop was chosen governor again, and Mr. Dudley, deputy governor, Mr. Endecott, sergeant major, and he and Mr. Bradstreet, commissioners, etc.

(3.)   Here arrived three ships from London in one day.   By the passengers we understood, as also by letters from Mr. Winslow, etc., how the hopes and endeavors of Dr. Child and other the petitioners, etc., had been blasted by the special providence of the Lord, who still wrought for us.   Dr. Child had a brother, a major of a regiment in Kent, who, being set on by his brother and William Vassall, (who went from Scituate to petition against the country, etc.) set out a pamphlet, wherein he published their petition, exhibited to our general court, and other proceedings of the court.   This was answered by Mr. Winslow in a book, entitled the *Salamander*, (pointing therein at Mr. Vassall, a man never at rest, but when he was in the fire of contention,) wherein he cleared the justice of our proceedings.[1]   As for those who went over to procure us trouble, God met with them all.   Mr. Vassall, finding no entertainment for his petitions, went to Barbados.

Dr. Child preferred a petition to the committee against us, and put in Mr. Thomas Fowle his name among others; but he, hearing of it, protested against it, (for God had brought him very low, both in his estate and in his reputation, since he

---

[1] The two publications referred to are Major John Child's *New England's Jonas cast up at London*, and Winslow's *New England's Salamander Discovered*. Both were published at London in 1647, and both were reprinted in the *Collections of the Massachusetts Historical Society*, the former in second series, IV., the latter in third series, II.

joined in the first petition). After this the Doctor, meeting with Mr. Willoughby[1] upon the exchange, (this Mr. Willoughby dwelt at Charlestown, but his father was a colonel of the city,) and falling in talk about New England, the Doctor railed against the people, saying they were a company of rogues and knaves; Mr. Willoughby answered, that he who spake so, etc., was a knave, whereupon the Doctor gave him a box on the ear. Mr. Willoughby was ready to have closed with him, etc., but being upon the exchange, he was stayed, but presently arrested him. And when the Doctor saw the danger he was in, he employed some friends to make his peace, who ordered him to give five pounds to the poor of New England, (for Mr. Willoughby would have nothing of him,) and to give Mr. Willoughby open satisfaction in the full exchange, and to give it under his hand, never to speak evil of New England men after, nor to occasion any trouble to the country, or to any of the people, all which he gladly performed; and besides God had so blasted his estate, as he was quite broken, etc.

Samuel Gorton arrived here. The court, being informed of it, made an order that he should be apprehended, etc., but he sending us the Earl of Warwick's letter, desiring only that he might have liberty to pass home, the court recalled their former order, and gave him a week's liberty to provide for his departure. This was much opposed by some; but the most considered, that, it being only at the Earl's request, (no command,) it could be no prejudice to our liberty, and our commissioner being still attending the parliament, it might much have disadvantaged our cause and his expedition, if the Earl should have heard that we had denied him so small a request. Yet it was carried only by a casting voice.

The Gortonists of Shaomett, hearing how matters were like to go against them in England, and [illegible] by Aquiday,

---

[1] Francis Willoughby returning to New England became a much respected citizen, attaining the office of deputy-governor, and at the Restoration strongly opposing the exercise of the royal prerogative.

began to consider how they might make their peace with us, and for that end sent two of their company to petition our general court, etc., but these messengers being come to Dedham, and hearing that the court was adjourned, they came no further; but one of them wrote a letter to our governor, in this tenor following:—

To the right worshipful Mr. John Winthrop, Governor of the Massachusetts,
  Humbly presented to your worship's consideration,
  That whereas I, with another, was chosen by the general court held at Providence the eighteenth of this month, and sent with an humble request to this honorable state concerning Shaomett business, but when we came at Dedham, hearing that the general court was adjourned, I your suppliant (being an inhabitant of Shaomett) seriously weighing my present condition there, I made bold to advise with Mr. Powell[1] concerning the same, who advised me to repair to your worship, which (on consideration) I could not, till I had some knowledge of your worship's favorable acceptation. My humble request therefore is, that your worship would be pleased to send me your mind in a few lines concerning the premises. So, craving your worship's favorable construction,
          I remain,
              Yours, most humbly,
                  RUFUS BARTON.
  Dedham, May 22, 1648.


This year corn was very scarce, and so it was in all countries of Europe. Our scarcity came by occasion of our transporting much to the West Indies, and the Portugal and Spanish Islands. The magistrates sent out to have a survey of the corn in the country, and finding it to fall very short, the next general court made an order to prohibit transportation except of such as should be brought in from other parts and such as were sold before to be transported, etc. Yet this restraint notwithstanding, etc., the price did not rise 12d. in the bushel,

---

[1] Michael Powell kept the ordinary, or tavern, at Dedham; but coming later to Boston, was one of the founders and ruling elders of the Second Church.

nor (through the good providence of the Lord) was the scarcity much felt among the people.

Mr. Eaton having again moved the governor to know the mind of the court touching the Dutch governor's proceedings, the court appointed a committee to consider of it, (after the court was adjourned,) and withal to consider of the articles of confederation, and some of the commissioners' orders; for there was some murmuring among the people about the inequality of some articles, as that we bearing more than half the charge upon all occasions, etc., should yet have no more commissioners than the smallest of the other, and that all charges should be levied by the poll, considering how great a part of our people were laborers and craftsmen, and of theirs the most were farmers and well stocked, etc.

28, (3.) (*May* 28.)] Soon after the court was adjourned, the governor received two letters from the Dutch governor, holding forth much assurance of his sincere affection to a firm peace and neighborly compliance with all the English, and that upon these grounds, 1. our unity in the true religion, 2. the ancient league between the two nations, 3. the community in danger, in respect of the common enemy, both Spaniards and Indians, 4. the reconciling former differences and preventing future, 5. the benefit of a mutual league, both offensive and defensive, against a common enemy; and offered to meet Mr. Bradford, the governor of Plymouth, and Mr. Winthrop, the governor of the Massachusetts, at Connecticut, at such time as we should appoint, and to refer all to us.

The governor returned answer to him, of what gladness he conceived in his forwardness to peace, and had no reason to doubt of his cordial intentions, etc., promising to further the meeting what lay in his power, etc.

There was some reason, why the Dutch governor's spirit should begin to fall, both in regard of the weakness the state of Holland (especially the West India Company) were fallen into, (which was not the least occasion of their late peace

with Spain,)[1] and also in respect of the doubts which he was
fallen into at this time, both from his own unruly people, and
also of their neighbor Indians, for neither would his people be
restrained from furnishing the Indians with guns, powder, etc.,
nor would the Indians endure to be without that trade; and
the great loss the company had sustained by late wreck of
three ships, and the old governor and many principal men
with him, made him doubtful of any great supply from Holland.

4. (4). (*June* 4.)] Here arrived one Sir Edmund Plowden,[2]
who had been in Virginia about seven years. He came first
with a patent of a county Palatine for Delaware Bay, but
wanting a pilot for that place, he went to Virginia and there
having lost the estate he brought over, and all his people
scattered from him, he came hither to return to England for
supply, intending to return and plant Delaware, if he could get
sufficient strength to dispossess the Swedes.

This year a new way was found out to Connecticut, by
Nashoway, which avoided much of the hilly way.

The magistrates, being informed at a court of assistants that
four or five Indians, who lived upon the spoil of their neighbors,
had murdered some Indians of Nipnett, who were subject to
this government, and robbed their wigwam, sent twenty men to
Nashoway to inquire of the truth of the matter, and to apprehend the murderers, if they could be found; but being fled to
Narragansett, they returned, and informed us certainly of the
persons murdered, and of the actors, etc., which was of this
good use, (though they could not apprehend them,) that the
Indians saw our care of them, and readiness to protect them,
and revenge their wrongs.

[1] The United Provinces ended the "Eighty Years' War" with Spain by the
treaty of Münster, January 30, 1648. The Dutch West India Company, whose
fortunes had fallen very low, was rechartered in 1647.

[2] An unsuccessful adventurer who planned a large enterprise, and secured
in 1634 a patent from the crown of Ireland, making him "Earl Palatine of the
province of New Albion." Of the great feudal domain projected, nothing ever
came. Its history is fully related by Professor Gregory B. Keen in Winsor's
*Narrative and Critical History of America*, III. 457-468.

After this, two Indians, of Cutshamekin's procuring, offering themselves to apprehend some of the murderers, we gave them commission, and withal wrote to Mr. Pincheon to assist them, etc. (they being near Springfield). Mr. Pincheon offered his assistance, but wrote to the governor, that the Indians murdered, nor yet the murderers, were not our subjects, and withal that it would endanger a war; whereupon the governor advising with the deputy, etc., wrote back presently to Mr. Pincheon, that then he should proceed no further, but send back the Indians, etc.

At this court one Margaret Jones of Charlestown was indicted and found guilty of witchcraft, and hanged for it. The evidence against her was, 1. that she was found to have such a malignant touch, as many persons, (men, women, and children,) whom she stroked or touched with any affection or displeasure, or, etc., were taken with deafness, or vomiting, or other violent pains or sickness, 2. she practising physic, and her medicines being such things as (by her own confession) were harmless, as aniseed, liquors, etc., yet had extraordinary violent effects, 3. she would use to tell such as would not make use of her physic, that they would never be healed, and accordingly their diseases and hurts continued, with relapse against the ordinary course, and beyond the apprehension of all physicians and surgeons, 4. some things which she foretold came to pass accordingly; other things she could tell of (as secret speeches, etc.) which she had no ordinary means to come to the knowledge of, 5. she had (upon search) an apparent teat in her secret parts as fresh as if it had been newly sucked, and after it had been scanned, upon a forced search, that was withered, and another began on the opposite side, 6. in the prison, in the clear day-light, there was seen in her arms, she sitting on the floor, and her clothes up, etc., a little child, which ran from her into another room, and the officer following it, it was vanished. The like child was seen in two other places, to which she had relation; and one maid that saw it, fell sick upon it, and was cured by the said

Margaret, who used means to be employed to that end. Her behavior at her trial was very intemperate, lying notoriously, and railing upon the jury and witnesses, etc., and in the like distemper she died. The same day and hour she was executed, there was a very great tempest at Connecticut, which blew down many trees, etc.

4. (*June.*)] The wife of one Willip of Exeter was found in the river dead, her neck broken, her tongue black and swollen out of her mouth, and the blood settled in her face, the privy parts swollen, etc., as if she had been much abused, etc.

A vessel of Connecticut being the last winter at Quorasoe,[1] in the possession of the Dutch, found there a negro, who had lost his legs, and had been sent thither out of Holland to perform such service to the governor, etc., as he was fit for (having been trained up to some learning in Holland). This man had attained to some good savor of religion, so as he grew weary of the Dutch of the island, who were very debauched, (only one man he found some piety in,) and there being some Indians in the island, he acquainted himself with them, and having attained some skill in their language, he began to instruct them and their children in the knowledge of God, etc., and the Lord so blessed his endeavors, as the Indians began to hearken to him, and yielded themselves to be taught at certain times which this negro appointed. This negro told the master of the English vessel, one Bull, a godly and discreet man, of all his proceedings, and what comfort he had in that one godly Dutchman, saying that he never was in his company but he found Jesus Christ warming him at the heart. He inquired of Bull about New England and our religion and churches, and asked if we were of those Christians, who advanced the doctrine of merits, etc., and much rejoiced when he heard the truth of our doctrine, etc., and showed himself very desirous to see New England; and so he left him at that time.

28.] The *Welcome*, of Boston, about 300 tons, riding before

[1] Curaçao.

Charlestown, having in her eighty horses and 120 tons of ballast, in calm weather, fell a rolling, and continued so about twelve hours, so as though they brought a great weight to the one side, yet she would heel to the other, and so deep as they feared her foundering. It was then the time of the county court at Boston, and the magistrates hearing of it, and withal that one Jones (the husband of the witch lately executed) had desired to have passage in her to Barbados, and could not have it without such payment, etc., they sent the officer presently with a warrant to apprehend him, one of them saying that the ship would stand still as soon as he was in prison. And as the officer went, and was passing over the ferry, one said to him, you can tame men sometimes, can't you tame this ship? The officer answered, I have that here, that (it may be) will tame her, and make her be quiet; and with that showed his warrant. And at the same instant, she began to stop and presently staid, and after he was put in prison, moved no more.

There appeared over the harbor at New Haven, in the evening, the form of the keel of a ship with three masts, to which were suddenly added all the tackling and sails, and presently after, upon the top of the poop, a man standing with one hand akimbo under his left side, and in his right hand a sword stretched out toward the sea. Then from the side of the ship which was from the town arose a great smoke, which covered all the ship, and in that smoke she vanished away; but some saw her keel sink into the water. This was seen by many, men and women, and it continued about a quarter of an hour.[1]

Divers letters passed between our governor and the Dutch governor about a meeting for reconciling the differences between our confederates of New Haven, etc., and him. But Mr. Bradford, the governor of Plymouth, (being one of the

---

[1] The spectral ship of New Haven, the tradition of which was taken up and characteristically developed by Cotton Mather, is one of the most weird of New England legends, and has become very familiar to the later generations.

two whom the Dutch governor desired to refer the differences
unto, being sent unto about it, came to Boston, and there
excused himself, by bodily infirmities and other reasons, that
he could not go to Hartford that summer, but promised (the
Lord assisting) to prepare against the middle of the (4) (*June*)
next summer. So the governor (Mr. Hopkins being then also
at Boston) despatched away letters presently to the Dutch
governor to certify him thereof, who returned answer soon
after, that he was very sorry the meeting did not hold, and
professed his earnest inclination to peace, and that he never
had any thought of war, and desired that in the mean time all
things might remain as they were, neither encroaching upon
others' pretended limits, desiring withal that he might meet the
commissioners of the colonies also to treat with them about
the Indian trade, which was much abused, etc.

15. (6.) (*August* 15.)] The synod met at Cambridge by adjournment from the (4) (*June*) last. Mr. Allen of Dedham
preached out of Acts 15, a very godly, learned, and particular
handling of near all the doctrines and applications concerning
that subject with a clear discovery and refutation of such
errors, objections, and scruples as had been raised about it by
some young heads in the country.

It fell out, about the midst of his sermon, there came a snake
into the seat, where many of the elders sate behind the preacher.
It came in at the door where people stood thick upon the stairs.
Divers of the elders shifted from it, but Mr. Thomson, one of
the elders of Braintree, (a man of much faith,) trode upon the
head of it, and so held it with his foot and staff with a small
pair of grains,[1] until it was killed. This being so remarkable,
and nothing falling out but by divine providence, it is out of
doubt, the Lord discovered somewhat of his mind in it. The
serpent is the devil; the synod, the representative of the
churches of Christ in New England. The devil had formerly
and lately attempted their disturbance and dissolution; but

[1] Pair of grains, a sort of fish-spear.

their faith in the seed of the woman overcame him and crushed his head.

The synod went on comfortably, and intended only the framing of a confession of faith, etc., and a form of church discipline (not entertaining any other business). For the first, they wholly agreed with that which the assembly in England had lately set forth. For the other, viz., for discipline, they drew it by itself, according to the general practice of our churches. So they ended in less than fourteen days.[1]

This month, when our first harvest was near had in, the pigeons came again all over the country, but did no harm, (harvest being just in,) but proved a great blessing, it being incredible what multitudes of them were killed daily. It was ordinary for one man to kill eight or ten dozen in half a day, yea five or six dozen at one shoot, and some seven or eight. Thus the Lord showed us, that he could make the same creature, which formerly had been a great chastisement, now to become a great blessing.

About the midst of this summer, there arose a fly out of the ground, about the bigness of the top of a man's little finger, of brown color. They filled the woods from Connecticut to Sudbury with a great noise, and eat up the young sprouts of the trees, but meddled not with the corn. They were also between Plymouth and Braintree, but came no further. If the Lord had not stopped them, they had spoiled all our orchards, for they did some few.

At the last meeting of the commissioners at New Haven, information was given them, that Sequashin, a sachem near

---

[1] At this synod was laid down the famous Cambridge platform upon which the Congregational polity of New England substantially rested until 1780. Twenty years of experience had taught the leaders that Congregationalism might be too absolute. Hence this grafting upon the original idea, of the council or synod, which differed from Presbyterianism in not being permanent, only resorted to in temporary emergencies, and yet was a decided check upon independency. The platform or *Book of Discipline*, as it was often called, was adopted, hardly with cordiality, but remained long in authority. See Palfrey, *History of New England*, I. 330.

Hartford, would have hired an Indian to kill some of the magistrates of Hartford, whereupon he was sent for, but came not, and being among other Indians about Pacomtuckett,[1] they sent for Unkas, who undertook to fetch him in, which he not being able to do by force, he surprised him in the night, and brought him to Hartford, where he was kept in prison divers weeks. But there not being sufficient proof to convict him, etc., he was discharged. Yet the Indians, from whom he was taken, took it so to heart against Uncas, as they intended to make war upon him, and the Narragansetts sent wampom to them to encourage them; and accordingly in this month, there were gathered together from divers parts about one thousand Indians armed, three hundred or more having guns, powder, and bullets, and were at Pacumtuckett preparing, etc., which the magistrates of Hartford hearing of, they sent three horsemen to them (one being very expert in the Indian language) to know their intent, and to tell them, that if they made war upon Uncas, the English must defend him. The Indian sachems entertained the messengers courteously; and having heard their message, they took time to give their answer, which was this, viz. they knew the English to be a wise and warlike people, and they intended not to fall out with them, therefore for the present they would desist, and consider further of the matter. And God had so disposed, as at the same instant they had intelligence of a defeat given to some of their confederates by other Indians, which called them to their aid, and also the Narragansett had failed to send them all the wampom he had promised. Thus the Lord delivered us from that war, which must needs have been very dangerous, especially to our brethren of Connecticut.

The Narragansett and Niantick dealing thus underhand contrary to their covenant, and being yet behind near one thousand fathom of the wampom they should have paid us long since, the commissioners, sitting at Plymouth, (7) (*September*) ordered four men to be sent to them, with an interpreter, with

[1] Pocumtuckett became later Deerfield.

instructions how to treat with them, both concerning their hiring other Indians to war upon Uncas, and also about the wampom behind. Captain Atherton and Captain Prichard, assisted with two others, voluntarily undertook this service, and went hence, 3 (8) (*October* 3). They were to have taken Benedict Arnold for their interpreter; but he being from home, they went to Mr. Williams, who sent for the sachems. But they had heard that many horsemen were come to take them, which made Pesicus fly over to Rhode Island. Then our messengers went to Niantick, where Ninicraft entertained them courteously, (there they staid the Lord's day,) and came back with them to Mr. Williams, and then Pesicus and Canonicus' son, being delivered of their fear, came to them, and being demanded about hiring the Mohawks against Uncas, they solemnly denied it; only they confessed, that the Mohawk, being a great sachem, and their ancient friend, and being come so near them, they sent some twenty fathom of wampom for him to tread upon, as the manner of Indians is. And Canonicus' son, called [*blank*,] used this asseveration, viz. Englishman's God doth know, that we did not send to stir up or hire the Mohawks against Uncas. Then they further promised, that they would not meddle with Uncas, nor stir up any other against him, before they had paid all their debt of wampom to the English, and then they would require satisfaction for all the wrongs Uncas had done them, and if the English would not see them satisfied, they would consider what to do. And for their wampom behind, etc., they desired the English to bear with them, in regard their want of corn last winter had made them lay out their wampom to the English for corn; but in the spring they would provide part of it, and the rest so soon as they could.

(8.) (*October.*)] A shallop having been fishing at Monhigen, and returning with other boats, and being to put in at Damarell's cove,[1] the other boats fell to their oars (the wind failing)

---

[1] Now Damariscove Island, near Monhegan, on the Maine coast.

and called upon this boat to do the like, that they might be harbored before night; but they were slothful, and neglected, etc., whereupon she missed her way, and was split upon a rock, and all the men (being four, and one Indian) and all the goods perished.

20.] In the time of our general court here arrived from Virginia one Mr. Haryson, pastor of the church of Nanseman there, and reported to us, that their church was grown to one hundred and eighteen persons, and many more looking towards it, which had stirred up the governor there, Sir William Berkley, to raise persecution against them, and he had banished their elder, Mr. Durand, and himself (viz. Mr. Haryson) was to depart the country by the third ship at furthest, which had caused [*him*] to come now to take advice of the magistrates and elders here about the matter. First he spake with the magistrates, and propounded two things, 1. whether their church ought not to remove, upon this persecution, 2. whether we would advise them to remove.

To the first our answer was, that seeing God had carried on his work so graciously hitherto, etc., and that there was so great hope of a far more plentiful harvest at hand, (many of the council being well inclined, etc., and one thousand of the people by conjecture,) they should not be hasty to remove, as long as they could stay upon any tolerable terms. 2. For the place they should remove to, if necessitated, Mr. Haryson acquainted us with a place allowed and propounded to them, and the occasion of it, which was thus: Captain Wm. Sayle of Summers Islands,[1] having been lately in England, had procured an ordinance of parliament for planting the Bahamas Islands (now called Eleutheria) in the mouth of the gulf of Florida, and wanting means to carry it on, had obtained of divers parliament men and others in London to undertake the work, which they did, and drew up a covenant and articles for all to enter into, who would come into the business. The first article

---

[1] Bermudas.

was for liberty of conscience, wherein they provided, that the civil magistrate should not have cognizance of any matter which concerned religion, but every man might enjoy his own opinion or religion, without control or question, (nor was there any word of maintaining or professing any religion or worship of God at all;) and the commission (by authority of the ordinance of parliament) to Captain Sayle to be governor three years was with limitation, that they should be subject to such orders and directions as from time to time they should receive from the company in England, etc.  Upon these terms they furnished him with a ship and all provisions and necessaries for the design, and some few persons embarked with him, and sailed to the Summers Islands, where they took in Mr. Patrick Copeland, elder of that church, a godly man of near eighty years of age, and so many other of the church there, as they were in the ship in all seventy persons.  But in the way to Eleutheria, one Captain Butler, a young man who came in the ship from England, made use of his liberty to disturb all the company.  He could not endure any ordinances or worship, etc., and when they arrived at one of the Eleutheria Islands, and were intended there to settle, he made such a faction, as enforced Captain Sayle to remove to another island, and being near the harbor, the ship struck and was cast away.  The persons were all saved, save one, but all their provisions and goods were lost, so as they were forced (for divers months) to lie in the open air, and to feed upon such fruits and wild creatures as the island afforded.  But finding their strength to decay, and no hope of any relief, Captain Sayle took a shallop and eight men, with such provisions as they could get, and set sail, hoping to attain either the Summers Islands, or Virginia, or New England; and so it pleased the Lord to favor them, that in nine days they arrived in Virginia, their provisions all spent, etc.  Those of the church relieved them, and furnished them with a bark and provisions to return to relieve their company left in Eleutheria.  Captain Sayle, finding the church in this state, persuaded them to remove to Eleutheria, which they began to listen unto, but after they had seen a copy of his commission and articles, etc. (though he undertook to them, that the company in England would alter any thing they should desire, yet) they paused upon it (for the church were very orthodox and zealous for the truth) and would not resolve before they had received advice from us. Whereupon letters were returned to them, dissuading them from joining with that people under those terms.

(9) (*November*) 2.] Here arrived a Dutch hoy of about 30 tons, with cordage and other goods, seven men in her. She came from the Isle of Wight hither in five weeks.

18.] One Bezaleel Payton of the church of Boston, coming from Barbados in a vessel of 60 tons, was taken with a great storm of wind and rain at east in the night, between Cape Cod and the bay, so as he was forced to put out two anchors; but the storm increasing, they were put from their anchors, and seeing no way but death before their eyes, they commended themselves to the Lord, who delivered them marvelously, for they were carried among Conyhasset rocks, yet touched none of them, and put on shore upon a beach, and presently there came a mighty sea, which lifted their vessel over the beach into a smooth water, and after the storm was over, they used means, and gate her safe out.

The like example of the blessing of prayer fell out not long after in saving a small open vessel of ours, wherein was one Richard Collicut of the church of Dorchester, who being eastward about trading was carried by a violent storm among the rocks, where they could find no place to get out. So they went to prayer, and presently there came a great sea, and heaved their vessel over into the open sea, in a place between two rocks.

# 1649

11, (11.) (*January* 11.)] About eight persons were drowned this winter, all by adventuring upon the ice, except three, whereof two (one of them being far in drink) would needs pass from Boston to Winisemett in a small boat and a tempestuous night. This man (using to come home to Winisemett drunken) his wife would tell him, he would one day be drowned, etc., but he made light of it. Another went aboard a ship to make merry the last day at night, (being the beginning of the Lord's day,) and returning about midnight with three of the ship's company, the boat was overset by means of the ice, they guiding her by a rope, which went from the ship to the shore. The seamen waded out, but the Boston man was drowned, being a man of good conversation and hopeful of some work of grace begun in him, but drawn away by the seamen's invitation. God will be sanctified in them that come near him. Two others were the children of one of the church of Boston. While their parents were at the lecture, the boy, (being about seven years of age,) having a small staff in his hand, ran down upon the ice towards a boat he saw, and the ice breaking, he fell in, but his staff kept him up, till his sister, about fourteen years old, ran down to save her brother (though there were four men at hand, and called to her not to go, being themselves hasting to save him) and so drowned herself and him also, being past recovery ere the men could come at them, and could easily reach ground with their feet. The parents had no more sons, and confessed they had been too indulgent towards him, and had set their hearts over much upon him.

This puts me in mind of another child very strangely drowned a little before winter. The parents were also members of the church of Boston. The father had undertaken to maintain the mill-dam, and being at work upon it, (with some help he had hired,) in the afternoon of the last day of the week, night came upon them before they had finished what they intended, and his conscience began to put him in mind of the Lord's day, and he was troubled, yet went on and wrought an hour within night. The next day, after evening exercise, and after they had supped, the mother put two children to bed in the room where themselves did lie, and they went out to visit a neighbor. When they returned, they continued about an hour in the room, and missed not the child, but then the mother going to the bed, and not finding her youngest child, (a daughter about five years of age,) after much search she found it drowned in a well in her cellar; which was very observable, as by a special hand of God, that the child should go out of that room into another in the dark, and then fall down at a trap door, or go down the stairs, and so into the well in the farther end of the cellar, the top of the well and the water being even with the ground. But the father, freely in the open congregation, did acknowledge it the righteous hand of God for his profaning his holy day against the checks of his own conscience.

# INDEX